THE GIFT OF FEAR

THE GIFT OF FEAR

SURVIVAL SIGNALS THAT PROTECT US FROM VIOLENCE

GAVIN DE BECKER

1837

Little, Brown and Company

BOSTON NEW YORK TORONTO LONDON

Every story in this book is true. While a few names have been changed to protect privacy, 90 percent are the actual names of the people involved.

The author is grateful for permission to include the following previously copyrighted material:

Excerpts from *Amphigorey* by Edward Gorey. Copyright © by Edward Gorey. Reprinted by permission of Donadio & Ashworth, Inc.

978-0-7394-9749-4

Printed in the United States of America

To the two people who taught me the most about
courage and kindness: my sisters, Chrysti and Melissa.
And for my mother, and grandfather, and father.

CONTENTS

1	In the Presence of Danger	3
2	The Technology of Intuition	25
3	The Academy of Prediction	42
4	Survival Signals	54
5	Imperfect Strangers	76
6	High-Stakes Predictions	89
7	Promises to Kill (*Understanding threats*)	103
8	Persistence, Persistence (*Dealing with people who refuse to let go*)	119
9	Occupational Hazards (*Violence in the workplace*)	141
10	Intimate Enemies (*Domestic violence*)	172

11	"I Was Trying to Let Him Down Easy" (*Date stalking*)	194
12	Fear of Children (*Violent Children*)	210
13	Better to Be Wanted by the Police Than Not to Be Wanted at All (*Attacks against public figures*)	231
14	Extreme Hazards	261
15	The Gift of Fear	277
	Acknowledgments	300
	Appendixes	304
	Recommended Reading	323
	Index	325

Note: Men of all ages and in all parts of the world are more violent than women. For this reason, the language in this book is mostly gender-specific to men. When it comes to violence, women can proudly relinquish recognition in the language, because here at least, politically correct would be statistically incorrect.

GdeB

THE GIFT OF FEAR

. 1 .

IN THE PRESENCE OF DANGER

"This above all, to refuse to be a victim."
— *Margaret Atwood*

He had probably been watching her for a while. We aren't sure — but what we do know is that she was not his first victim. That afternoon, in an effort to get all her shopping done in one trip, Kelly had overestimated what she could comfortably carry home. Justifying her decision as she struggled with the heavy bags, she reminded herself that making two trips would have meant walking around after dark, and she was too careful about her safety for that. As she climbed the few steps to the apartment building door, she saw that it had been left unlatched (again). Her neighbors just don't get it, she thought, and though their lax security annoyed her, this time she was glad to be saved the trouble of getting out the key.

She closed the door behind her, pushing it until she heard it latch. She is certain she locked it, which means he must have already been inside the corridor.

Next came the four flights of stairs, which she wanted to do in one trip. Near the top of the third landing, one of the bags gave way, tearing open and dispensing cans of cat food. They rolled down the stairs almost playfully, as if they were trying to get away from her. The can in the lead paused at the second floor landing, and Kelly watched as it literally turned the corner, gained some speed, and began its seemingly mindful hop down the next flight of steps and out of sight.

"Got it! I'll bring it up," someone called out. Kelly didn't like that voice. Right from the start something just sounded wrong to her, but then this friendly-looking young guy came bounding up the steps, collecting cans along the way.

He said, "Let me give you a hand."

"No, no thanks, I've got it."

"You don't look like you've got it. What floor are you going to?"

She paused before answering him. "The fourth, but I'm okay, really."

He wouldn't hear a word of it, and by this point he had a collection of cans balanced between his chest and one arm. "I'm going to the fourth floor too," he said, "and I'm late — not my fault, broken watch — so let's not just stand here. And give me that." He reached out and tugged on one of the heavier bags she was holding. She repeated, "No, really, thanks, but no, I've got it."

Still holding on to the grocery bag, he said, "There's such thing as being *too* proud, you know."

For a moment, Kelly didn't let go of that bag, but then she did, and this seemingly insignificant exchange between the cordial stranger and the recipient of his courtesy was the signal — to him and to her — that she was willing to trust him. As the bag passed from her control to his, so did she.

"We better hurry," he said as he walked up the stairs ahead of Kelly. "We've got a hungry cat up there."

Even though he seemed to want nothing more at that moment than to be helpful, she was apprehensive about him, and for no good reason, she thought. He was friendly and gentlemanly, and she felt guilty about her suspicion. She didn't want to be the kind of person who distrusts everybody, so they were next approaching the door to her apartment.

"Did you know a cat can live for three weeks without eating?" he asked. "I'll tell you how I learned that tidbit: I once forgot that I'd promised to feed a cat while a friend of mine was out of town."

Kelly was now standing at the door to her apartment, which she'd just opened.

"I'll take it from here," she said, hoping he'd hand her the groceries, accept her thanks, and be on his way. Instead, he said, "Oh no, I didn't come this far to let you have another cat food spill." When she still hesitated to let him in her door, he laughed understandingly. "Hey, we can leave the door open like ladies do in old movies. I'll just put this stuff down and go. I promise."

She did let him in, but he did not keep his promise.

■ ■ ■

At this point, as she is telling me the story of the rape and the whole three-hour ordeal she suffered, Kelly pauses to weep quietly. She now knows that he killed one of his other victims, stabbed her to death.

All the while, since soon after we sat down knee to knee in the small garden outside my office, Kelly has been holding both my hands. She is twenty-seven years old. Before the rape, she was a counselor for disturbed children, but she hasn't been back to work in a long while. That friendly-looking young man had caused three hours of suffering in her apartment and at least three months of suffering in her memory. The confidence he scared off was still hiding, the dignity he pierced still healing.

Kelly is about to learn that listening to one small survival signal saved her life, just as failing to follow so many others had put her at risk in the first place. She looks at me through moist but clear eyes and says she wants to understand every strategy he used. She wants me to tell her what her intuition saw that saved her life. But she will tell me.

"It was after he'd already held the gun to my head, after he raped me. It was after that. He got up from the bed, got dressed, then closed the window. He glanced at his watch, and then started acting like he was in a hurry."

"I gotta be somewhere. Hey, don't look so scared. I promise I'm not going to hurt you." Kelly absolutely knew he was lying. She knew he planned to kill her, and though it may be hard to imagine, it was the first time since the incident began that she felt profound fear.

He motioned to her with the gun and said, "Don't you move or do anything. I'm going to the kitchen to get something to drink, and then I'll leave. I promise. But you stay right where you are." He had little reason to be concerned that Kelly might disobey his instructions because she had been, from the moment she let go of that bag until this moment, completely under his control. "You know I won't move," she assured him.

But the instant he stepped from the room, Kelly stood up and walked after him, pulling the sheet off the bed with her. "I was literally right behind him, like a ghost, and he didn't know I was there. We walked down the hall together. At one point he stopped, and so did I. He was looking at my stereo, which was playing some music, and he reached out and made it louder. When he moved on toward the kitchen, I turned and walked through the living room."

Kelly could hear drawers being opened as she walked out her front door, leaving it ajar. She walked directly into the apartment across the hall (which she somehow knew would be unlocked). Holding a finger up to signal her surprised neighbors to be quiet, she locked their door behind her.

"I knew if I had stayed in my room, he was going to come back from the kitchen and kill me, but I don't know how I was so certain."

"Yes, you do," I tell her.

She sighs and then goes over it again. "He got up and got dressed, closed the window, looked at his watch. He promised he wouldn't hurt me, and that promise came out of nowhere. Then he went into the kitchen to get a drink, supposedly, but I heard him opening drawers in there. He was looking for a knife, of course, but I knew way before that." She pauses. "I guess he wanted a knife because using the gun would be too noisy."

"What makes you think he was concerned about noise?" I ask.

"I don't know." She takes a long pause, gazing off past me, looking back at him in the bedroom. "Oh . . . I do know. I get it, I get it. Noise was the thing — that's why he closed the window. That's how I knew."

Since he was dressed and supposedly leaving, he had no other reason to close her window. It was that subtle signal that warned her, but it was fear that gave her the courage to get up without hesitation and follow close behind the man who intended to kill her. She later described a fear so complete that it replaced every feeling in her body. Like an animal hiding inside her, it opened to its full size and stood up using the muscles in her legs. "I had nothing to do with it," she explained. "I was a passenger moving down that hallway."

What she experienced was real fear, not like when we are startled, not like the fear we feel at a movie, or the fear of public speaking. This fear is the powerful ally that says, "Do what I tell you to do." Sometimes, it tells a person to play dead, or to stop breathing, or to run or scream or fight, but to Kelly it said, "Just be quiet and don't doubt me and I'll get you out of here."

Kelly told me she felt new confidence in herself, knowing she had acted on that signal, knowing she had saved her own life. She said she was tired of being blamed and blaming herself for letting him into her apartment. She said she had learned enough in our meetings to never again be victimized that way.

"Maybe that's the good to come from it," she reflected. "The weird thing is, with all this information I'm actually less afraid walking around now than I was before it happened — but there must be an easier way people could learn."

The thought had occurred to me. I know that what saved Kelly's life can save yours. In her courage, in her commitment to listen to intuition, in her determination to make some sense out of it, in her passion to be free of unwarranted fear, I saw that the information should be shared not just with victims but with those who need never become victims at all. I want this book to help you be one of those people.

Because of my sustained look at violence, because I have predicted the behavior of murderers, stalkers, would-be assassins, rejected boyfriends, estranged husbands, angry former employees, mass killers, and others, I am called an expert. I may have learned many lessons, but my basic premise in these pages is that you too are an expert at predicting violent behavior. Like every creature, you can know when you are in the presence of danger. You have the gift of a brilliant internal guardian that stands ready to warn you of hazards and guide you through risky situations.

I've learned some lessons about safety through years of asking people who've suffered violence, "Could you have seen this coming?" Most often they say, "No, it just came out of nowhere," but if I am quiet, if I wait a moment, here comes the information: "I felt uneasy when I first met that guy . . ." or "Now that I think of it, I was suspicious when he approached me," or "I realize now I had seen that car earlier in the day."

Of course, if they realize it now, they knew it then. We all see the signals because there is a universal code of violence. You'll find some of what you need to break that code in the following chapters, but most of it is in you.

■ ■ ■

In a very real sense, the surging water in an ocean does not move; rather, energy moves through it. In this same sense, the energy of violence moves through our culture. Some experience it as a light but unpleasant breeze, easy to tolerate. Others are destroyed by it, as if by a hurricane. But nobody — nobody — is untouched. Violence is a part of America, and more than that, it is a part of our species. It is around us, and it is in us. As the most powerful people in history, we have climbed to the top of the world food chain, so to speak. Facing not one single enemy or predator who poses to us any danger of consequence, we've found the only prey left: ourselves.

Lest anyone doubt this, understand that in the last two years alone, more Americans died from gunshot wounds than were killed during the entire Vietnam War. By contrast, in all of Japan (with a population of 120 million people), the number of young men shot to death in a year is equal to the number killed in New York City in a single busy weekend. Our armed robbery rate is one hundred times higher than Japan's. In part, that's because we are a nation with more firearms than adults, a nation where 20,000 guns enter the stream of commerce every day. No contemplation of your safety in America can be sincere without taking a clear-eyed look down the barrel of that statistic. By this time tomorrow, 400 more Americans will suffer a shooting injury, and another 1,100 will face a criminal with a gun, as Kelly did. Within the hour, another 75 women will be raped, as Kelly was.

Neither privilege nor fame will keep violence away: In the last 35 years, more public figures have been attacked in America than in the 185 years before that. Ordinary citizens can encounter violence at their jobs to the point that homicide is now the leading cause of death for women in the workplace. Twenty years ago, the idea of someone going on a shooting spree at work was outlandish; now it's in the news nearly every week, and managing employee fear of co-workers is a frequent topic in the boardroom.

While we are quick to judge the human rights record of every other country on earth, it is we civilized Americans whose murder rate is ten times that of other Western nations, we civilized Americans who kill women and children with the most alarming frequency. In (sad) fact, if a full jumbo jet crashed into a mountain killing everyone on board, and if that happened every month, month in and month out, the number of people killed still wouldn't equal the number of women murdered by their husbands and boyfriends each year.

We all watched as bodies were carried away from the Oklahoma City bombing, and by the end of that week we learned to our horror that nineteen children had died in the blast. You now know that seventy children died that same week at the hands of a parent, just like every week — and most of them were under five years old. Four million luckier children were physically abused last year, and it was not an unusual year.

Statistics like this tend to distance us from the tragedies that surround each incident because we end up more impressed by the numbers than by the reality. To bring it closer to home, you personally know a woman who has been battered, and you've probably seen the warning signs. She or her husband works with you, lives near you, amazes you in sports, fills your prescriptions at the pharmacy, or advises on your taxes. You may not know, however, that women visit emergency rooms for injuries caused by their husbands or boyfriends more often than for injuries from car accidents, robberies, and rapes combined.

Our criminal-justice system often lacks justice, and more often lacks reason. For example, America has about three thousand people slated for execution, more by far than at any time in world history, yet the most frequent cause of death listed for those inmates is "natural causes." That's because we execute fewer than 2 percent of those sentenced to die. It is actually safer for these men to live on death row than to live in some American neighborhoods.

I explore capital punishment here not to promote it, for I am not an advocate, but rather because our attitude toward it raises a question that is key to this book: Are we really serious about fighting crime and violence? Often, it appears we are not. Here's just one example of what we accept: If you add up how long their victims would otherwise have lived, our country's murderers rob us of almost a million years of human contribution every year.

I've presented these facts about the frequency of violence for a reason: to increase the likelihood that you will believe it is at least possible that you or someone you care for will be a victim at some time. That belief is a key element in recognizing when you are in the presence of danger. That belief balances denial, the powerful and cunning enemy of successful predictions. Even having learned these facts of life and death, some readers will still compartmentalize the hazards in order to exclude themselves: "Sure, there's a lot of violence, but that's in the inner city"; "Yeah, a lot of women are battered, but I'm not in a relationship now"; "Violence is a problem for younger people, or older people"; "You're only at risk if you're out late at night"; "People bring it on themselves," and on and on. Americans are experts at denial, a choir whose song could be titled "Things Like That Don't Happen in This Neighborhood."

Denial has an interesting and insidious side effect. For all the peace of mind deniers think they get by saying it isn't so, the fall they take when victimized is far, far greater than that of those who accept the possibility. Denial is a save-now-pay-later scheme, a contract written entirely in small print, for in the long run, the denying person knows the truth on some level, and it causes a constant low-grade anxiety. Millions of people suffer that anxiety, and denial keeps them from taking action that could reduce the risks (and the worry).

If we studied any other creature in nature and found the record of intraspecies violence that human beings have, we would be repulsed by it. We'd view it as a great perversion of natural law — but we wouldn't deny it.

As we stand on the tracks, we can only avoid the oncoming train if we are willing to see it and willing to predict that it won't stop. But instead of improving the technologies of prediction, America improves the technologies of conflict: guns, prisons, SWAT teams, karate classes, pepper spray, stun guns, Tasers, Mace. And now more than ever, we need the most accurate predictions. Just think about how we live: We are searched for weapons before boarding a plane, visiting city hall, seeing a television show taping, or attending a speech by the president. Our government buildings are surrounded by barricades, and we wrestle through so-called tamper-proof packaging to get a couple aspirin. All of this was triggered by the deeds of fewer than ten dangerous men who got our attention by frightening us. What other quorum in American history, save those who wrote our constitution, could claim as much impact on our day-to-day lives? Since fear is so central to our experience, understanding when it is a gift — and when it is a curse — is well worth the effort.

We live in a country where one person with a gun and some nerve can derail our democratic right to choose the leaders of the most powerful nation in history. The guaranteed passport into the world of great goings-on is violence, and the lone assailant with a grandiose idea and a handgun has become an icon of our culture. Yet comparatively little has been done to learn about that person, particularly considering his (and sometimes her) impact on our lives.

We don't need to learn about violence, many feel, because the police will handle it, the criminal-justice system will handle it, experts will handle it. Though it touches us all and belongs to us all, and though we each have something profound to contribute to the solution, we have left this critical inquiry to people who tell us that violence cannot be predicted, that risk is a game of odds, and that anxiety is an unavoidable part of life.

Not one of these conventional "wisdoms" is true.

▪ ▪ ▪

Throughout our lives, each of us will have to make important behavioral predictions on our own, without experts. From the wide list of people who present themselves, we'll choose candidates for inclusion in our lives — as employers, employees, advisers, business associates, friends, lovers, spouses.

Whether it is learned the easy way or the hard way, the truth remains that your safety is yours. It is not the responsibility of the police, the government, industry, the apartment building manager, or the security company. Too often, we take the lazy route and invest our confidence without ever evaluating if it is earned. As we send our children off each morning, we assume the school will keep them safe, but as you'll see in chapter 12, it might not be so. We trust security guards — you know, the employment pool that gave us the Son of Sam killer, the assassin of John Lennon, the Hillside Strangler, and more arsonists and rapists than you have time to read about. Has the security industry earned your confidence? Has government earned it? We have a Department of Justice, but it would be more appropriate to have a department of violence prevention, because that's what we need and that's what we care about. Justice is swell, but safety is survival.

Just as we look to government and experts, we also look to technology for solutions to our problems, but you will see that your personal solution to violence will not come from technology. It will come from an even grander resource that was there all the while, within you. That resource is intuition.

It may be hard to accept its importance, because intuition is usually looked upon by us thoughtful Western beings with contempt. It is often described as emotional, unreasonable, or inexplicable. Husbands chide their wives about "feminine intuition" and don't take it seriously. If intuition is used by a woman to explain some choice she made or a concern she can't let go of, men roll their eyes and write it off. We much prefer logic, the grounded, explainable, unemotional thought process that ends in a supportable conclusion. In fact, Americans worship logic, even when it's wrong, and deny intuition, even when it's right.

Men, of course, have their own version of intuition, not so light and inconsequential, they tell themselves, as that feminine stuff. Theirs is more viscerally named a "gut feeling," but it isn't just a feeling. It is a process more extraordinary and ultimately more logical in the natural order than the most fantastic computer calculation. It is our most complex cognitive process and at the same time the simplest.

Intuition connects us to the natural world and to our nature. Freed from the bonds of judgment, married only to perception, it carries us to predictions we will later marvel at. "Somehow I knew," we will say about the chance meeting we predicted, or about the unexpected phone call from a distant friend, or the unlikely turnaround in someone's behavior, or about the violence we steered clear of, or, too often, the violence we elected not to steer clear of. "Somehow I knew . . ." Like Kelly knew, and you can know.

The husband and wife who make an appointment with me to discuss the harassing and threatening phone calls they are getting want me to figure out who is doing it. Based on what the caller says, it's obvious he is someone they know, but who? Her ex-husband? That weird guy who used to rent a room from them? A neighbor angry about their construction work? The contractor they fired?

The expert will tell them who it is, they think, but actually they will tell me. It's true I have experience with thousands of cases, but they have *the* experience with this one. Inside them, perhaps trapped where I can help find it, is all the information needed to make an accurate evaluation. At some point in our discussion of possible suspects, the woman will invariably say something like this: "You know, there is one other person, and I don't have any concrete reasons for thinking it's him. I just have this feeling, and I hate to even suggest it, but . . ." And right there I could send them home and send my bill, because that is who it will be. We will follow my client's intuition until I have "solved the mystery." I'll be much praised for my skill, but most often, I just listen and give them permission to listen to themselves. Early on in these meetings, I say, "No theory is too remote to explore, no person is beyond consideration, no gut feeling is too unsubstantiated." (In fact, as you are about to find out, every intuition is firmly substantiated.) When clients ask, "Do the people who make these threats ever do such-and-such?" I say, "Yes, sometimes they do," and this is permission to explore some theory.

When interviewing victims of anonymous threats, I don't ask, "Who do you think sent you these threats?" because most victims can't imagine that anyone they know sent the threats. I ask instead, "Who *could* have sent them?" and together we make a list of everyone who had the ability, without regard to motive. Then I ask clients to assign a motive, even a ridiculous one, to each person on the list. It is a creative process that puts them under no pressure to be correct. For this very reason, in almost every case, one of their imaginative theories will be correct.

Quite often, my greatest contribution to solving the mystery is my refusal to call it a mystery. Rather, it is a puzzle, one in which there are enough pieces available to reveal what the image is. I have seen these pieces so often that I may recognize them sooner than some people, but my main job is just to get them on the table.

As we explore the pieces of the human violence puzzle, I'll show you their shapes and their colors. Given your own lifelong study of human behavior — and your own humanness — you'll see that the pieces are already familiar to you. Above all, I hope to leave you knowing that every puzzle can be solved long before all the pieces are in place.

■ ■ ■

People do things, we say, "out of the blue," "all of a sudden," "out of nowhere." These phrases support the popular myth that predicting human behavior isn't possible. Yet to successfully navigate through morning traffic, we make amazingly accurate high-stakes predictions about the behavior of literally thousands of people. We unconsciously read tiny untaught signals: the slight tilt of a stranger's head or the momentarily sustained glance of a person a hundred feet away tells us it is safe to pass in front of his two-ton monster. We expect all the drivers to act just as we would, but we still alertly detect those few who might not — so that we are also predicting their behavior, unpredictable though we may call it. So here we are, traveling along faster than anyone before the 1900s ever traveled (unless they were falling off a cliff), dodging giant, high-momentum steel missiles, judging the intent of their operators with a fantastic accuracy, and then saying we can't predict human behavior.

We predict with some success how a child will react to a warning, how a witness will react to a question, how a jury will react to a witness, how a consumer will react to a slogan, how an audience will react to a scene, how a spouse will react to a comment, how a reader will react to a phrase, and on and on. Predicting violent behavior is easier than any of these, but since we fantasize that human violence is an aberration done by others unlike us, we say we can't predict it. Watching Jane Goodall's documentary showing a group of chimpanzees stalking and killing another group's males, we say the unprovoked attack is territorialism or population control. With similar certainty, we say we understand the cause and purpose of violence by every creature on earth — except ourselves.

The human violence we abhor and fear the most, that which we call "random" and "senseless," is neither. It always has purpose and meaning, to the perpetrator, at least. We may not choose to explore or understand that purpose, but it is there, and as long as we label it "senseless," we'll not make sense of it.

Sometimes a violent act is so frightening that we call the perpetrator a monster, but as you'll see, it is by finding his humanness — his similarity to you and me — that such an act can be predicted. Though you're about to learn new facts and concepts about violent people, you will find most of the information resonating somewhere in your own experience. You will see that even esoteric types of violence have detectable patterns and warning signs. You'll also see that the more mundane types of violence, those we all relate to on some level, such as violence between angry intimates, are as knowable as affection between intimates. (In fact, the violence has fewer varieties than the love.)

A television news show reports on a man who shot and killed his wife at her work. A restraining order had been served on him the same day as his divorce papers, coincidentally also his birthday. The news story tells of the man's threats, of his being fired from his job, of his putting a gun to his wife's head the week before the killing, of his stalking her. Even with all these facts, the reporter ends with: "Officials concede that no one could have predicted this would happen."

That's because we want to believe that people are infinitely complex, with millions of motivations and varieties of behavior. It is not so. We want to believe that with all the possible combinations of human beings and human feelings, predicting violence is as difficult as picking the winning lottery ticket, yet it usually isn't difficult at all. We want to believe that human violence is somehow beyond our understanding, because as long as it remains a mystery, we have no duty to avoid it, explore it, or anticipate it. We need feel no responsibility for failing to read signals if there are none to read. We can tell ourselves that violence just happens without warning, and usually to others, but in service of these comfortable myths, victims suffer and criminals prosper.

The truth is that every thought is preceded by a perception, every impulse is preceded by a thought, every action is preceded by an impulse, and man is not so private a being that his behavior is unseen, his patterns undetectable. Life's highest-stakes questions can be answered: Will a person I am worried about try to harm me? Will the employee I must fire react violently? How should I handle the person who refuses to let go? What is the best way to respond to threats? What are the dangers posed by strangers? How can I know a babysitter won't turn out to be someone who harms my child? How can I know whether some friend of my child might be dangerous? Is my own child displaying the warning signs of future violence? Finally, how can I help my loved ones be safer?

I commit that by the end of this book, you will be better able to answer these questions, and you will find good reason to trust your already keen ability to predict violence.

How can I say all this so confidently? Because I've had four decades of lessons from the most qualified teachers.

When I called and told Kelly I had decided to devote a year to writing this book (it turned out to take two), I also thanked her for what she'd taught me, as I always do with clients. "Oh, I don't think you learned anything new from my case," she said, "but which one *did* teach you the most?"

With many to choose from, I told Kelly I didn't know, but as soon as I'd said good-bye and hung up the phone, I realized I did know. Thinking back, it was as if I was in that room again.

■ ■ ■

A woman was pointing a gun at her husband, who was standing with his hands held out in front of him. She was anxiously changing her grip on the small semiautomatic pistol. "Now I'm going to kill you," she repeated quietly, almost as if to herself. She was an attractive, slender woman of thirty-three, wearing black slacks and a man's white shirt. There were eight bullets in the gun.

I was standing off to the side in a doorway, watching the scene unfold. As I had been before and would be many times again, I was responsible for predicting whether or not a murder would occur, whether or not the woman in this case would keep her promise to kill. The stakes were high, for in addition to the man at risk, there were also two young children in the house.

Threats like hers, I knew, are easy to speak, harder to honor. Like all threats, the words betrayed her by admitting her failure to influence events in any other way, and like all people who threaten, she had to advance or retreat. She might be satisfied with the fear her words and actions caused, might accept the attention she had garnered at gunpoint and leave it at that.

Or, she might pull the trigger.

For this young woman, the forces that inhibit violence and those that might provoke it were rising and falling against each other like stormy waves. She was by turns hostile, then silent. At one moment, violence seemed the obvious choice; at the next, it seemed the last thing she'd ever do. But violence *is* the last thing some people do.

All the while, the pistol stayed steadily pointed at her husband.

Except for the rapid, shallow breaths he was taking, the man in the gun sights didn't move. His hands were held out stiffly in front of him as if they could stop bullets. I remember wondering for a moment if it would hurt to be shot, but another part of my mind jerked me back to the job I'd taken on. I could not miss a detail.

The woman appeared to relax and then she became silent again.

Though some observers might have viewed this as a favorable indicator, I had to assess if her quiet pauses were used for a rallying of reason or a contemplation of murder. I noticed that she was not wearing shoes, but discarded the observation as irrelevant to my task. Details are snapshots, not portraits, and I had to quickly determine which bore on my prediction and which did not. The mess of papers on the floor near an overturned table, the phone knocked off the hook, a broken glass likely thrown when the argument was more innocent — all assessed and quickly discarded.

I then saw a detail of great significance, though it was just a quarter-inch movement. (In these predictions, the gross movements may get our attention, but they are rarely the ones that matter most.) The fraction of an inch her thumb traveled to rest on the hammer of the gun carried the woman further along the path to homicide than anything she had said or could have said. From this new place, she began an angry tirade. A moment later, she pulled the hammer of the pistol back, a not-so-subtle underscoring that earned her new credibility. Her words were chopped and spit across the room, and as her rage escalated, it might have seemed I had to hurry and complete the prediction. In fact, I had plenty of time. That's because the best predictions use all the time available. When effective, the process is completed just behind the line that separates foresight and hindsight, the line between what might happen and what has just happened.

It's like your high-stakes prediction about whether the driver of an advancing car will slow down enough to allow safe passage — a fantastically complex process, but it happens just in time. Though I didn't know it that day, I was automatically applying and reapplying the single most important tool of any prediction: pre-incident indicators.

Pre-incident indicators are those detectable factors that occur before the outcome being predicted. Stepping on the first rung of a ladder is a significant pre-incident indicator to reaching the top; stepping on the sixth even more so. Since everything a person does is created twice — once in the mind and once in its execution — ideas and impulses are pre-incident indicators for action. The woman's threats to kill revealed an idea that was one step toward the outcome;

her introduction of the gun into the argument with her husband was another, as was its purchase some months earlier.

The woman was now backing away from her husband. To someone else, this may have looked like a retreat, but I intuitively knew it was the final pre-incident indicator before the pulling of the trigger. Because guns are not intimate weapons, her desire for some distance from the person she was about to shoot was the element that completed my prediction, and I quickly acted.

I backed quietly down the hall through the kitchen, by the burning and forgotten dinner, into the small bedroom where a young girl was napping. As I crossed the room to wake the child, I heard the gunshot that I had predicted just a moment before. I was startled, but not surprised. The silence that followed, however, did concern me.

My plan had been to take the child out of the house, but I abandoned that and told her to stay in bed. At two years old, she probably didn't understand the seriousness of the situation, but I was ten and knew all about these things.

▪ ▪ ▪

It wasn't the first time I'd heard that gun go off in the house; my mother had accidentally fired it toward me a few months earlier, the bullet passing so close to my ear that I felt it buzz in the air before striking the wall.

On my way back to our living room, I stopped when I smelled the gunpowder around me. I listened, trying to figure out what was happening without going back into that room. It was too quiet.

As I stood straining to hear any tiny sound, there came instead an enormous noise: several more gunshots fired quickly. These I had not predicted. I quickly rounded the corner into the living room.

My stepfather was crouched down on both knees, my mother leaning over him, seemingly offering care. I could see blood on his hands and legs, and when he looked up at me, I tried to reassure him with my calm. I knew he'd never been through anything like this before, but I had.

The gun was on the floor near me, so I leaned over and picked it up by the barrel. It was uncomfortably hot to the touch.

In terms of predicting what was coming next, the scene before me was good news. My initial thought had been to grab the gun and run out the back door, but because of a new prediction, I hid it behind a cushion on the couch. I had concluded that my mother had discharged much of her hostility and frustration along with those gunshots. At least for the moment, she was not only reasonable, but was shifting to the role of supportive wife, nursing her husband's injury as if she'd played no part in it. Far from being someone to be apprehensive about, she was now a person we were grateful to have in charge. She would make sure my stepfather was all right, she would deal with the police and the ambulance, and she would put our lives back in place as surely as if she could draw those bullets back into the gun.

I went to check on my little sister, who was now sitting up expectantly in her bed. Having learned that the time after a major incident offered a period of safety and the best rest, I lay down next to her. I couldn't take a vacation from all predictions, of course, but I lowered the periscope a bit, and after a while we fell asleep.

By the time our family moved from that house a year later, there were nine bullets embedded in the walls and floors. The house is still there. I imagine the bullets are as well.

▪ ▪ ▪

When the U.S. attorney general and the director of the FBI gave me an award for designing MOSAIC™, the assessment system now used for screening threats to justices of the U.S. Supreme Court, I am certain neither realized it was actually invented by a ten-year-old boy, but it was. The way I broke down the individual elements of violence as a child became the way the most sophisticated artificial intuition systems predict violence today. My ghosts had become my teachers.

I am often asked how I got into my work. If viewed in cinematic terms, the answer would cut quickly from scene to scene: running at eleven years old alongside a limousine, clamoring with other fans to get a glimpse of Elizabeth Taylor and Richard Burton, would cut to me inside that limousine working for the famous couple within eight years. Watching President Kennedy's inauguration on television would cut to standing with another president at his inauguration twenty years later, and with another twelve years after that. Watching in shock the reports of Kennedy's murder would cut to working with our government on predicting and preventing such attacks. Watching in shock the reports of Senator Robert Kennedy's murder would cut to developing the assessment system now used to help screen threats to U.S. senators.

Trying unsuccessfully to stop one of my mother's husbands from hitting her would cut to training hundreds of New York City police detectives in new ways to evaluate domestic violence situations. Visiting my mother in a psychiatric ward after one of her suicide attempts would cut to touring mental hospitals as an adviser to the governor of California. Above all, living with fear would cut to helping people manage fear.

My childhood wasn't a movie, of course, though it did have chase sequences, fight scenes, shoot-outs, skyjacking, life-and-death suspense, and suicide. The plot didn't make much sense to me as a boy, but it does now.

It turns out I was attending an academy of sorts, and though hopefully on different subjects, so were you. No matter what your major, you too have been studying people for a long time, carefully developing theories and strategies to predict what they might do.

Even some of my clients will be surprised to learn what you just learned about my earliest training, but those who visit my office are surprised in many ways. It is, after all, a very unusual firm. The clients of Gavin de Becker, Incorporated, are a wide-ranging group: federal government agencies (including the U.S. Marshals Service, the Federal Reserve Board, and the Central Intelligence Agency), prosecutors, battered women's shelters, giant corporations, universities, television stars, television stations, police departments, cities, states, movie studios, cultural figures, religious leaders, champion athletes, politicians, recording artists, movie stars, and college students. Clients include the world's most famous and the world's most anonymous.

People from my office attend presidential inaugurations on one coast, the Oscars and the Emmys on the other. They stroll observantly through crowds of angry protesters one day and are whisked into an underground garage at the federal courthouse the next. We have toured Africa, Europe, Asia, the Middle East, South America, and the South Pacific learning about violence in those places. We have flown in Gulfstream jets and hot-air balloons, paddled down the Amazon, been driven in armored limousines, ridden on elephants and rickshas, been smothered by hostile crowds and smothered by adoring crowds. We have testified before Senate committees and toured secret government installations. We've had staff meetings while floating down a jungle river in the dead of night. We've ridden in presidential motorcades one week and in buses used to transport prisoners the next. We have advised the targets of assassination attempts and the families of those who were assassinated, including the widow of a slain foreign president. We have been chased by tabloid reporters and we have chased them right back. We've been on both sides of the *60 Minutes* cameras, hiding out with their crews for one story about a national fraud, answering Ed Bradley's probing questions on a murder case for another.

We are called by our government when some zealot shoots an abortion doctor or opens fire on federal employees. We are called by Larry King when he needs a guest to discuss whether O. J. Simpson fits the profile of a stalking spousal killer, and we are called by Simpson's prosecutors for the same reason. We visit murder scenes to counsel frightened survivors — sometimes just minutes after the crime. We advise people who have been threatened, and we have ourselves been frequent targets of death threats. As I said, it is an unusual firm, one that could only exist in America and, in most regards, need only exist in America.

What binds all of this together is prediction. My firm predicts human behavior, behavior in one category, mostly: violence. Far more often, we predict safety. We counsel cultural and religious leaders on how to navigate between being hated too much and being loved too much. We advise corporations and government agencies on managing employees who might act out violently. We advise famous people who are the targets of unwanted pursuers, stalkers, and would-be assassins. Most people do not realize that media figures are at the center of a swirl of desperate and often alarming pursuers.

Fewer still realize that the stalking of regular citizens is an epidemic affecting hundreds of thousands every year.

Among all the weird ventures in America, could you ever have imagined a literal warehouse of alarming and unwelcome things that stalkers have sent to the objects of their unwanted pursuit, things like thousand-page death threats, phone book–thick love letters, body parts, dead animals, facsimile bombs, razor blades, and notes written in blood? Would you have imagined that there is a building containing more than 350,000 obsessive and threatening communications? Many of my forty-six associates work in just such a building. There they cast light on the darkest parts of our culture, seeking every day to improve our understanding of hazard, and every day helping people manage fear.

Though fewer than fifty of our twenty thousand cases have been reported in the news, and though most of our work is guardedly nonpublic, we have participated in many of the highest-stakes predictions that individuals and nations ever make. To be the best at this, we have systematized intuition, captured and tamed just a tiny part of its miracle.

You have some of that miracle, and through an exploration of high-stakes predictions — those involving the outcome of violence or death — you'll learn ways to have a safer life. After discussing how intuition works for you and how denial works against you, I'll show that fear, which can be central to your safety, is frequently misplaced. I'll explore the role of threats in our lives and show how you can tell the difference between a real warning and mere words. I'll identify the specific survival signals we get from people who might harm us.

Since the signals are best concealed when an attacker is not known to us, I'll start with the dangers posed by strangers. This is the violence that captures our fear and attention, even though only 20 percent of all homicides are committed by strangers. The other 80 percent are committed by people we know, so I'll focus on those we hire, those we work with, those we fire, those we date, those we marry, those we divorce.

I'll also discuss the tiny but influential minority whose violence affects us all: assassins. Through the story of a man who didn't quite complete his plans to kill a famous person (though he did kill five other people), I'll provide a look at public life you've never seen before.

In chapter 15, you'll see that if your intuition is informed accurately, the danger signal will sound when it should. If you come to trust this fact, you'll not only be safer, but it will be possible to live life nearly free of fear.

■ 2 ■

THE TECHNOLOGY OF INTUITION

> "Technology is not going to save us. Our computers, our tools, our machines are not enough. We have to rely on our intuition, our true being."
>
> — *Joseph Campbell*

"I walked into that convenience store to buy a few magazines and for some reason, I was suddenly . . . afraid, and I turned right around and walked out. I don't know what told me to leave, but later that day I heard about the shooting."

Airline pilot Robert Thompson is telling me about dodging death right here on the ground. I ask him what he saw, what he reacted to.

"Nothing, it was just a gut feeling. [A pause.] Well, now that I think back, the guy behind the counter looked at me with a very rapid glance, just jerked his head toward me for an instant, and I guess I'm used to the clerk sizing you up when you walk in, but he was intently looking at another customer, and that must have seemed odd to me. I must have seen that he was concerned."

When free of judgment, we inherently respect the intuition of others. Sensing that someone else is in that special state of assessing hazard, we are alerted, just as when we see the cat or dog awaken suddenly from a nap and stare intently into a dark hallway.

Thompson continues. "I noticed that the clerk was focused on a customer who was wearing a big, heavy jacket, and of course, I now realize that it was very hot, so that's probably where the guy was hiding the shotgun. Only after I saw on the news what kind of car they were looking for did I remember that there were two men sitting in a station wagon in the parking lot with the engine running. Now it's all clear, but it didn't mean a thing to me at the time."

"Actually, it did then too," I tell him. Combining what amounted to fear on the face of the clerk, with the man in the heavy coat on the hot day, with the men in the car with its engine running, with Thompson's unconscious knowledge of convenience store robberies from years of news reports, with his unconscious memory of frequent police visits to that store, which he'd driven past hundreds of times, and with countless other things we might never discover about Thompson's experience and knowledge, it is no wonder he left that store just moments before a police officer happened in and was shot dead by a man he surprised in the middle of a robbery.

What Robert Thompson and many others want to dismiss as a coincidence or a gut feeling is in fact a cognitive process, faster than we recognize and far different from the familiar step-by-step thinking we rely on so willingly. We think conscious thought is somehow better, when in fact, intuition is soaring flight compared to the plodding of logic. Nature's greatest accomplishment, the human brain, is never more efficient or invested than when its host is at risk. Then, intuition is catapulted to another level entirely, a height at which it can accurately be called graceful, even miraculous. Intuition is the journey from A to Z without stopping at any other letter along the way. It is knowing without knowing why.

At just the moment when our intuition is most basic, people tend to consider it amazing or supernatural. A woman tells a simple story as if it were mystical: "I couldn't believe it! I absolutely knew when the phone rang that it would be my college roommate, calling after all these years." Though people act as if predictions of who is calling are miraculous, they rarely are. In this case, her old roommate was reminded of her by reports of the explosion of the space shuttle. Is it a miracle that both women happened to watch the same news event along with a billion others? Is it a miracle that their strongest association with space travel was the angry belief they shared in college that women would never be astronauts? And a woman astronaut died in the space shuttle explosion that morning, and the two women thought of each other, even after a decade.

These noncritical intuitions, which at first impress us, are often revealed to be somewhat rudimentary, especially in contrast to what the mind delivers when we might be in danger.

In *A Natural History of the Senses,* author Diane Ackerman says, "The brain is a good stagehand. It gets on with its work while we're busy acting out our scenes. When we see an object, the whole peninsula of our senses wakes up to appraise the new sight. All the brain's shopkeepers consider it from their point of view, all the civil servants, all the accountants, all the students, all the farmers, all the mechanics." We could add the soldiers and guards to Ackerman's list, for it is they who evaluate the context in which things occur, the appropriateness and significance of literally everything we sense. These soldiers and guards separate the merely unusual from the significantly unusual. They weigh the time of day, day of the week, loudness of the sound, quickness of the movement, flavor of the scent, smoothness of the surface, the entire mosaic of each moment. They discard the irrelevant and value the meaningful. They recognize the survival signals we don't even (consciously) know are signals.

After years of praising intuition as the cornerstone of safety, I just recently learned to my surprise and appreciation that the root of the word *intuition, tuere,* means "to guard, to protect." That is what it did for Robert Thompson. Shaken by his narrow miss, he later wondered why the police officer did not intuit what he did. It may be that the officer saw different things. Thompson saw only one car in the parking lot, but the officer saw two, likely giving the appearance of a business patronized by a few customers. Though the clerk's face had sent Thompson a fear signal, the police officer probably saw relief in that same face as he entered the store. It is also likely that the seasoned officer suffered the disadvantage that sometimes comes with being expert at something. He was operating with the accurate but (in this case) misleading knowledge that armed robberies are less frequent in the daytime than at night.

Many experts lose the creativity and imagination of the less informed. They are so intimately familiar with known patterns that they may fail to recognize or respect the importance of the new wrinkle. The process of applying expertise is, after all, the editing out of unimportant details in favor of those known to be relevant. Zen master Shunryu Suzuki said, "The mind of the beginner is empty, free of the habits of the expert, ready to accept, to doubt, and open to all the possibilities." People enjoying so-called beginner's luck prove this all the time.

Even men of science rely on intuition, both knowingly and unknowingly. The problem is, we discourage them from doing it. Imagine that you go to see a doctor, a specialist in some particular malady, and before you even sit down in his examining room, he says, "You're fine; please pay my receptionist on the way out." You might understandably feel that the opinion he rendered intuitively was not worth paying for, though it might be the exact same diagnosis you would get after his poking and prodding you with fancy equipment. A friend of mine who is a doctor has to prove his scientific acumen to patients before they'll accept his intuition. "I call it the tap dance. After I do a few steps, patients say, 'Okay, I see you can dance,' and then they believe me."

The amateur at the convenience store teaches us that intuition heeded is far more valuable than simple knowledge. Intuition is a gift we all have, whereas retention of knowledge is a skill. Rare is the expert who combines an informed opinion with a strong respect for his own intuition and curiosity. Curiosity is, after all, the way we answer when intuition whispers, "There's something there." I use it all the time in my work because it can unlock information that clients are hiding from themselves.

Often I will carry a conversation back to details a client provided but then rushed past. I am particularly interested in those that are not required elements of the story, those that might seem unimportant but for the fact that they were mentioned. I call these extra details satellites, shot off into space, later to beam back valuable information. I always follow them.

A client who recounted getting anonymous death threats after a long and contentious lawsuit felt quite certain they were from the man she had sued, but her story included some extra details: "After the case was settled, I knew that the guy we'd sued was still really angry, but I was surprised he would stoop to sending me death threats. I was discussing the settlement one day with Tony — he used to be an intern for my lawyer, but he's not working for my lawyer anymore — anyway, I said to him, 'I hope the case being over really ends the matter,' and I thought it would, but then the threat letters started coming."

What's the satellite in the story? *I was discussing the settlement one day with Tony — he used to be an intern for my lawyer, but he's not working for my lawyer anymore. . . .* These details about a person my client made a remark to are not key elements in the story, but her inclusion of them was a signal for me.

"Tell me about the guy who used to work for your lawyer."

"Oh, Tony? He got fired, one of the many casualties of the case, I guess. He was so sweet to me. He'd taken a real interest in the case, but apparently he'd let other responsibilities slide. Even after he was fired, he kept coming to court to give me support, which I really appreciated. When the case settled, my lawyer threw a party for us all, but Tony wasn't invited. It was sad, because he called me and said, 'I hope we can still stay in touch even though the case is over.' [A pause.] You don't think . . . ?"

My client then described several odd things Tony had done, followed by the revelation (more accurately, the recollection) that Tony had once told her he was helping an acquaintance who was getting threats from an ex-boyfriend. So an extraneous character in a story — a seemingly unimportant detail — became a suspect, and ultimately the proven threatener. On some level, my client knew all along he was the best suspect, but she denied it, preferring to indict her nasty opponent over her friendly ally.

How many times have you said after following one course, "I knew I shouldn't have done that"? That means you got the signal and then didn't follow it. We all know how to respect intuition, though often not our own. For example, people tend to invest all kinds of intuitive ability in dogs, a fact I was reminded of recently when a friend told me this story: "Ginger had a really bad reaction to our new building contractor; she even growled at him. She seemed to sense that he isn't trustworthy, so I'm going to get some bids from other people."

"That must be it," I joked with her. "The dog feels you should get another general contractor because this one's not honest."

"The irony," I explained, "is that it's far more likely Ginger is reacting to your signals than that you are reacting to hers. Ginger is an expert at reading you, and you are the expert at reading other people. Ginger, smart as she is, knows nothing about the ways a contractor might inflate the cost to his own profit, or about whether he is honest, or about the benefits of cost-plus-fifteen-percent versus a fixed bid, or about the somewhat hesitant recommendation you got from a former client of that builder, or about the too-fancy car he arrived in, or about the slick but evasive answer he gave to your pointed question." My friend laughed at the revelation that Ginger, whose intuition she was quick to overrate, is actually a babbling idiot when it comes to remodel work. In fact, Ginger is less than that because she can't even babble. (If there are dogs out there intuitive enough to detect what's being read here by their masters, I take it all back.)

Contrary to what people believe about the intuition of dogs, your intuitive abilities are vastly superior (and given that you add to your experience every day, you are at the top of your form right now). Ginger does sense and react to fear in humans because she knows instinctively that a frightened person (or animal) is more likely to be dangerous, but she has nothing you don't have. The problem, in fact, is that extra something you have that a dog doesn't: It is judgment, and that's what gets in the way of your perception and intuition. With judgment comes the ability to disregard your intuition unless you can explain it logically, the eagerness to judge and convict your feelings rather than honor them. Ginger is not distracted by the way things could be, used to be, or should be. She perceives only what is. Our reliance on the intuition of dogs is often a way to find permission to have an opinion we might otherwise be forced to call (God forbid) unsubstantiated.

Can you imagine an animal reacting to the gift of fear the way some people do, with annoyance and disdain instead of attention? No animal in the wild, suddenly overcome with fear, would spend any of its mental energy thinking, "It's probably nothing." Yet we chide ourselves for even momentarily giving validity to the feeling that someone is behind us on a seemingly empty street, or that someone's unusual behavior might be sinister. Instead of being grateful to have a powerful internal resource, grateful for the self-care, instead of entertaining the possibility that our minds might actually be working for us and not just playing tricks on us, we rush to ridicule the impulse. We, in contrast to every other creature in nature, choose not to explore — and even to ignore — survival signals. The mental energy we use searching for the innocent explanation to everything could more constructively be applied to evaluating the environment for important information.

Every day people engaged in the clever defiance of their own intuition become, in midthought, victims of violence and accidents. So when we wonder why we are victims so often, the answer is clear: It is because we are so good at it.

A woman could offer no greater cooperation to her soon-to-be attacker than to spend her time telling herself, "But he seems like such a nice man." Yet this is exactly what many people do. A woman is waiting for an elevator, and when the doors open she sees a man inside who causes her apprehension. Since she is not usually afraid, it may be the late hour, his size, the way he looks at her, the rate of attacks in the neighborhood, an article she read a year ago — it doesn't matter why. The point is, she gets a feeling of fear. How does she respond to nature's strongest survival signal? She suppresses it, telling herself: "I'm not going to live like that; I'm not going to insult this guy by letting the door close in his face." When the fear doesn't go away, she tells herself not to be so silly, and she gets into the elevator.

Now, which is sillier: waiting a moment for the next elevator, or getting into a soundproofed steel chamber with a stranger she is afraid of?

Even when intuition speaks in the clearest terms, even when the message gets through, we may still seek an outside opinion before we'll listen to ourselves. There is a story about a psychiatrist whose patient reported: "Recently, when my wife goes to bed, I find some excuse to stay downstairs until she's asleep. If she's still awake when I get to our room, I'll stay in the bathroom for a long time so that I'm sure she's asleep by the time I get into bed. Do you think I'm unconsciously trying to avoid having sex with my wife?" The psychiatrist astutely asked, "What was the unconscious part?"

When victims explain to me after the fact that they "unconsciously" knew they were in danger, I could ask the same question: "What was the unconscious part?"

The strange way people evaluate risk sheds some light on why we often choose not to avoid danger. We tend to give our full attention to risks that are beyond our control (air crashes, nuclear-plant disasters) while ignoring those we feel in charge of (dying from smoking, poor diet, car accidents), even though the latter are far more likely to harm us. In *Why the Reckless Survive,* Dr. Melvin Konner's exceptional book about you and me (and all other human beings), he points out that "we drink and drive without our seat belts and light up another cigarette . . . and then cancel the trip to Europe on the one-in-a-million chance of an Arab terrorist attack." Many Americans who wouldn't travel to see the pyramids for fear of being killed in Egypt stay home, where that danger is twenty times greater.

While we knowingly volunteer for some risks, we object to those imposed on us by others. Konner notes that we seem to be saying, "If I want to smoke myself to death, it's my own business, but if some company is trying to put something over on me with asbestos or nerve gas, I'll be furious." We will tolerate familiar risks over strange ones. The hijacking of an American jet in Athens looms larger in our concern than the parent who kills a child, even though one happens rarely, and the other happens daily.

We deny because we're built to see what we want to see. In his book *The Day the Universe Changed,* historian James Burke points out that "it is the brain which sees, not the eye. Reality is in the brain before it is experienced, or else the signals we get from the eye would make no sense." This truth underscores the value of having the pieces of the violence puzzle in our heads before we need them, for only then can we recognize survival signals.

We certainly care enough about this topic to learn the signals: A Harris poll reveals that an overwhelming majority of Americans perceives the greatest risks in the areas of crime and personal safety. If this is true, then we must ask some new questions about violence and about ourselves. For example, is it reasonable that we know more about why a man buys a particular brand of shaving lotion than about why he buys a gun? And why are we fascinated when a famous person is attacked by a stalker, which happens once every two or three years, yet uninterested when a woman is killed by a stalking husband or boyfriend, which happens once every two hours? Why does America have thousands of suicide prevention centers and not one homicide prevention center?

And why do we worship hindsight (as in the news media's constant rehash of the day, the week, the year) and yet distrust foresight, which actually might make a difference in our lives?

One reason is that we don't have to develop our own predictive skills in a world where experts will tell us what to do. Katherine, a young woman of twenty-seven, asks me (the expert) a question nearly all women in our society must consider: "How can I tell if a man I date is turning into a problem? Is there a checklist of warning signs about stalkers?"

Instead of answering her question directly, I ask her to give me an example of what she means.

"Well," she says, "I dated this guy named Bryan, who got sort of obsessed with me and wouldn't let go when I wanted to stop seeing him. We met at a party of a friend of mine, and he must have asked somebody there for my number. Before I even got home, he'd left me three messages. I told him I didn't want to go out with him, but he was so enthusiastic about it that I really didn't have any choice. In the beginning, he was superattentive, always seemed to know what I wanted. It was flattering, but it also made me a little uncomfortable. Like when I mentioned needing more space for my books, he showed up one day with shelves and all the stuff and just put them up. I couldn't say no. And he read so much into whatever I said. Once he asked if I'd go to a basketball game with him, and I said maybe. He later said, 'You promised.' Also, he talked about serious things so early, like living together and marriage and children. He started with jokes about that stuff the first time we went out, and later he wasn't joking. Or when he suggested that I have a phone in my car. I wasn't sure I even wanted a car phone, but he borrowed my car one day and just had one installed. It was a gift, so what could I say? And, of course, he called me whenever I was in the car. And he was so adamant that I never speak to my ex-boyfriend on that car phone. Later he got angry if I spoke to my ex at all. Finally, when I told him I didn't want to be his girlfriend, he refused to hear it. He basically insisted that I stay in a relationship with him, and when I wouldn't, he forced me into a relationship of sorts by always calling, showing up, sending gifts, talking to my friends, coming to my work uninvited. We'd only known each other for about a month, but he acted like it was the most important relationship of his life. So what are the warning signs of that kind of guy?"

Katherine had, of course, answered her own question (more on date stalking in chapter 11). My best advice might not have been satisfying to her: "Listen to yourself." Experts rarely tell us we already know the answers. Just as we want their checklist, they want our check.

Perhaps the greatest experts at day-to-day high-stakes predictions are police officers. Those with experience on the streets have learned about violence and its warning signs, but unchecked denial can eclipse all that knowledge. Police survival expert Michael Cantrell learned this many times in his career.

When Cantrell was in his fourth year as a policeman, his partner, whom I'll call David Patrick, told him about a dream he'd had in which "one of us gets shot."

"Well, you should pay close attention to that dream," Cantrell responded, "because it isn't going to be me."

Patrick brought up the topic again, announcing one day: "I'm sure I will be shot." Cantrell came to believe him, particularly given Patrick's lax officer-survival strategies. On one of their rides together, they'd pulled over a car with three men inside. Though the driver was cordial, Cantrell intuitively felt danger because the other two men just stared straight ahead. He was dismayed that his partner wasn't alert to the possible hazards and seemed more interested in getting a pipe lit as he stood at the side of the patrol car. Cantrell asked the driver to get out of the car, and as the man opened the door, Cantrell saw a handgun on the floor and yelled out "Gun!" to his partner, but Patrick still did not respond attentively.

They survived that hazard, but unable to shake the feeling that his partner's premonition was an accurate prediction, Cantrell eventually discussed it with his supervisor. The sergeant told him he was overreacting. Each of the several times Cantrell asked to discuss it, the sergeant chided him, "Look, in all my time with the department, I've never even drawn my gun, and we haven't had a shooting here for as long as I can remember."

On one of Cantrell's days off, Patrick sat with other officers at the patrol briefing listening to the description of two men who had been involved in several armed robberies. Within a few hours, Patrick (riding alone) observed two men who fit the description discussed in the briefing. One of them stood at a pay phone but didn't appear to be talking to anyone. The other man repeatedly walked over and looked in the window of a supermarket. Patrick had more than enough reason to call for backup but may have been concerned that he'd be embarrassed if it turned out these weren't the wanted criminals. The men saw Patrick and they walked off down the street. He followed alongside in his patrol car. Without calling in any description or request for assistance, he waved the men over. Patrick got out of his car and asked one of them to turn around for a pat-down. Even though Patrick had seen enough to be suspicious, even though he recognized and consciously considered that these might be the two wanted men, he still continued to ignore the survival signals. When he finally registered a signal of great danger from the man next to him, it was much too late to act on. Out of the corner of his eye, Patrick saw the slowly rising handgun that, an instant later, was fired into his face. The man pulled the trigger six times as Patrick fell. The second man produced a gun and shot Patrick once in the back.

After the two criminals ran off, Patrick was able to get to his radio. When the tape of that radio call was played for Cantrell, he could clearly hear blood gurgling in Patrick's mouth as he gasped, "I've been shot. I've been shot."

Amazingly, Patrick recovered and went back to police work for a short while. Still reluctant to take responsibility for his safety or his recklessness, he later told Cantrell, "If you'd been with me, this wouldn't have happened."

Remember that sergeant who accused Cantrell of overreacting? He had decided there was a low level of risk based on just two factors: He had never drawn his gun during his career, and none of the department's officers had been shot in recent memory. If this second factor were a valid predictor, then the shooting of Patrick should have changed the sergeant's evaluation of hazard. Apparently it didn't, because a few months later, he was himself shot in a convenience store.

Cantrell has left law enforcement for the corporate world, but every week he volunteers his time to teach the gift of fear to police officers. People now listen to him when he tells them to listen to themselves.

Aside from outright denial of intuitive signals, there is another way we get into trouble. Our intuition fails when it is loaded with inaccurate information. Since we are the editors of what gets in and what is invested with credibility, it is important to evaluate our sources of information. I explained this during a presentation for hundreds of government threat assessors at the Central Intelligence Agency, making my point by drawing on a very rare safety hazard: kangaroo attacks. I told the audience that about twenty people a year are killed by the normally friendly animals, and that kangaroos always display a specific set of indicators before they attack:

1) They will give what appears to be a wide and genial smile (they are actually showing their teeth).
2) They will check their pouches compulsively several times to be sure they have no young with them (they never attack while carrying young).
3) They will look behind them (since they always retreat immediately after they kill).

After these signals, they will lunge, brutally pummel an enemy, and gallop off.

I asked two audience members to stand up and repeat back the three warning signs, and both flawlessly described the smile, the checking of the pouch for young, and the looking back for an escape route. In fact, everyone in that room (and now you) will remember those warning signs for life. If you are ever face-to-face with a kangaroo, be it tomorrow or decades from now, those three pre-incident indicators will be in your head.

The problem, I told the audience at the CIA, is that I made up those signals. I did it to demonstrate the risks of inaccurate information. I actually know nothing about kangaroo behavior (so forget the three signals if you can — or stay away from hostile kangaroos).

In our lives, we are constantly bombarded with kangaroo signals masquerading as knowledge, and our intuition relies on us to decide what we will give credence to. James Burke says, "You are what you know." He explains that fifteenth-century Europeans *knew* that everything in the sky rotated around the earth. Then Galileo's telescope changed that truth.

Today, Burke notes, we live according to still another truth, and "like the people of the past, we disregard phenomena which do not fit our view because they are 'wrong' or outdated. Like our ancestors, we know the real truth."

When it comes to safety, there is a lot of "real truth" to go around, and some of it puts people at risk. For example, is it always best for a woman being stalked by an ex-husband to get a restraining order? This certainly is the conventional wisdom, yet women are killed every day by men they have court orders against, the often useless documents found by police in the purse or pocket of the victims. (More on this in chapter 10.)

Perhaps the greatest false truth is that some people are just not intuitive, as if this key survival element was somehow left out of them.

Cynthia is a substitute schoolteacher, a funny, beautiful woman totally unlike the dull and much-harassed substitutes most of us recall from our school years. One day while we were having lunch, Cynthia bemoaned to me that she just wasn't intuitive. "I never see the signs until it's too late; I don't have that inner voice some people have."

And yet, I reminded her, several times a week she enters a room full of six- and seven-year-old children she's never met before and quickly makes automatic, unconscious assessments of their future behavior. With amazing accuracy, she predicts who among thirty will seek to test her the most, who will encourage the other children to behave or misbehave, whom the other children will follow, what discipline strategies will work best, and on and on.

"That's true," she said. "Every day I have to predict what the kids will do, and I succeed for reasons I can't explain." After a thoughtful pause she added: "But I can't predict the behavior of adults."

This is interesting, because the range of behavior children might engage in is far, far greater than it is for adults. Few adults will suddenly throw something across the room and then break into uncontrolled laughter. Few women will, without apparent reason, lift their skirts above their heads or reach over to the next desk at work and grab the eyeglasses right off someone's face. Few adults will pour paint on the floor and then smear it around with their feet. Yet each of these behaviors is familiar to substitute teachers.

Predicting the routine behavior of adults in the same culture is so simple, in fact, that we rarely even bother to do it consciously. We react only to the unusual, which is a signal that there might be something worth predicting. The man next to us on the plane for five hours garners little of our attention until, out of the corner of one eye, we see that he is reading the magazine in our hand. The point is that we intuitively evaluate people all the time, quite attentively, but they only get our conscious attention when there is a reason. We see it all, but we edit out most of it. Thus, when something does call out to us, we ought to pay attention. For many people, that is a muscle they don't exercise.

At lunch, I told Cynthia I'd show her an example of listening to intuition. We were at a restaurant neither of us had been to before. The waiter was a slightly too subservient man whom I took to be of Middle-Eastern descent.

I said, "Take our waiter, for example. I've never met him and don't know a thing about him, but I can tell you he's not just the waiter — he's actually the owner of this restaurant. He is from Iran, where his family ran successful restaurants before they moved to America."

Because there was no expectation that I'd be right on any of this, I had simply said what came into my head. I thought I was making it up, creating it. More likely, I was calling it up, discovering it.

Cynthia and I went on talking, but in my head I was tearing apart the theories I had just expressed with such certainty. Across the room I saw a print of an elephant on the wall and thought, "Oh, he's from India, not Iran; that makes sense, because an Iranian would be more assertive than this guy. And he's definitely not the owner."

By the time he next visited our table, I'd concluded that all my predictions were wrong. I reluctantly asked him who owned the restaurant.

"I do."

"Is it your first place?"

"Yes, but my family owned several successful restaurants in Iran. We sold them to come to America." Turning to Cynthia he said, "And you are from Texas." Cynthia, who has no Texas accent whatever, asked how he knew.

"You have Texas eyes."

No matter how I so accurately guessed his status at the restaurant, his country of origin, and his family history, and no matter how he knew Cynthia was from Texas, we did know. But is that methodology something I'd bet my life on? I do it every day, and so do you, and I'd have done no better with conscious logic.

Cynthia also talked about what she called "car body language," her ability to predict the likely movements of cars. "I know when a car is about to edge over into my lane without signaling. I know when a car will or won't turn left in front of me." Most people gladly accept this ability and travel every day with absolute confidence in their car-reading skill. Clearly they are actually expert at reading people, but because we can't see the whole person, we read his intent, level of attentiveness, competence, sobriety, caution, all through the medium of the tiny movements of that big metal object around him.

So, we think: We can predict what kangaroos and children and cars might do, but we cannot predict human behavior to save our lives.

▪ ▪ ▪

China Leonard's story is not about violence. It is, however, about life and death, and about the denial of intuition. She and her young son, Richard, had just settled into the preop room at St. Joseph's Hospital, where Richard was soon to have minor ear surgery. He usually had a barrage of questions for doctors, but when the anesthesiologist, Dr. Joseph Verbrugge Jr., came into the room, the boy fell silent. He didn't even answer when Dr. Verbrugge asked if he was nervous. "Look at me!" the doctor demanded, but Richard didn't respond.

The boy obviously disliked the abrupt and unpleasant doctor, and China felt the same way, but she also felt something more than that. A strong intuitive impulse crossed her mind: "*Cancel the operation,*" it boldly said, "*Cancel the operation.*" She quickly suppressed that impulse and began a mental search for why it was unsound. Setting aside her intuition about Dr. Verbrugge in favor of logic and reason, she assured herself that you can't judge someone by his personality. But again, that impulse: "*Cancel the operation.*" Since China Leonard was not a worrier, it took some effort to silence her inner voice. "Don't be silly," she thought, "St. Joseph's is one of the best hospitals in the state, it's a teaching hospital; it's owned by the Sisters of Charity, for Christ's sake. You just have to assume this doctor is good."

With her intuition successfully beaten down, the operation went forward as scheduled, and Richard died during the minor procedure. It is a sad story that teaches us that the words "I know it" are more valuable than the words "I knew it."

Later, it was revealed that some of Dr. Verbrugge's colleagues had also been concerned about him. They said he was inattentive to his work, and, most seriously, there were at least six occasions when colleagues reported that he appeared to be sleeping during surgeries. For the hospital staff, these were clear signals, but I can't be certain what China and her son detected. Their concern — whatever it was — was justified by the boy's death, and I accept that as good enough.

There were people right at the operating table who heard and then vetoed their intuition. The surgeon told Verbrugge that Richard's breathing was distressed, but Verbrugge did nothing effective. A nurse said she was getting concerned with the boy's distress but "chose to believe" that Verbrugge was competent.

One of the doctors who reviewed how people had performed in that operating room could have been speaking about denial in general when he astutely said: "It's like waking up in your house with a room full of smoke, opening the window to let the smoke out, and then going back to bed."

▪ ▪ ▪

I've seen many times that after the shock of violence has begun to heal, victims will be carried in their minds back to that hallway or parking lot, back to the sights, smells, and sounds, back to the time when they still had choices, before they fell under someone's malevolent control, before they refused the gift of fear. Often they will say about some particular detail, "I realize this now, but I didn't know it then." Of course, if it is in their heads now, so was it then. What they mean is that they only now accept the significance. This has taught me that the intuitive process works, though often not as well as its principal competitor, the denial process.

With denial, the details we need for the best predictions float silently by us like life preservers, and while the man overboard may enjoy the comfortable belief that he is still in his stateroom, there is soon a price to pay for his daydream. I know a lot about this; I spent half my childhood and half my adulthood practicing prediction while perfecting denial.

■ 3 ■

THE ACADEMY OF PREDICTION

"I am capable of what every other human is capable of. This is one of the great lessons of war and life."

— *Maya Angelou*

Before I was thirteen, I saw a man shot, I saw another beaten and kicked to unconsciousness, I saw a friend struck near lethally in the face and head with a steel rod, I saw my mother become a heroin addict, I saw my sister beaten, and I was myself a veteran of beatings that had been going on for more than half my life. The stakes of my predictions back then were just as high as they are today — life and death — and I viewed it as my responsibility to be sure we all got through those years alive. We didn't, and for a long while I viewed that as my responsibility too, but my point in telling you all this is not about me; it is about you. It is about you because, though triggered by different occurrences, you felt the exact same emotions that I felt. While some were painful and some were frightening, no experience of mine had any more impact on me than those of yours that had the greatest impact on you.

People sometimes say they cannot imagine what a given experience must have been like, but you can imagine every human feeling, and as you'll see, it is that ability that makes you an expert at predicting what others will do.

You want to know how to spot violently inclined people, how to be safe in the presence of danger. Well, since you know all about human beings, this expedition begins and ends in familiar territory. You have been attending your academy for years, and to pick up your diploma in predicting violence, there is just one truth you must accept: that there is no mystery of human behavior that cannot be solved inside your head or your heart.

Nicholas Humphrey of Cambridge University explains that evolution gave us introspection specifically so we could "model other human beings and therefore predict their behavior." To succeed at this, we have to be what Humphrey calls "natural psychologists." We have to know, he says, "what it's like to be human."

Way back when she was still anonymous, I assisted a young prosecutor named Marcia Clark on her brilliant prosecution of assassin Robert Bardo. Bardo had killed actress Rebecca Schaeffer, and Clark sent him to prison for life. When I interviewed him there, his relative normalcy took me out of the safe realm of *US* and *THEM* — experts and assassins — and into the world of our shared humanness. It may be unwelcome news, but you and I and Bardo have much more in common than we have in contrast.

Distinguished psychiatrist Karl Menninger has said, "I don't believe in such a thing as the criminal mind. Everyone's mind is criminal; we're all capable of criminal fantasies and thoughts." Two of history's great minds, Albert Einstein and Sigmund Freud, went even further. In an extraordinary correspondence, they explored the topic of human violence. Einstein's letter concluded that "man has in him the need to hate and destroy."

In his reply, Freud agreed "unreservedly," adding that human instincts could be divided into two categories: "those which seek to preserve and unite, and those which seek to destroy and kill." He wrote that the phenomenon of life evolves from their "acting together and against each other."

Proving the opinions of Einstein and Freud is the fact that violence and homicide occur in all cultures. In their book on the origins of violence, *Demonic Males,* Richard Wrangham and Dale Peterson say that modern humans are "the dazed survivors of a continuous, 5-million-year habit of lethal aggression." Those scientific explorers who set out to find communities that would disprove man's universal violence all came home disappointed. South Pacific islanders were incorrectly romanticized as nonviolent in Margaret Mead's *Coming of*

Age in Samoa. The Fijians, correctly perceived today as the friendliest people in the world, were not that long ago among humanity's most violent. The !Kung of the Kalahari were called "the harmless people" in a book by the same title, but Melvin Konner, whose search for the answers took him more than once to study hunter-gatherers in Africa, concluded that "again and again, ethnographers have discovered Eden in the outback, only to have the discovery foiled by better data."

Though we live in space-age times, we still have stone-age minds. We are competitive and territorial and violent, just like our simian ancestors. There are people who insist this isn't so, who insist that they could never kill anyone, but they invariably add a telling caveat: "Unless, of course, a person tried to harm someone I love." So the resource of violence is in everyone; all that changes is our view of the justification.

Studying and interviewing those who use violence to reach their goals, I long ago learned that I must find in them some part of myself, and, more disturbingly at times, find in myself some part of them. There must be a place to hook the line before I drop down into the dark mine of some dark mind; there must be something familiar to hold on to.

A man kills a cow with an ax, cuts open the carcass, and then climbs inside to see what it feels like; later he uses the ax to kill his eight-year-old stepbrother. Another man murders his parents by shooting out their eyes with a shotgun. We use the word *inhuman* to describe these murderers, but I know them both, and they are not inhuman — they are precisely human. I know many other people like them; I know their parents and the parents of their victims. Their violent acts were repugnant, to be sure, but not inhuman.

When a bank robber shoots a security guard, we all understand why, but with aberrant killers, people resist the concept of a shared humanness. That's because *US* and *THEM* is far more comfortable. In my work I don't have that luxury. The stakes of some predictions require that I intimately recognize and accept what I observe in others no matter who they are, no matter what they have done, no matter what they might do, no matter where it takes me in myself. There may be a time in your life when you too won't have the luxury of saying you don't recognize someone's sinister intent. Your survival may depend on your recognizing it.

Though anthropologists have long focused on the distinctions between people, it is recognizing the sameness that allows us to most accurately predict violence. Of course, accepting someone's humanness does not mean excusing his behavior. This lesson is probably starkest when you spend time with the world's most violent and dangerous people, the ones you might call monsters, the ones who committed acts you might think you couldn't have imagined. Many of them are locked up at Atascadero State Hospital in California. I founded and fund a program there called Patient Pets, which allows patients to care for small animals. Many of these men will be locked up for life without visitors, and a mouse or bird might be all they have.

I recall the way the patients reacted to the death of a particular guinea pig who had been one of the first pets in the program. When they noticed the old animal was sick, they wanted to find a way to keep her from dying, though most knew that wasn't possible. The program's coordinator, Jayne Middlebrook, sent me this report:

> One patient, Oliver, made it his job to be sure the ailing animal had everything she needed. Oliver asked to keep her in his room, "so she won't be alone at night, just in case she decides to die then." Eventually, the old guinea pig was unable to move and her breathing was labored. Oliver gathered several patients in my office, and the guinea pig died in his arms, surrounded by an unlikely group of mourners. There was not a dry eye in the ward as the patients said their good-byes and silently left the office.
>
> I have often shared with you the effects these events have on the patients, some of whom, moved by the death of one of the animals, cried for the first time about the harms they had committed on others. Now I want to share some of my own feelings. As I sat in my office watching the patients, all felons, many guilty of brutal crimes, most lost in a variety of addictions (you choose), mental illness (pick one), and regarded as the bottom of the barrel, I saw a glimmer of compassion, a bit of emotion, and

> the glimpse of humanity that society believes these men lack (and in most situations, they do). It is true that the majority of these men are exactly where they belong; to unleash them on society would be unthinkable, but we cannot disregard their humanness, because if we do, I believe, we become less human in the process.

So, even in a gathering of aberrant murderers there is something of you and me. When we accept this, we are more likely to recognize the rapist who tries to con his way into our home, the child molester who applies to be a baby-sitter, the spousal killer at the office, the assassin in the crowd. When we accept that violence is committed by people who look and act like people, we silence the voice of denial, the voice that whispers, "This guy doesn't look like a killer."

Our judgment may classify a person as either harmless or sinister, but survival is better served by our perception. Judgment results in a label, like calling Robert Bardo a monster and leaving it at that. Such labels allow people to comfortably think it's all figured out. The labels also draw a bold line between that "wacko" and us, but perception carries you much further.

Scientists, after all, do not observe a bird that destroys its own eggs and say, "Well, that never happens; this is just a monster." Rather, they correctly conclude that if this bird did it, others might, and that there must be some purpose in nature, some cause, some predictability.

▪ ▪ ▪

People who commit terrible violences choose their acts from among many options. I don't have to provide a list of horrors to demonstrate this — you can find the proof in your own mind. Imagine what you believe is the worst thing anyone might ever do to another human being; imagine something worse than anything you've ever seen in a movie, or read about or heard about. Imagine something *original.* Pause in your reading and conjure this awful thing.

Now, by virtue of the fact that you could conceive it, rest assured it has likely been done to someone, because everything that can be done by a human being to another human being has been done. Acts of extraordinary horror and violence happen, and we cannot learn why they happen by looking at rare behavior as if it is something outside ourselves. That idea you just conjured was in you, and thus it is part of us. To really work toward prediction and prevention, we must accept that these acts are done by people included in the "we" of humanity, not by interlopers who somehow sneaked in.

One evening a few years ago, legendary FBI behavioral scientist Robert Ressler, the man who coined the term "serial killer," visited my home for dinner. (Ressler wrote the book *Whoever Fights Monsters . . .*, the title of which comes from a Nietzsche quote I have often considered: "Whoever fights monsters should see to it that in the process he does not become a monster. For when you look long into an abyss, the abyss also looks into you.") Having just read an advance copy of *The Silence of the Lambs,* I was discussing its fictional (I thought) character who killed young women to harvest their skin for a "woman suit." Ressler matter-of-factly responded, "Oh, the Ed Gein case," and he described the man who stole corpses from cemeteries, skinned them, and cured the skin in order to wear it. Ressler knew that nothing human is foreign. He had learned enough about so-called monsters to know that you don't find them in gothic dungeons or humid forests. You find them at the mall, at the school, in the town or city with the rest of us.

But how do you find them before they victimize someone? With animals, it depends on perspective: The kitten is a monster to the bird, and the bird is a monster to the worm. With man, it is likewise a matter of perspective, but more complicated, because the rapist might first be the charming stranger, the assassin first the admiring fan. The human predator, unlike the others, does not wear a costume so different from ours that he can always be recognized by the naked eye.

The blind eye, of course, will never recognize him, which is why I devote this chapter and the next to removing the blinders, to revealing the truths and the myths about the disguises someone might use to victimize you.

I'll start with a hackneyed myth you'll recognize from plenty of TV news reports: "Residents here describe the killer as a shy man who kept to himself. They say he was a quiet and cordial neighbor."

Aren't you tired of this? A more accurate and honest way for TV news to interpret the banal interviews they conduct with neighbors would be to report, "Neighbors didn't know anything relevant." Instead, news reporters present noninformation as if it is information. They might as well say (and sometimes do), "The tollbooth operator who'd taken his quarters for years described the killer as quiet and normal." By the frequency of this cliché, you could almost believe that apparent normalcy is a pre-incident indicator for aberrant crime. It isn't.

One thing that does predict violent criminality is violence in one's childhood. For example, Ressler's research confirmed an astonishingly consistent statistic about serial killers: 100 percent had been abused as children, either with violence, neglect, or humiliation.

You wouldn't think so by the TV news reports on the early family life of one accused serial killer, Ted Kaczynski, believed to be the Unabomber. They told us that his mother was "a nice woman, well-liked by neighbors," as if that has any bearing on anything. Neighbors usually have only one qualification for being in news reports: They are willing to speak to reporters. Don't you think something more than the neighbors knew about might have gone on in that home when Ted and his brother, David, were children?

Just look at a few facts about the family: The Kaczynskis raised two boys, both of whom dropped out of society as adults and lived antisocial, isolated lives. One of them lived for a time in a ditch he dug in the ground — and that was the *sane* one, David, who didn't end up killing anybody. If prosecutors are right, then the "crazy" one, Ted, grew up to become a brutal remote-control serial killer. Yet neighbors tell reporters that they saw nothing unusual, and reporters tell us the family was normal, and the myth that violence comes out of nowhere is perpetuated.

I don't mean here to indict all parents who raise violent children, for there are cases in which awful acts are committed by people with organic mental disorders, those the National Alliance of Mental Illness correctly terms "No-fault Diseases." (It is also true that many people with mental illnesses were abused as children.) Genetic predispositions may also play some role in violence, but whatever cards are dealt to a family, parents have at a minimum what Daniel Goleman, author of *Emotional Intelligence,* calls "a window of opportunity."

That window was slammed shut during the childhoods of most violent people. To understand who these mistreated children become, we must start where they started: as regular people. One of them grew up to rape Kelly and kill another woman, one of them murdered Rebecca Schaeffer, one of them killed a police officer just after Robert Thompson left that convenience store, and one of them wrote the book you are reading. Difficult childhoods excuse nothing, but they explain many things — just as your childhood does. Thinking about that introspectively is the best way to sharpen your ability to predict what others will do. Ask and answer why you do what you do.

■ ■ ■

When assassin Robert Bardo told me he was treated at home like the family cat, fed and left in his room, it occurred to me to ask him to compare his childhood with his current life in prison.

Bardo: It's the same in the sense that I'm always withdrawing within myself in my cell, just like back at home.
GdeB: Are there any differences between what you do here and what you did when you were a child?
Bardo: Well, I have to be more social here.
GdeB: Didn't you have any requirement at home to be social?
Bardo: No, I learned that in prison.

As long as there are parents preparing children for little more than incarceration, we'll have no trouble keeping our prisons full. While society foots the bill, it is individual victims of crime who pay the highest price.

In studying Bardo's childhood of abuse and neglect, I could not ignore the similarity of some of our early experiences. I was also struck by the extraordinary intersection of our adult experiences, both drawn as we were to opposite sides of assassination.

The revelation reminded me of Stacey J., a would-be assassin I know well. For years, my office has prevented him from successfully encountering the client of mine with whom he is obsessed. I came to know his family through the many times I had to call and ask them to fly to Los Angeles and take him home, or the times they called our office to warn that Stacey was on his way to see my client, or that he had stolen a car, or was missing from a mental hospital. Once, I found him slumped in a phone booth, clothes torn, bleeding from a wound on each leg, wounds all over his face, and completely crazy from a week off medication. On the way to the emergency room, he described the origins of his interest in assassination: "When John Kennedy was killed, that's when I knew; that's when it all started." Stacey and I had both been profoundly affected by the same event, each of us sitting at ten years old in front of a television at the exact same moment in time. In part because of what we saw back then, we now found ourselves together, one of us stalking a public figure, the other protecting a public figure.

In the fifteen years my office has monitored his behavior, Stacey has mellowed some, but from time to time he still requires our attention or the attention of the Secret Service (for threats he has made to kill Ronald Reagan). When I see him, some years doing well, other years doing terribly, overweight and damaged by the side-effects of medication, I think of him at ten, and I wonder about the paths of people's lives.

▪ ▪ ▪

Though I did not end up a violent man myself, I did become a kind of ambassador between the two worlds, fluent in both languages. I'm able to tell you something about how many criminals think because it's similar to how I thought during much of my life. For example, because my childhood became all about prediction, I learned to live in the future. I didn't feel things in the present because I wanted to be a moving target, gone to the future before any blow could really be felt. This ability to live in tomorrow or next year immunized me against the pain and hopelessness of the worst moments, but it also made me reckless about my own safety. Recklessness and bravado are features of many violent people. Some might call it daring or bravery, but as you'll see in the chapter about assassins, "heroism" has two sides.

As a child, I was left with the pastimes that cross time: worrying and predicting. I could see a vision of the future better than most people because the present did not distract me. This single-mindedness is another characteristic common to many criminals. Even things that would frighten most people could not distract me as a boy, for I had become so familiar with danger that it no longer caused alarm. Just as a surgeon loses his aversion to gore, so does the violent criminal. You can spot this feature in people who do not react as you might to shocking things. When everyone else who just witnessed a hostile argument is shaken up, for example, this person is calm.

Another characteristic common to predatory criminals (and many other people as well) is their perceived need to be in control. Think of someone you know whom you might call a control freak. That person, like most violent people, grew up in a chaotic, violent, or addictive home. At a minimum, it was a home where parents did not act consistently and reliably, a place where love was uncertain or conditional. For him or her, controlling others became the only certain way to predict their behavior. People can be very motivated to become control experts because an inability to predict behavior is absolutely intolerable for human beings and every other social animal. (The fact that most people act predictably is literally what holds human societies together.)

In sharing these few features, I do not mean to say that all men who are reckless or brave, who are calm when others are alarmed, and who seek to be in control are likely to be violent; these are simply three small pieces of the human violence puzzle to more fully inform your intuition.

Another is that murderers are not as different from us as we'd like to think. I'll protect the anonymity of the friend who told me about an experience she had in her twenties. She was so angry at an ex-boyfriend that she fantasized about killing him, though she knew she'd never really do anything like that. As she was driving to work one morning, an amazing coincidence occurred: Her ex-boyfriend was crossing the street directly in the path of her car. His being there seemed like a signal, and as her anger welled up, this woman pushed the accelerator to the floor. The car was going about fifty miles an hour when it struck him, but having moved enough at the last moment to save his life, he was hit in the leg only. Were it not for the loudness of her car, this woman would be marked today as a common killer. Instead, she is among the world's most famous and admired people, someone you know of whom you certainly wouldn't have pegged as being like a murderer.

You probably know more people who've tried to kill someone than you realize, as I learned again when Mark Wynn told me a story about his violent (now former) stepfather: "My brother and I decided we'd had enough, but we didn't have a gun to shoot him with and we knew we couldn't stab him. We had seen a TV commercial for Black Flag bug spray, and since it was lethal, we found our father's wine bottle on the nightstand and filled it with the bug spray. Later, he came into the living room with the bottle and started kicking it back. He didn't realize he was drinking poison and he finished every drop. Then we just waited for him to roll over on the floor and die."

What makes Mark Wynn's story doubly interesting is that he is Sergeant Mark Wynn, a founder of Nashville's Domestic Violence Division, considered the most innovative in the nation. Solely because his stepfather survived, Mark is not a murderer, and though he attended "crime school," as he puts it, he did not grow up to be a criminal. (More on why some do and why others do not in chapter 12.)

I assure you, you've sat next to someone sometime whose history, if you knew it, would amaze you. He might even have committed the kind of crime we see on the TV news, the kind of act about which we ask, "Who could do such a thing?" Well, now you know . . . anyone could do it.

■ ■ ■

Though our experiences as children will affect much of what we do, a violent history does not ensure a violent future. There is a story about playwright David Mamet, a pure genius of human behavior: When told about the complaints of two famous cast members in one of his plays, he joked: "If they didn't want to be stars, they shouldn't have had those awful childhoods."

It is not an original revelation that some who have weathered great challenges when they were young created great things as adults. From artists to scientists, even to President Clinton (who, when he was a small boy, was shot at by his stepfather), people with secret childhoods can make the most public contributions. The boy who suffers violence and sees preventable death might grow up to help people avoid violence and preventable deaths. The boy whose father is killed by robbers might grow up to be a Secret Service agent protecting the president (father). The girl whose mother dies of Alzheimer's might become a world-famous neurologist. The boy who escapes chaos by going into his imagination might grow up to enrich millions of filmgoers with that same imagination. These people are in their jobs for more than the paychecks. There are reasons we all do what we do, and those reasons are sometimes displayed.

Unfortunately, many children of violence will contribute something else to our nation: more violence — against their children, against their wives, against you or me, and that's why the topics of childhood and our shared humanness appear in a book written to help you be safer.

When you can find no other common ground to aid in your predictions, remember that the vast majority of violent people started as you did, felt what you felt, wanted what you wanted. The difference is in the lessons they learned. It saddens me to know that as I write these words and as you read them, some child is being taught that violence has a place, learning that when it comes to cruelty, it is better to give than to receive.

Had it not been for the reminders in my work, I might have cared about none of this, but I've met too many people who were brutalized as children and gave it back to society tenfold. They may have grown up looking like everyone else, but they send subtle signals that can reveal their intent.

■ 4 ■

SURVIVAL SIGNALS

"People should learn to see and so avoid all danger.
Just as a wise man keeps away from mad dogs,
so one should not make friends with evil men."
— *Buddha*

Kelly had been apprehensive from the moment she heard the stranger's voice, and now she wants me to tell her why. More than anything else, it was just the fact that someone was there, because having heard no doors open before the man appeared, Kelly knew (at least intuitively) that he must have been waiting out of sight near the entry hall. Only as we spoke did she realize that when he said he was going to the fourth floor, he didn't offer why. It was Kelly who had filled in the blanks, concluding that he was visiting the Klines, who lived across the hall from her. Now, as we are talking, she realizes that if the Klines had admitted a guest over the intercom, she'd have heard the loud buzz of the electric lock being released, and Mrs. Kline would have been at the top of the stairs, already well into a high-volume conversation with her visitor. It was because of all this that Kelly's intuition sent her the signal to be wary.

Kelly tells me that she didn't listen to herself because there wasn't anything she saw in the man's behavior to explain the alarm she felt. Just as some things must be seen to be believed, some must be believed to be seen. The stranger's behavior didn't match Kelly's image of a rapist's behavior, and she could not consciously recognize what she didn't recognize. Neither can you, so one way to reduce risk is to learn what risk looks like.

The capable face-to-face criminal is an expert at keeping his victim from seeing survival signals, but the very methods he uses to conceal them can reveal them.

FORCED TEAMING

Kelly asks me what signals her attacker displayed, and I start with the one I call "forced teaming." It was shown through his use of the word "we" ("We've got a hungry cat up there"). Forced teaming is an effective way to establish premature trust because a *we're-in-the-same-boat* attitude is hard to rebuff without feeling rude. Sharing a predicament, like being stuck in a stalled elevator or arriving simultaneously at a just-closed store, will understandably move people around social boundaries. But forced teaming is not about coincidence; it is intentional and directed, and it is one of the most sophisticated manipulations. The detectable signal of forced teaming is the projection of a shared purpose or experience where none exists: "Both of us"; "We're some team"; "How are we going to handle this?"; "Now we've done it," etc.

David Mamet's film *House of Games* is a wonderful exploration of cons and con artists that shows forced teaming at work. A young soldier enters a Western Union office late one evening; he is anxious about whether the money he needs for a bus ticket will arrive there before Western Union closes. Another man is there, apparently in the same predicament. The two commiserate while waiting, and then the man tells the soldier, "Hey, if my money comes in first, I'll give you whatever amount you need. You can send it to me when you get back to the base." The soldier is moved by this kindness, but the stranger brushes it off, saying, "You'd do the same for me."

In fact, the stranger is *not* in the same boat, is not expecting any money to be wired. He is a con artist. Predictably, the soldier's money is the only to arrive, and when the Western Union office closes, he insists that the stranger accept some of his cash. The best cons make the victim want to participate.

Kelly did not consciously recognize what her intuition clearly knew, so she couldn't apply the simple defense for forced teaming, which is to make a clear refusal to accept the concept of partnership: "I did not ask for your help and I do not want it." Like many of the best defenses, this one has the cost of appearing rude. Kelly now knows it is a small cost, comparatively speaking.

Safety is the preeminent concern of all creatures and it clearly justifies a seemingly abrupt and rejecting response from time to time. Anyway, rudeness is relative. If while waiting in some line, a person steps on our foot a second time, and we bark, "Hey!" we don't call our response rude. We might even feel we showed restraint. That's because the appropriateness of our response is relative to the behavior that provoked it. If people would view forced teaming as the inappropriate behavior it is, we might feel less concern about appearing rude in response.

Forced teaming is done in many contexts for many reasons, but when applied by a stranger to a woman in a vulnerable situation (such as alone in a remote or unpopulated area), it is always inappropriate. It is not about partnership or coincidence — it is about establishing rapport, and that may or may not be all right, depending on *why* someone seeks rapport.

Generally speaking, rapport building has a far better reputation than it deserves. It is perceived as admirable when in fact it is almost always done for self-serving reasons. Even though the reasons most people seek rapport aren't sinister, such as pleasantly conversing with someone you've just met at a party, that doesn't mean a woman must participate with every stranger who approaches her. Perhaps the most admirable reason to seek rapport would be to put someone at ease, but if that is a stranger's entire intent, a far simpler way is to just leave the woman alone.

CHARM AND NICENESS

Charm is another overrated ability. Note that I called it an ability, not an inherent feature of one's personality. Charm is almost always a directed instrument, which, like rapport building, has motive. To charm is to compel, to control by allure or attraction. Think of charm as a verb, not a trait. If you consciously tell yourself, "This person is trying to charm me," as opposed to "This person is charming," you'll be able to see around it. Most often, when you see what's behind charm, it won't be sinister, but other times you'll be glad you looked.

So many signals, I tell Kelly, are in the face. She intuitively read the face of her attacker, as she is now reading mine, as I am now reading hers. University of California at San Francisco psychologist Paul Eckman says, "The face tells us subtleties in feelings that only a poet can put into words." One way to charm is with the smile, which Eckman calls the most important signal of intent. He adds that it is also "the typical disguise used to mask the emotions."

University of California at Los Angeles psychiatrist Leslie Brothers says, "If I am trying to deceive someone, that person has to be just a bit smarter than I am in order to see through my deceit. That means you have sort of an arms race."

The predatory criminal does all he can to make that arms race look like détente. "He was so nice" is a comment I often hear from people describing the man who, moments or months after his niceness, attacked them. We must learn and then teach our children that niceness does not equal goodness. Niceness is a decision, a strategy of social interaction; it is not a character trait. People seeking to control others almost always present the image of a nice person in the beginning. Like rapport building, charm, and the deceptive smile, unsolicited niceness often has a discoverable motive.

Kelly nods and reminds me that her attacker was "very nice." I tell her about a rhyme by Edward Gorey, the master of dark humor:

The proctor buys a pupil ices
And hopes the boy will not resist,
When he attempts to practice vices
Few people even know exist.

Yes, the proctor is nice enough to buy some sweets for the boy, and he is nice in lots of other ways, but that is not a credential of his good intent.

Way back in 1859, in a book called *Self Help* (which pioneered a new genre), Samuel Smiles said personality itself is "plainly a vehicle for self-advancement." He wrote that "men whose acts are at direct variance with their words command no respect, and what they say has but little weight." Unfortunately, this isn't as true in our time. Unlike when people lived in small communities and could not escape their past behavior, we live in an age of anonymous onetime encounters, and many people have become expert at the art of fast persuasion. Trust, formerly earned through actions, is now purchased with sleight of hand, and sleight of words.

I encourage women to explicitly rebuff unwanted approaches, but I know it is difficult to do. Just as rapport building has a good reputation, explicitness applied by women in this culture has a terrible reputation. A woman who is clear and precise is viewed as cold, or a bitch, or both. A woman is expected, first and foremost, to respond to every communication from a man. And the response is expected to be one of willingness and attentiveness. It is considered attractive if she is a bit uncertain (the opposite of explicit). Women are expected to be warm and open, and in the context of approaches from male strangers, warmth lengthens the encounter, raises his expectations, increases his investment, and, at best, wastes time. At worst, it serves the man who has sinister intent by providing much of the information he will need to evaluate and then control his prospective victim.

TOO MANY DETAILS

People who want to deceive you, I explain to Kelly, will often use a simple technique that has a simple name: too many details. The man's use of the story about the cat he left unfed in a friend's apartment: too many details. His reference to leaving the door open, "like ladies do in old movies": too many details. His volunteering that he is always late ("broken watch, not my fault"): too many details.

When people are telling the truth, they don't feel doubted, so they don't feel the need for additional support in the form of details. When people lie, however, even if what they say sounds credible to you, *it doesn't sound credible to them,* so they keep talking.

Each detail may be only a small tack he throws on the road, but together they can stop a truck. The defense is to remain consciously aware of the context in which details are offered.

Context is always apparent at the start of an interaction and usually apparent at the end of one, but too many details can make us lose sight of it. Imagine gazing out the window of a train as it pulls away from the station. Details move by you, or you by them, slowly at first. As the train gets going a little faster, you see more details, but each one more briefly: an empty playground, a phrase painted in graffiti, some kids playing in the street, a construction site, the steeple of a church, until the train reaches a speed that requires you to let the individual components become . . . a neighborhood. This same transition can occur as a conversation becomes . . . a robbery. Every type of con relies upon distracting us from the obvious.

Kelly had so many details thrown at her that she lost sight of this simple context: The man was an absolute stranger. Whenever the train got going fast enough that she was uncomfortable, whenever she might have seen what was happening, like his taking the shopping bag from her hand even though she said no, he slowed the train down with some new irrelevance. He used catchy details to come to be perceived as someone familiar to her, someone she could trust. But she knew him artificially; she knew the con, not the con man.

The person who recognizes the strategy of Too Many Details sees the forest while simultaneously being able to see the few trees that really matter. When approached by a stranger while walking on some city street at night, no matter how engaging he might be, you must never lose sight of the context: He is a stranger who approached you. A good exercise is to occasionally remind yourself of where you are and what your relationship is to the people around you. With a date who stays beyond his welcome, for example, no matter how jokey or charming he may be, a woman can keep herself focused on context simply by thinking, "I have asked him to leave twice." The defense for too many details is simple: Bring the context into conscious thought.

TYPECASTING

Another strategy used by Kelly's rapist is called typecasting. A man labels a woman in some slightly critical way, hoping she'll feel compelled to prove that his opinion is not accurate. "You're probably too snobbish to talk to the likes of me," a man might say, and the woman will cast off the mantle of "snob" by talking to him. A man tells a woman, "You don't look like someone who reads the newspaper," and she sets out to prove that she is intelligent and well-informed. When Kelly refused her attacker's assistance, he said, "*There's such thing as being too proud, you know,*" and she resisted the label by accepting his help.

Typecasting always involves a slight insult, and usually one that is easy to refute. But since it is the response itself that the typecaster seeks, the defense is silence, acting as if the words weren't even spoken. If you engage, you can win the point, but you might lose something greater. Not that it matters what some stranger thinks anyway, but the typecaster doesn't even believe what he says is true. He just believes that it will work.

LOAN SHARKING

The next signal I explain to Kelly is one I call loan sharking: "He wanted to be allowed to help you because that would place you in his debt, and the fact that you owe a person something makes it hard to ask him to leave you alone." The more traditional loan shark gladly lends one amount but cruelly collects much more. Likewise, the predatory criminal generously offers assistance but is always calculating the debt. The defense is to bring two rarely remembered facts into consciousness: He approached me, and I didn't ask for any help. Then, though a person may turn out to be just a kindly stranger, watch for other signals.

We are all familiar with the stranger who offers to help a woman with her groceries; most often he is a fairly unsophisticated loan shark looking to pick someone up. The debt he records in his ledger can usually be paid off quite easily, just a little talk will do it. But he has something in common with the predatory criminal who imposes his counterfeit charity into someone's life: motive. There is no spiritually minded movement dedicated to lightening the burden of American women by carrying their groceries. At its best, loan sharking is a strategy on a par with asking a woman, "Do you come here often?" At its worst, it exploits a victim's sense of obligation and fairness.

I haven't focused here on the criminal who simply walks up, displays a weapon, and demands money. That's because he is distinctly more obvious than those who use the strategies I've described.

It's important to clarify that forced teaming, too many details, charm, niceness, typecasting, and loan sharking are all in daily use by people who have no sinister intent. You might have already recognized several of these strategies as those commonly used by men who want little more than an opportunity to engage a woman in conversation. I don't mean to cramp the style of some crude Casanova, but times have changed, and we men can surely develop some approaches that are not steeped in deceit and manipulation.

THE UNSOLICITED PROMISE

For the next signal, I ask Kelly to go back to that moment when she was reluctant to let her attacker into her apartment. He had said, "I'll just put this stuff down and go. *I promise.*"

The unsolicited promise is one of the most reliable signals because it is nearly always of questionable motive. Promises are used to convince us of an intention, but they are not guarantees. A guarantee is a promise that offers some compensation if the speaker fails to deliver; he commits to make it all right again if things don't go as he says they would. But promises offer no such collateral. They are the very hollowest instruments of speech, showing nothing more than the speaker's desire to convince you of something. So, aside from meeting all unsolicited promises with skepticism (whether or not they are about safety), it's useful to ask yourself: Why does this person need to convince me? The answer, it turns out, is not about him — it is about you. The reason a person promises something, the reason he needs to convince you, is that he can see that you are not convinced. You have doubt (which is a messenger of intuition), likely because there is reason to doubt. The great gift of the unsolicited promise is that the speaker tells you so himself!

In effect, the promise holds up a mirror in which you get a second chance to see your own intuitive signal; the promise is the image and the reflection of your doubt. Always, in every context, be suspicious of the unsolicited promise. When Kelly's rapist told her he would leave after he got something to drink from the kitchen, he detected her doubt, so he added, "I promise."

Here's the defense: When someone says "I promise," you say (at least in your head) "You're right, I am hesitant about trusting you, and maybe with good reason. Thank you for pointing it out."

DISCOUNTING THE WORD "NO"

It is late, and I suggest to Kelly that we'll discuss the rest tomorrow, but she wants another signal before we stop. Like every victim of a truly awful crime, she is anxious to make some sense of it, to understand it, to control it. So I speak to her about one more signal, perhaps the most universally significant one of all: a man's ignoring or discounting the concept of *no.* Kelly's rapist ignored it several times, in various forms. First she said no, she didn't want his help. Then she showed him no when she didn't immediately let go of the bag.

Actions are far more eloquent and credible than words, particularly a short and undervalued word like "no," and particularly when it's offered tentatively or without conviction. So when Kelly said no but then agreed, it wasn't really no anymore. "No" is a word that must never be negotiated, because the person who chooses not to hear it is trying to control you.

In situations in which unsolicited offers of assistance are appropriate, such as approaches by a salesman or flight attendant, it is simply annoying if you have to decline three times. With a stranger, however, refusal to hear no can be an important survival signal, as with a suitor, a friend, a boyfriend, even a husband.

Declining to hear "no" is a signal that someone is either seeking control or refusing to relinquish it. With strangers, even those with the best intentions, never, ever relent on the issue of "no," because it sets the stage for more efforts to control. If you let someone talk you out of the word "no," you might as well wear a sign that reads, "You are in charge."

The worst response when someone fails to accept "no" is to give ever-weakening refusals and then give in. Another common response that serves the criminal is to negotiate ("I really appreciate your offer, but let me try to do it on my own first"). Negotiations are about possibilities, and providing access to someone who makes you apprehensive is not a possibility you want to keep on the agenda. I encourage people to remember that "no" is a complete sentence.

The criminal's process of victim selection, which I call "the interview," is similar to a shark's circling potential prey. The predatory criminal of every variety is looking for someone, a vulnerable someone who will allow him to be in control, and just as he constantly gives signals, so does he read them.

The man in the underground parking lot who approaches a woman as she puts groceries in the trunk of her car and offers assistance may be a gentleman or he may be conducting an interview. The woman whose shoulders tense slightly, who looks intimidated and shyly says, "No, thanks, I think I've got it," may be his victim. Conversely, the woman who turns toward him, raises her hands to the Stop position, and says directly, "I don't want your help," is less likely to be his victim.

A decent man would understand her reaction or, more likely, wouldn't have approached a woman alone in the first place, unless she really had some obvious need. If a man doesn't understand the reaction and stomps off dejected, that's fine too. In fact, any reaction — even anger — from a decent man who had no sinister intent is preferable to continued attention from a violent man who might have used your concern about rudeness to his advantage.

A woman alone who needs assistance is actually far better off choosing someone and asking for help, as opposed to waiting for an unsolicited approach. The person you choose is nowhere near as likely to bring you hazard as is the person who chooses you. That's because the possibility that you'll inadvertently select a predatory criminal for whom you are the right victim type is very remote. I encourage women to ask other women for help when they need it, and it's likewise safer to accept an offer from a woman than from a man. (Unfortunately, women rarely make such offers to other women, and I wish more would.)

I want to clarify that many men offer help without any sinister or self-serving intent, with no more in mind than kindness and chivalry, but I have been addressing those times that men refuse to hear the word "no," and that is not chivalrous — it is dangerous.

When someone ignores that word, ask yourself: Why is this person seeking to control me? What does he want? It is best to get away from the person altogether, but if that's not practical, the response that serves safety is to dramatically raise your insistence, skipping several levels of politeness. "I said *NO!*"

When I encounter people hung up on the seeming rudeness of this response (and there are many), I imagine this conversation after a stranger is told no by a woman he has approached:

Man: What a bitch. What's your problem, lady? I was just trying to offer a little help to a pretty woman. What are you so paranoid about?

Woman: You're right. I shouldn't be wary. I'm overreacting about nothing. I mean, just because a man makes an unsolicited and persistent approach in an underground parking lot in a society where crimes against women have risen four times faster than the general crime rate, and three out of four women will suffer a violent crime; and just because I've personally heard horror stories from every female friend I've ever had; and just because I have to consider where I park, where I walk, whom I talk to, and whom I date in the context of whether someone will kill me or rape me or scare me half to death; and just because several times a week someone makes an inappropriate remark, stares at me, harasses me, follows me, or drives alongside my car pacing me; and just because I have to deal with the apartment manager who gives me the creeps for reasons I haven't figured out, yet I can tell by the way he looks at me that given an opportunity he'd do something that would get us both on the evening news; and just because these are life-and-death issues most men know nothing about so that I'm made to feel foolish for being cautious even though I live at the center of a swirl of possible hazards *doesn't mean a woman should be wary of a stranger who ignores the word "no."*

Whether or not men can relate to it or believe it or accept it, that is the way it is. Women, particularly in big cities, live with a constant wariness. Their lives are literally on the line in ways men just don't experience. Ask some man you know, "When is the last time you were concerned or afraid that another person would harm you?" Many men cannot recall an incident within years. Ask a woman the same question and most will give you a recent example or say, "Last night," "Today," or even "Every day."

Still, women's concerns about safety are frequently the subject of critical comments from the men in their lives. One woman told me of constant ridicule and sarcasm from her boyfriend whenever she discussed fear or safety. He called her precautions silly and asked, "How can you live like that?" To which she replied, "How could I not?"

I have a message for women who feel forced to defend their safety concerns: tell Mister I-Know-Everything-About-Danger that he has nothing to contribute to the topic of your personal security. Tell him that your survival instinct is a gift from nature that knows a lot more about your safety than he does. And tell him that nature does not require his approval.

It is understandable that the perspectives of men and women on safety are so different — men and women live in different worlds. I don't remember where I first heard this simple description of one dramatic contrast between the genders, but it is strikingly accurate: At core, men are afraid women will laugh at them, while at core, women are afraid men will kill them.

▪ ▪ ▪

I referred Kelly to IMPACT, which I believe is the best self-defense course for women. She is now an instructor there, helping others to heed the signals. At IMPACT, which is available in most major cities, women have actual physical confrontations with male instructors who play assailants. (The men wear heavily padded outfits that can withstand direct punches and kicks.) Women learn not only physical defense tactics but also about how to deal with strangers who make unwanted approaches. (See appendix 2 for more information about IMPACT.)

Most new IMPACT students are very concerned that they must avoid making a man angry, reasoning that this could turn someone whose intent was favorable into someone dangerous. Be aware, however, that it is *impossible* in this context to transform an ordinary, decent man into a rapist or killer. Thankfully, though, it is possible to transform yourself into a person who responds to the signals and is thus a less likely victim.

▪ ▪ ▪

I recently got a close look at several of the strategies outlined above. I was on a flight from Chicago to Los Angeles, seated next to a teenage girl who was traveling alone. A man in his forties who'd been watching her from across the aisle took off the headphones he was wearing and said to her with partylike flair, "These things just don't get *loud* enough for me!" He then put his hand out toward her and said, "I'm Billy." Though it may not be immediately apparent, his statement was actually a question, and the young girl responded with exactly the information Billy hoped for: She told him her full name. Then she put out her hand, which he held a little too long. In the conversation that ensued, he didn't directly ask for any information, but he certainly got lots of it.

He said, "I hate landing in a city and not knowing if anybody is meeting me." The girl answered this question by saying that she didn't know how she was getting from the airport to the house where she was staying. Billy asked another question: "Friends can really let you down sometimes." The young girl responded by explaining, "The people I'm staying with [thus, not family] are expecting me on a later flight."

Billy said, "I love the independence of arriving in a city when nobody knows I'm coming." This was the virtual opposite of what he'd said a moment before about hating to arrive and not be met. He added, "But you're probably not that independent." She quickly volunteered that she'd been traveling on her own since she was thirteen.

"You sound like a woman I know from Europe, more like a

woman than a teenager," he said as he handed her his drink (scotch), which the flight attendant had just served him. "You sound like you play by your own rules." I hoped she would decline to take the drink, and she did at first, but he persisted, "Come on, you can do whatever you want," and she took a sip of his drink.

I looked over at Billy, looked at his muscular build, at the old tattoo showing on the top of his wrist, and at his cheap jewelry. I noted that he was drinking alcohol on this morning flight and had no carry-on bag. I looked at his new cowboy boots, new denim pants and leather jacket. I knew he'd recently been in jail. He responded to my knowing look assertively, "How you doin' this morning, pal? Gettin' out of Chicago?" I nodded.

As Billy got up to go to the bathroom, he put one more piece of bait in his trap: Leaning close to the girl, he gave a slow smile and said, "Your eyes are *awesome.*"

In a period of just a few minutes, I had watched Billy use forced teaming (they both had nobody meeting them, he said), too many details (the headphones and the woman he knows from Europe), loan sharking (the drink offer), charm (the compliment about the girl's eyes), and typecasting ("You're probably not that independent"). I had also seen him discount the girl's "no" when she declined the drink.

As Billy walked away down the aisle, I asked the girl if I could talk to her for a moment, and she hesitantly said yes. It speaks to the power of predatory strategies that she was glad to talk to Billy but a bit wary of the passenger (me) who asked permission to speak with her. "He is going to offer you a ride from the airport," I told her, "and he's not a good guy."

I saw Billy again at baggage claim as he approached the girl. Though I couldn't hear them, the conversation was apparent. She was shaking her head and saying no, and he wasn't accepting it. She held firm, and he finally walked off with an angry gesture, not the "nice" guy he'd been up till then.

There was no movie on that flight, but Billy had let me watch a classic performance of an interview that by little more than the context (forty-year-old stranger and teenage girl alone) was high stakes.

Remember, the nicest guy, the guy with no self-serving agenda whatsoever, the one who wants nothing from you, won't approach you at all. You are not comparing the man who approaches you to all men, the vast majority of whom have no sinister intent. Instead, you are comparing him to other men who make unsolicited approaches to women alone, or to other men who don't listen when you say no.

In my firm, when we make complex, high-stakes predictions, part of the approach also involves comparison. Let's imagine we are predicting whether a former boyfriend might act out violently toward the woman he is stalking. We first seek to identify characteristics that separate him from the population as a whole. To do this, imagine a circle containing 240 million Americans. At the center are the few thousand men who kill those they stalk. Figuratively working from an outer ring of 240 million people, we eliminate all those who are the wrong gender, too young, too old, or otherwise disqualified. We then seek to determine if this man's behavior is most similar to those at the center of the circle.

A prediction about safety is not, of course, merely statistical or demographic. If it were, a woman crossing a park alone one late afternoon could calculate risk like this: There are 200 people in the park; 100 are children, so they cause no concern. Of the remaining 100, all but 20 are part of couples; 5 of those 20 are women, meaning concern would appropriately attach to about 15 people she might encounter (men alone). But rather than acting just on these demographics, the woman's intuition will focus on the behavior of the 15 (and on the context of that behavior). Any man alone may get her attention for an instant, but among those, only the ones doing certain things will be moved closer to the center of the predictive circle. Men who look at her, show special interest in her, follow her, appear furtive, or approach her will be far closer to the center than those who walk by without apparent interest, or those playing with a dog, or those on a bicycle, or those asleep on the grass.

Speaking of crossing a park alone, I often see women violating some of nature's basic safety rules. The woman who jogs along enjoying music through Walkman headphones has disabled the survival sense most likely to warn her about dangerous approaches: her hearing. To make matters worse, those wires leading up to her ears display her vulnerability for everyone to see. Another example is that while women wouldn't walk around blindfolded, of course, many do not use the full resources of their vision; they are reluctant to look squarely at strangers who concern them. Believing she is being followed, a woman might take just a tentative look, hoping to see if someone is visible in her peripheral vision. It is better to turn completely, take in everything, and look squarely at someone who concerns you. This not only gives you information, but it communicates to him that you are not a tentative, frightened victim-in-waiting. You are an animal of nature, fully endowed with hearing, sight, intellect, and dangerous defenses. You are not easy prey, so don't act like you are.

■ ■ ■

Predictions of stranger-to-stranger crimes must usually be based on few details, but even the simplest street crime is preceded by a victim selection process that follows some protocol. More complicated crimes, such as those committed by the serial rapist and killer whom Kelly escaped from, require that a series of specific conditions be met. Some aspects of victim selection (being the right appearance or "type," for example) are generally outside the victim's influence, but those that involve making oneself available to a criminal, such as accessibility, setting, and circumstance (all part of context), are determinable. In other words, you can influence them. Most of all, you can control your response to the tests the interviewer applies. Will you engage in conversation with a stranger when you'd rather not? Can you be manipulated by guilt or by the feeling that you owe something to a person just because he offered assistance? Will you yield to someone's will simply because he wants you to, or will your resolve be strengthened when someone seeks to control your conduct? Most importantly, will you honor your intuition?

Seeing the interview for what it is while it is happening doesn't mean that you view every unexpected encounter as if it is part of a crime, but it does mean that you react to the signals if and as they occur. Trust that what causes alarm probably should, because when it comes to danger, intuition is always right in at least two important ways:

1) It is always in response to something.
2) It always has your best interest at heart.

Having just said that intuition is always right, I can imagine some readers resisting, so I'll clarify. Intuition is always right in the ways I noted, but our interpretation of intuition is not always right. Clearly, not everything we predict will come to pass, but since intuition is always in response to something, rather than making a fast effort to explain it away or deny the possible hazard, we are wiser (and more true to nature) if we make an effort to identify the hazard, if it exists.

If there's no hazard, we have lost nothing and have added a new distinction to our intuition, so that it might not sound the alarm again in the same situation. This process of adding new distinctions is one of the reasons it is difficult at first to sleep in a new house: Your intuition has not yet categorized all those little noises. On the first night, the clinking of the ice maker or the rumbling of the water heater might be an intruder. By the third night, your mind knows better and doesn't wake you. You might not think intuition is working while you sleep, but it is. A book salesman I know who often returns late at night from out-of-town trips: "I can drive into the garage, open and close the back door, walk up the stairs, open the bedroom door, toss down my luggage, get undressed, and get into bed — and my wife won't wake up. But if our four-year-old opens the door to his room in the middle of the night, my wife bolts out of bed in an instant."

▪ ▪ ▪

Intuition is always learning, and though it may occasionally send a signal that turns out to be less than urgent, everything it communicates to you is meaningful. Unlike worry, it will not waste your time. Intuition might send any of several messengers to get your attention, and because they differ according to urgency, it is good to know the ranking. The intuitive signal of the highest order, the one with the greatest urgency, is fear; accordingly, it should always be listened to (more on that in chapter 15). The next level is apprehension, then suspicion, then hesitation, doubt, gut feelings, hunches, and curiosity. There are also nagging feelings, persistent thoughts, physical sensations, wonder, and anxiety. Generally speaking, these are less urgent. By thinking about these signals with an open mind when they occur, you will learn how you communicate with yourself.

There is another signal people rarely recognize, and that is humor.

In one story that offers an excellent example, all the information was there like a great unharvested crop left to dry in the sun. The receptionist was off that day, so Bob Taylor and others at the California Forestry Association sorted through the mail. When they came upon the package, they looked it over and chatted about what to do with it. It was addressed to the former president of the association, and they debated whether to just forward it to him. When Gilbert Murray, the current president, arrived, they brought him in on their discussion. Murray said, "Let's open it."

Taylor got up and cracked a joke: "I'm going back to my office before the bomb goes off." He walked down the hall to his desk, but before he sat down, he heard the enormous explosion that killed his boss. Because of intuition, that bomb didn't kill Bob Taylor.

All the information he needed was there and dismissed by the others, but not before Taylor's intuition sent a signal to everyone in the clearest language: "I'm going back to my office before the bomb goes off."

I have learned to listen to the jokes clients make when we are discussing some possible hazard. If, as I stand to leave the office of a corporate president, he says, "I'll call you tomorrow — if I haven't been shot," I sit back down to get more information.

Humor, particularly dark humor, is a common way to communicate true concern without the risk of feeling silly afterward, and without overtly showing fear. But how does this type of remark evolve? One doesn't consciously direct the mind to search all files for something funny to say. Were that the case, Bob Taylor might have looked at this package addressed to a man who'd resigned a year earlier and more cleverly said, "It's probably a fruitcake that's been lost in the mail since Christmas," or any of thousands of comments. Or he could have made no comment at all. But with this type of humor, an idea comes into consciousness that, in context, seems so outlandish as to be ridiculous. And that's precisely why it's funny. The point is, though, that the idea came into consciousness. Why? Because all the information was there.

That package sent by the Unabomber to the California Forestry Association was very heavy. It was covered with tape, had too much postage, and aroused enough interest that morning that several people speculated on whether it might be a bomb. They had noted the Oakland firm named on the return address, and had they called directory assistance, they'd have found it to be fictitious. Still, it was opened.

A few weeks earlier, advertising executive Thomas Mosser received such a package at his New Jersey home. Just before he opened it, he was curious enough to ask his wife if she was expecting a parcel. She said she was not. Mosser had asked a good question, but a moment later, he ignored the answer he'd sought. He was killed when he opened the package (also sent by the Unabomber).

Postal inspector Dan Mihalko: "I've heard many times that people would make a comment, 'This looks like a bomb,' and still open it. That's one for the psychologists to answer. Perhaps they don't want to call the police and be embarrassed if it turns out to be nothing."

The Unabomber himself has mocked some of the twenty-three people hurt by his bombs. Two years after being injured, Yale computer scientist David Gelenter received a letter from the Unabomber: "If you had any brains you would have realized that there are a lot of people out there who resent the way techno-nerds like you are changing the world and you wouldn't have been dumb enough to open an unexpected package from an unknown source. People with advanced degrees aren't as smart as they think they are."

In fairness to the victims, I note that mail bombs are very rare and aren't the type of hazard one is normally concerned about, but the point is that these victims *were* concerned enough to comment on it. Anyway, people are just as likely to make jokes about more common crimes before sacrificing themselves to some avoidable harm.

While a group of employees at the Standard Gravure plant sat eating lunch, they heard sounds from outside. Some thought they were firecrackers, but one made a quip about an angry co-worker: "That's probably just Westbecher coming back to finish us off." A moment later, it was indeed Joseph Westbecher who burst into the room spraying bullets, one of which hit the man who'd made the joke. Listen to humor, particularly dark humor. It can be good for more than a laugh.

THE MESSENGERS OF INTUITION

Nagging feelings
Persistent thoughts
Humor
Wonder
Anxiety
Curiosity
Hunches
Gut feelings
Doubt
Hesitation
Suspicion
Apprehension
Fear

The first messenger from Kelly's intuition was apprehension. China Leonard got the unheeded message about her son's surgery through a strong persistent thought. Michael Cantrell had nagging feelings about his partner's recklessness. Bob Taylor's survival signal about the bomb package came through dark humor. Robert Thompson got the loudest signal — fear — when he entered and then exited that convenience store.

That's the same messenger a young woman named Nancy heeded as she sat in the passenger seat of a parked sports car. Her friend had left the car running when he got out to withdraw money from an ATM. Suddenly and without knowing why, Nancy felt great fear.

She felt in danger, but where from? To her credit, she didn't wait for an answer to that question. Her breathing stopped and her arms started: She scrambled to find the door locks, but it was too late. A man opened the driver's door, got in, put a gun against her stomach, and drove the car away, kidnapping Nancy.

She hadn't seen the man, so why the fear signal? A tiny image in the side-view mirror on the opposite side of the car, a glimpse of a three-inch section of denim — that was her signal that a man in blue jeans was too close to the car and moving too fast. That was her accurately interpreted signal that he might imminently get into the car with sinister intent. All this was gleaned from a tiny patch of blue, meaningful only in context, which she had no time to figure out but which her intuition already had figured out. If one had tried to convince Nancy to lock the car on the basis of just this fleeting blue image, she might have argued, but fear is far more persuasive than logic.

Nancy survived her five-hour ordeal by following another intuition: She engaged the dangerous stranger in constant conversation. Inside her head, she heard the repeated word "calm, calm, calm." Outwardly, she acted as if she were speaking with a close friend. When her kidnapper ordered her out of the car behind a remote warehouse miles from the city, Nancy felt he wouldn't shoot a person he had come to know, and she was right.

▪ ▪ ▪

I have discussed at length the warning signs that can help you avoid being a victim of violence, but even if you make excellent predictions, you might still find yourself in danger. Though I am often asked for advice on how a person should respond to a robber or car-jacker, for example, I cannot offer a checklist of what to do for each type of hazard you could encounter, because cookie-cutter approaches are dangerous. Some people say about rape, for example, *do not resist,* while others say *always resist.* Neither strategy is right for all situations, but one strategy is: Listen to your intuition. I don't know what might be best for you in some hazardous situation because I don't have all the information, but you will have all the information.

Do not listen to the TV news checklist of what to do, or the magazine article's checklist of what to do, or the story about what your friend did. Listen to the wisdom that comes from having heard it all by listening to yourself.

■ ■ ■

The stories in this chapter have been about dangers posed by strangers, but what about dangers that might come from those people we choose to bring into our lives as employees, employers, people we date, and people we marry? These relationships do not start with the first meeting — we meet many people we don't keep in our lives. *Our relationships actually start with predictions,* predictions that determine — literally — the quality and course of our lives. So it is time to take a look at the quality of those predictions.

▪ 5 ▪

IMPERFECT STRANGERS

"A rock pile ceases to be a rock pile
the moment a single man contemplates it,
bearing within him the image of a cathedral."
— *Antoine de Saint-Exupéry*

See if you can imagine this: It is the year 2050, and predictions about people are perfect. They are made with a high-tech chemical test. You can accept a ride from a total stranger, you can ask a homeless person you've never seen before to watch your house while you are out of town. You can do this free of fear that they might harm you because predictions of intent and character are totally reliable.

You are skimming along in your hovercraft one afternoon, taking your six-year-old daughter to the park, when you are paged to come to an urgent business meeting. You go to the park anyway and look around for some stranger with whom you can leave your daughter. There is a middle-aged woman sitting on a bench reading a book, and as you sit down next to her, she smiles. Using a device nearly everyone carries these days, you conduct an instant high-tech test on her, as she does on you, and you both pass with flying colors. Without hesitation, you ask if she'll watch your daughter for a few hours while you skim over to a meeting. She agrees, you exchange some information about how to contact each other, and off you go without any concern, because you have predicted to your satisfaction that this stranger is emotionally healthy, competent, drug-free, and trustworthy.

The story sounds far-fetched, but in our time we already make every single one of these predictions about baby-sitters. We just don't do it as quickly or as accurately.

With present-day technology, how much time would you have to spend with a stranger before she wouldn't be a stranger anymore? How many of your low-tech tests would a baby-sitter have to pass before you'd trust her? We undertake this common yet very high-stakes prediction by reviewing an application and asking a few questions, but let's really look at this prediction. For starters, we wouldn't just interview a woman we met in a park. No, we'd want someone who was recommended by a person we know, because we like to rely on predictions made by others. Our friend Kevin is so bright and honorable, we think, that if he endorses somebody, well, that person must be okay. What often happens, however, is that we attach *Kevin's* attributes to the person he recommended, and we don't listen to our own uncertainty. As we drive away from home, leaving our child behind with someone we met just a half hour ago, we feel the tug that says, "You never really know about people."

In our interview with the baby-sitter, we watch her attentively for any signs of . . . of what? Drug use? Well, that can be tested with great reliability; tens of thousands of drug-screen tests are done every week by employers who have less at stake than parents do when hiring a baby-sitter. Though most people believe the drug question is a critical one, have you ever heard of a parent requiring a drug screen of a baby-sitter candidate? Or a Breathalyzer test to see if she's been drinking? Most parents don't even contact all the baby-sitter's references, so it's no wonder they drive away feeling, "You never really know about people."

I am not, by the way, suggesting drug tests or polygraphs for baby-sitters, but I am pointing out that we rarely bring even a tenth of the available resources to high-stakes predictions. For example, the question people really want answered by a prospective baby-sitter is: Have you ever mistreated a child? But they never ask it! Why not? Because people feel that asking a question so direct is rude or ridiculous, since it wouldn't be answered truthfully by someone who had mistreated children. *Ask the question anyway,* and how it is answered will make you more comfortable or less comfortable with that applicant. Imagine you asked, "Have you ever abused a child?" and the applicant responded with "Define abuse," or "What have you heard?" It is entirely fair and appropriate to ask someone to whom you'll entrust your child to discuss the very issues you care about most. Good applicants will certainly understand, and bad applicants may reveal themselves.

Having not sought any of the information he or she really wants to know, a parent might see the applicant stroke the family cat and think: "She likes animals, that's a good sign." (Or worse still: "Tabby likes her, that's a good sign.") People want so badly to get someone hired for a job that they spend more time qualifying a candidate than disqualifying a candidate, but this is one process in which it's better to look for the storm clouds than to look for the silver lining.

Let's go back to 2050 for a moment. Not only do you have no hesitation about accepting a ride from a stranger, but there's a city-run transportation computer to facilitate precisely that. Rather than drive yourself from Los Angeles to San Diego, you enter your destination into the computer along with what time you want to leave, and it identifies several other people who are going from your area to San Diego at the same time. A perfect stranger will stop by your house and pick you up, and you'll get back from San Diego the same way. That's what could happen if predictions were perfect. Since they are not, a hundred thousand cars carry the passengers that twenty-five thousand could carry just as well. Fear of each other and lack of confidence in our predictions makes any alternative seem impossible.

But what if we had that transportation computer today, and in addition to identifying the people who are making the trip you want to make at the time you want to make it, it also provided some demographic information? You could ride to San Diego in an old van with two unemployed men in their thirties, or you could ride in a late-model station wagon with a housewife and her one-year-old child. You'd likely conclude that the ride with the housewife and her baby would be safer (noisier, perhaps, but safer). What else would you want to know about candidates for ride-alongs? Their criminal histories, driving histories, condition of their vehicles? The point is, if you could learn enough about each candidate, you would actually be comfortable relying upon your prediction because that's exactly how strangers become people you trust anyway. You learn enough about them. They pass several of your tests and suddenly they aren't strangers anymore.

Some animals perceive danger chemically — maybe even part of the way we do it is chemical; I don't know. But will the day really come when we'll be able to make predictions about people not by judging their appearance or clothing or smile or assurances, but by applying a chemical test? I believe the answer is yes, though I won't still be around to say I told you so. In the meantime, since we have to keep doing predictions the old-fashioned way, it's all the more important that we understand what's really going on.

■ ■ ■

Psychologist John Monahan is a pioneer in the field of prediction who has influenced my work and life a great deal. In his beautifully written book *Predicting Violent Behavior,* he begins by asking the simplest question: In which direction would this book fall if you let it go?

> The reader could technically state only that every other solid object he or she has let go of in the past has (eventually) fallen down rather than risen up or remained suspended. What allows for the prediction that this object, if released in the future, will also fall down is that we possess a theory — gravity — that can plausibly let us generalize from the past class of cases to the current individual case. The catch, of course, is that we understand gravity much better than we understand violence.

My friend John and I might have a spirited discussion on that, for I know much more about violence than I do about gravity. I believe behavior, like gravity, is bound by some essential rules. Admittedly they may not always apply, but remember, they don't always apply with gravity either. Where you are (such as in space, or in water) affects how objects will behave. The relationship of objects to each other and to their environment (i.e., magnets, airplanes, etc.) also bears on such predictions. With behavior, as with gravity, context will govern, but there are some broad strokes that can be fairly applied to most of us:

- We seek connection with others.
- We are saddened by loss and try to avoid it.
- We dislike rejection.
- We like recognition and attention.
- We will do more to avoid pain than we will do to seek pleasure.
- We dislike ridicule and embarrassment.
- We care what others think of us.
- We seek a degree of control over our lives.

These assumptions are hardly groundbreaking, and though we might expect something more esoteric about people who are violent, these mundane concepts apply to most of them, just as they do to you. You see, this list contains a few of the ingredients in the human recipe, and how much of one ingredient or how little of another will influence the final result. With the man who goes on a shooting spree at work, it is not that he has some mysterious extra component or that he necessarily has something missing. It is usually the balance and interaction of the same ingredients that influence us all. Am I saying the shooting spree at work can be predicted in part by weighing the balance of factors as common as the eight general assumptions listed above? Yes.

Certainly there are hundreds of other variables that my office considers in predicting violence, and I could present them here with charts and graphs and templates and computer printouts. I could use psychiatric terms that would require a psychiatrist to interpret, but my purpose here is to simplify, to identify in your experience the factors that matter most.

As I discussed earlier, no matter how aberrant the person whose behavior you seek to predict, no matter how different from him you may be or want to be, you must find in him a part of yourself, and in yourself a part of him. When you undertake a high-stakes prediction, keep looking until you find some common ground, something you share with the person whose behavior you seek to predict — this will help you see the situation as he perceives it. For example, the anonymous caller may seem to enjoy the fear he is causing in his victim. Getting pleasure from the fear of others is something most of us cannot relate to — until we recall the glee of every teenager who startles a friend or sibling by jumping out of the dark. Anyway, with the frightening caller, fear may not be the issue as much as liking attention. When the caller causes people to feel fear, they are very attentive. It might not be his favorite way of getting attention if he perceived better options or if he felt he brought other assets to his relationship with his victim, but it has likely worked for him in the past. I don't mean to imply that the threat caller is so introspective that he consciously considered all this, but neither is our behavior usually the result of conscious decision making.

Though it is true that people have more in common than in contrast, you will encounter some who have vastly different standards of behavior and vastly different ways of perceiving the same events. For example, some people operate without listening to their consciences; they do not care about the welfare of others, period. In the corporate boardroom we might call this negligence; on the street we call it criminality. The ability to act in spite of conscience or empathy is one characteristic associated with psychopaths. Robert D. Hare's insightful book *Without Conscience* identifies several other features. Such people are:

- Glib and superficial
- Egocentric and grandiose
- Lacking remorse or guilt
- Deceitful and manipulative
- Impulsive
- In need of excitement
- Lacking responsibility
- Emotionally shallow

Many errors in predicting behavior come from the belief that others will perceive things as we do. The psychopath described above will not. To successfully predict his behavior, you must see a situation your way *and* his way. It will be easy, of course, to see it your way — that's automatic. Seeing a situation from another person's perspective is an acquired skill, but you have already acquired it. Imagine that you are about to fire someone whose behavior, personality, and philosophy of life could not be further from your own. Even with all the differences, you would still know if he'd view the firing as fair, completely unfair, part of a vendetta, or motivated by discrimination or greed, etc. Particularly if you worked closely with this person, you could recite his perception of events much as he would. Though you may not share his view, you can still bring it into focus.

Predicting human behavior is really about recognizing the play from just a few lines of dialogue. It is about trusting that a character's behavior will be consistent with his perception of the situation. If the play is true to humanness, each act will follow along as it should, as it does in nature.

Imagine you are watching a bird as it floats to earth, about to land. The sun is casting the bird's shadow on the ground, and both bird and shadow move toward the landing point. We know that the bird cannot possibly arrive there before its shadow. Likewise, human action cannot land before impulse, and impulse cannot land before that which triggers it. Each step is preceded by the step before it. You cannot shoot the gun without first touching it, nor take hold of it without first intending to, nor intend to without first having some reason, nor have a reason without first reacting to something, nor react to something without first giving it meaning, and on and on. At many points before aiming a gun and pulling the trigger, particularly if the context is not unique, there are thoughts and emotions that others in similar situations also experienced.

Think of any situation that many have shared, say, getting to an airport late (but not too late) for a flight. Based on your experience, you can predict some of the thoughts, emotions, and thus behaviors of a harried traveler. Is he likely to stroll? At the ticket counter will he cordially allow others to get in line ahead of him? Will he savor the interesting architecture of the airport?

Because we are familiar with the airport situation, we find it easy to predict what the traveler will do. It is precisely because some people are not familiar with violent behavior that they feel they cannot predict it, yet they daily predict *non*violent behavior and *the process is identical.* In his book *Information Anxiety,* Richard Saul Wurman explains that "we recognize all things by the existence of their opposite — day as distinguishable from night, failure from success, peace from war." We could add "safety from hazard."

When a woman is comfortable with a stranger in her home, someone delivering furniture, for example, her comfort communicates that she has already predicted that he is not dangerous to her. Her intuition asked and answered several questions in order to complete that prediction. It evaluated favorable and unfavorable aspects of his behavior. Since we are more familiar with favorable behaviors, if you list them and then simply note their opposites, you will be predicting dangerousness. We call this the "rule of opposites," and it is a powerful predictive tool.

FAVORABLE	UNFAVORABLE
Does his job and no more	Offers to help on unrelated tasks
Respectful of privacy	Curious, asks many questions
Stands at an appropriate distance	Stands too close
Waits to be escorted	Walks around the house freely
Keeps his comments to the job at hand	Tries to get into discussions on other topics; makes personal comments
Mindful of the time; works quickly	No concern about time; in no hurry to leave
Doesn't care if others are home	Wants to know if others are home
Doesn't care if others are expected	Wants to know if others are expected
Doesn't pay undue attention to you	Stares at you

All types of behavioral predictions, not just those about danger, can be improved by applying the rule of opposites.

Just as we can predict behavior once we know the situation or context, we can also recognize the context by the behavior. A man insists on being first in the ticket line at the airport, looks frequently at his watch, appears exasperated by the slowness of the ticket agent.

After getting his ticket, he runs awkwardly along, carrying his bags. He appears rushed and stressed. He looks expectantly at each gate he approaches. Is he:

a) A politician seeking votes who will stop and chat with each passerby?
b) A charity volunteer who will solicit donations?
c) A person late for his flight who will proceed directly to the gate?

A hostile employee is fired the day he returns from a leave of absence. He refuses to vacate the building. He tells his supervisor, "You haven't heard the last of me," and then recites the supervisor's home address. He says, "I'll be visiting you with my buddies, Smith and Wesson." Security guards are called to remove him, and the following morning, his supervisor's car windshield is smashed.

Is this fired employee likely to:

a) Send a check for repair of the windshield?
b) Enroll the next day in medical school?
c) Start making late-night hang-up calls to the supervisor's home?

A couple of days after the man is fired, his supervisor finds a dead snake in his mailbox at home.

Was it placed there by:

a) A neighborhood prankster?
b) A member of the Snake Protective League trying to raise social consciousness?
c) The man fired a couple of days before?

I've used these obvious examples to demonstrate one of the greatest resources for predicting human behavior: You will rarely fail to place people in the most likely category when you frame the choice between contrasting options. This may seem obvious, but it is a powerful assessment tool.

A woman in an underground parking lot is approached by a stranger who offers help loading groceries into her car. She could refine her predictions about the man, and enjoy a creative exercise, by asking herself, Is this man:

a) A member of a citizen volunteer group whose mission is to patrol underground parking lots in search of women to help?
b) The owner of a supermarket chain looking for the star of his next national advertising campaign?
c) A guy who has some sexual interest in me?

By the time you consciously develop even the first possible category for your multiple-choice list, you likely already know the correct answer and you have already considered the level of immediate hazard intuitively. Intuition, remember, knows more about the situation than we are consciously aware of. In the parking lot, it knows when the woman first saw that man, as opposed to when she first registered seeing him; it may know when he first saw her; it may know how many other people are around. It knows about the lighting, about how sound carries here, about her ability to escape or defend herself should she need to, and on and on.

Similarly, when assessing the fired employee, intuition knows how long he held on to resentments in the past. It remembers sinister statements he made that were followed by some unsolved vandalism. It recalls his disconcerting story about getting even with a neighbor.

The reason for creating three options is that it frees you from the need to be correct; you know that at least two of your options will be wrong, and this freedom from judgment clears a path to intuition. In practice, this turns out to be less an exercise in creativity than an exercise in discovery; what you may think you are making up, you are *calling* up. Many believe the process of creativity is one of assembling thoughts and concepts, but highly creative people will tell you that the idea, the song, the image, was *in* them, and their task was to get it out, a process of discovery, not design.

This was said most artfully by Michelangelo when asked how he created his famous statue of David. He said, "It is easy — you just chip away the stone that doesn't look like David."

Well, you can know it will be a man long before the statue is complete. It is an irony of prediction that if you just wait long enough to commit, every prediction will be accurate. By the eleventh hour, most factors are apparent, and they are less likely to change because there is less opportunity for intervening influences. The key is to complete a prediction far enough in advance to get some benefit, in other words, while you still have time to prepare or to influence outcome.

Why, after all, do we make any prediction? To avoid an outcome or exploit an outcome. To do either, prediction must be followed by preparation. Prediction without preparation is just curiosity. Predicting that Lucky Dancer will run fastest is only valuable when you have time to exploit the outcome by placing a bet at the racetrack. Conversely, if you are standing in the path of the galloping horse, you use the same prediction to avoid the outcome of being trampled, and you get out of the way.

The amount of preparation appropriate for a given outcome is determined by evaluating the importance of avoiding or exploiting it and the cost and effectiveness of the strategies you'll use.

In deciding what preparations or precautions to apply, one also measures the perceived reliability of the prediction. If I predicted that you would be struck by lightning tomorrow and said that I could ensure your safety for $50,000, you wouldn't be interested. Though it is very important to avoid being struck by lightning, the reliability of my prediction is low, and thus the cost is much too high. If, however, a doctor says you need immediate heart-transplant surgery or you will die, the $50,000 cost is suddenly reasonable. The outcome of death is the same with lightning or heart failure, but we perceive the reliability of the medical prediction as much higher.

This same process of comparing reliability, importance, cost, and effectiveness (which my office calls the RICE evaluation) is how people go about making many daily decisions.

Society makes its precautionary decisions using the same RICE evaluation. Avoiding the assassination of a big-city mayor is less important to society than avoiding the assassination of a presidential candidate. That's why we spend more in a week on a presidential candidate's protection than we spend in a year for most mayors. We may consider our prediction that a presidential candidate might be shot to be more accurate than that a mayor might be shot, but it isn't necessarily so. In fact, mayors have been shot more often and more lethally than presidential candidates. When we add governors to the mix, we find that nearly all have protective details, some quite extensive, but I am unaware of any governor ever killed in office. (Two governors have been shot while in office, but neither because he was governor: George Wallace, because he was a presidential candidate; and John Connelly, because he was in the car when President Kennedy was assassinated.) So, though a mayor is more likely to be killed as a result of holding the office, I am sorry to tell my mayor-readers that we care more about avoiding that outcome for governors.

With societies, as with individuals, when the RICE evaluation is made irrationally, it is always because of emotion. For example, avoiding the outcome of hijacking is so important around the world that passengers are screened for weapons more than *one billion* times each year. Only a few hundred people are actually arrested on weapons charges, almost none of whom had any intention of hijacking a plane. Ironically, the only deaths associated with airline hijacking in America have occurred *since* we instituted weapons screening. So, given the effectiveness, we pay a lot to do something that might prevent just a few incidents. We do this because of emotion: worry, specifically. To be clear, I support screening of airline passengers, but this is as much for the fear-reducing benefits and deterrence as for the actual detecting of weapons.

The likelihood of burglary in your area may be remote, but the importance of avoiding it makes the cost of having locks on the door seem reasonable. Some people consider burglary to be more likely, or consider avoiding it more important, so they purchase security systems. Others don't feel that way. Our approaches to caution and precaution all boil down to a personal RICE evaluation. Ask yourself about the reliability of the safety predictions you make in your life, the importance of avoiding a bad outcome, and the cost and effectiveness of available precautions. With those answers, you can decide what resources to apply to personal safety.

When you are at imminent risk, intuition forgets about all this logical thought and just sends the fear signal. You are given the opportunity to react to a prediction that has already been completed by the time it comes into consciousness. These intuitive predictions are involuntary, but often we must make predictions consciously. How can those be improved? Ingmar Bergman said, "Imagine I throw a spear into the dark. That is my intuition. Then I have to send an expedition into the jungle to find the spear. That is my intellect."

Simply by throwing the spear, we greatly improve conscious predictions. By nothing more than the act of inquiry, or even curiously wondering about what a person might do, we enter into a conscious alliance with our intuition, an alliance with the self. Logic and judgment may sometimes be reluctant to follow that spear into the jungle, but the concepts in the next chapter should help persuade them.

▪ 6 ▪

HIGH-STAKES PREDICTIONS

"Once the principle of movement has been supplied, one thing follows on after another without interruption."

— *Aristotle*

I recall the case of a man who drove to a hotel near his home and requested a room on the highest floor. Though he had no luggage, he was escorted up to the eighteenth floor by a bellman. As a tip, he handed over all the money in his pocket (sixty-one dollars). He then asked if there would be paper and a pen in the room. Five minutes later, he jumped out the window, committing suicide.

Was this suicide foreseeable by the reception person who checked him in, or by the bellman? Both had an opportunity to observe the guest's conduct and demeanor, but they were predicting entirely different outcomes. They were answering such questions as: Can he pay for his room? Is he the authorized user of his credit card? How can I get another tip like that? The pre-incident indicators for those predictions do not include the ones relevant to suicide, such as: Why does he have no luggage? Why does a person who lives nearby check in to a hotel? Why did he seek a room on a high floor? Why did he want a pen and paper? Why did he give away all the money he had?

People do all these things for differing reasons, of course. The man might have lost his luggage. He might be staying in a hotel even though he lives nearby because his home is being fumigated (but then, wouldn't he have luggage?). He might be staying in a hotel because he just had an argument with his wife (and ran out too quickly to gather any belongings). He might have requested a room on a high floor for the view, and he might have asked about pen and paper to write a note to someone (his wife?). He might have given all his money as a tip because he's generous. A question that could give meaning to his other behavior is: Does he appear depressed? But that's not an issue on the minds of hotel staff.

While I'm sure some lawyer could make a case for the hotel's liability, the real point is that to consciously predict something, one must know what outcome is being predicted, or see enough pre-incident indicators to bring that possible outcome into consciousness. Here, some Zen wisdom applies: *Knowing the question is the first step toward knowing the answer.*

THE LANGUAGE OF PREDICTION

If you were surrounded by a pack of unfamiliar dogs that caused you fear, you could have no better companion than Jim Canino. He's an expert in canine behavior who has worked with hundreds of dogs that people considered vicious or unpredictable. Though you and Jim could observe the same actions by a dog, he'd be more likely to recognize the significance of those actions, and more likely to accurately predict the dog's behavior. That's because he knows the dog's predictive language. For example, you may believe that a dog that is barking at you is likely to bite you, but Jim knows that barking is simply a call to other dogs. Growling is the signal to respect. In the predictive language of dogs, the growl means "Nobody's coming, and I have to handle this on my own."

When someone speaks to you in a language you don't understand, though you hear the sounds clearly, they carry limited meaning. For instance, look at the following paragraph:

Flemeing, r o b e r t do. Bward, CCR, L-john john john john john john john john john john, GGS, stosharne, :powell. Kckkm, cokevstner, michL fir fir fir fir fir, hawstevking, bjacksrowne, steV1der, dgeLnrs.

This may look like gibberish, but your intuition has probably told you it is not. That paragraph contains the names of fifteen famous people, but in a slightly different language than the rest of this book.

Flemeing is Ian Fleming (E *in* Fleming). R o b e r t do is Robert De Niro (Robert D-near-O). Bward is Warren Beatty (War in B-D). CCR is Caesar (C's-R). L-john john john john john john john john john john is Elton John (L–ten john). GGS is Jesus (G's-S).

You now know enough of that language to get the remaining nine names. These word puzzles show that meaning is often in front of us to be harvested. Sometimes we need only believe it is there.

These puzzles show something else too, something about the differences between intuition and conscious prediction. If the solution to one of these puzzles does not come right away, it is then a matter of letting the answer surface in you, because stare though you may, there is no additional information forthcoming from the puzzle itself. If you solve one, the answer was available in you somewhere. Many people resist this idea, believing that they solve the puzzles by moving the letters around and trying them in different order, as if they were anagrams. But they are not anagrams and they have no consistent rules, and people often get them immediately, without having the time to figure them out.

I show a series of these intuitive puzzles when I give speeches and ask audience members to call out the answers as they come to them. Most of the correct answers — sometimes nearly all of them — come from women. It's also so that most of the *incorrect* answers come from women. That's because women are willing to call out what comes to them — they are willing to guess. The men, conversely, won't risk being wrong in front of a roomful of people, so they won't call out an answer until they are sure it's correct. The result is that while each man is plodding through his personal logic test for each puzzle, the women have called out all the answers. Woman are more comfortable relying on intuition because they do it all the time.

Intuition is just listening; prediction is more like trying to solve the puzzles with logic. You may have greater confidence in conscious predictions because you can show yourself the methodology you used, but that doesn't necessarily increase their accuracy. Even though this is a chapter about improving conscious predictions, don't believe for a moment that when it comes to human behavior the conscious predictions are any better than the unconscious ones.

▪ ▪ ▪

We predict the behavior of other human beings based on our ability to read certain signals that we recognize. In Desmond Morris's *Bodytalk,* he describes the meaning of gestures and body movements and notes in which parts of the world various meanings apply. Amazingly, sixty-six of the signals are listed as being valid worldwide, universal to all human beings in every culture on earth. The majority of them are presented unconsciously. Everywhere in the world, the chin jutted forward is a sign of aggression, the head slightly retracted is a sign of fear, the nostrils flared while taking a sharp breath is a sign of anger. If a person anywhere on the planet holds his arms forward with the palms facing down while making small downward movements, he means "Calm down." In every culture, stroking the chin means "I am thinking."

Just as these movements are unconscious, so is our reading of them usually unconscious. If I asked you to list just fifteen of the sixty-six worldwide gestures or physical movements, you'd find it difficult, but you absolutely know them all and respond to each intuitively. Earlier I mentioned the predictive language of dogs, which is all nonverbal. Desmond Morris has identified one of the nonverbal parts of human language, but we have many others. Often, knowing the language of a given prediction is more important than understanding exactly what a person says. The key is understanding the meaning and the perspective beneath and behind the words people choose. When predicting violence, some of the languages include:

The language of rejection
The language of entitlement
The language of grandiosity
The language of attention seeking
The language of revenge
The language of attachment
The language of identity seeking

Attention seeking, grandiosity, entitlement, and rejection are often linked. Think of someone you know who is always in need of attention, who cannot bear to be alone or to be unheard. Few people like being ignored, of course, but to this person it will have a far greater meaning. Imagine Al Sharpton or Rush Limbaugh unable to garner attention by the methods they do today. Believing they deserve it (entitlement and grandiosity), knowing they need it (fear of rejection), and committed to being seen and listened to (attention seeking), they might strongly resist a loss of audience. If the need in them is great enough (and you be the judge), they might do some pretty extreme things to draw interest.

Think of a person you know whose self-evaluation is lofty or grandiose, perhaps even with good reason. When he volunteers for something and later learns that he was not chosen or wasn't even seriously considered, the news will have a different meaning to him than it would to a modest, humble person. Such a person might also feel humiliated more quickly than a modest person.

In each prediction about violence, we must ask what the context, stimuli, and developments might mean to the person involved, not just what they mean to us. We must ask if the actor will perceive violence as moving him toward some desired outcome or away from it. The conscious or unconscious decision to use violence, or to do most anything, involves many mental and emotional processes, but they usually boil down to how a person perceives four fairly simple issues: justification, alternatives, consequences, and ability. My office abbreviates these elements as JACA, and an evaluation of them helps predict violence.

PERCEIVED JUSTIFICATION (J)

Does the person feel justified in using violence? Perceived justification can be as simple as being sufficiently provoked ("Hey, you stepped on my foot!") or as convoluted as looking for an excuse to argue, as with the spouse that starts a disagreement in order to justify an angry response. The process of developing and manufacturing justification can be observed. A person who is seeking to feel justification for some action might move from "What you've done angers me" to "What you've done is wrong." Popular justifications include the moral high ground of righteous indignation and the more simple equation known by its biblical name: an eye for an eye.

Anger is a very seductive emotion because it is profoundly energizing and exhilarating. Sometimes people feel their anger is justified by past unfairnesses, and with the slightest excuse, they bring forth resentments unrelated to the present situation. You could say such a person has prejustified hostility, more commonly known as having a chip on his shoulder.

The degree of provocation is, of course, in the eye of the provoked. John Monahan notes that "how a person appraises an event may have a great influence on whether he or she ultimately responds to it in a violent manner." What he calls "perceived intentionality" (e.g., "You didn't just bump into me, you meant to hit me") is perhaps the clearest example of a person looking for justification.

PERCEIVED ALTERNATIVES (A)

Does the person perceive that he has available alternatives to violence that will move him toward the outcome he wants? Since violence, like any behavior, has a purpose, it's valuable to know the goal of the actor. For example, if a person wants his job back, violence is not the most effective strategy, since it precludes the very outcome he seeks. Conversely, if he wants revenge, violence *is* a viable strategy, though usually not the only one. Alternatives to violence might be ridicule, smear campaigns, lawsuits, or inflicting some other nonphysical harm on the targeted person or organization. Knowing the desired outcome is the key. If a person's desired outcome is to inflict physical injury, then there are few alternatives to violence. If the desired outcome is to punish someone, there might be many. It is when he perceives no alternatives that violence is most likely. David wouldn't have fought Goliath if he had perceived alternatives. Justification alone wouldn't have been enough to compensate for his low ability to prevail over his adversary. More than anything, he fought because he had no choice. A person (or an animal) who feels there are no alternatives will fight even when violence isn't justified, even when the consequences are perceived as unfavorable, and even when the ability to prevail is low.

PERCEIVED CONSEQUENCES (C)

How does the person view the consequences associated with using violence? Before resorting to force, people weigh the likely consequences, even if unconsciously or very quickly. Consequences might be intolerable, such as for a person whose identity and self-image would be too damaged if he used violence. Context can change that, as with the person who is normally passive but becomes violent in a crowd or mob. (Violence can be made tolerable by the support or encouragement of others.) It is when consequences are perceived as favorable, such as for an assassin who wants attention and has little to lose, that violence is likely.

PERCEIVED ABILITY (A)

Does the person believe he can successfully deliver the blows or bullet or bomb? People who have successfully used violence in the past have a higher appraisal of their ability to prevail using violence again. People with weapons or other advantages perceive (often correctly) a high ability to use violence.

■ ■ ■

To see the JACA elements in practice on a large scale, look at world conflict. The Palestinians have the goal of reclaiming and protecting their land rights. Some also have the goal of avenging past wrongs and punishing the Israelis. In either case, those who bring violence to the issue feel *justified* in doing so. They perceive no *alternatives* that will move them toward their goals as effectively as violence. They view the *consequences* of violence as favorable (pressure on the Israelis, world attention to their plight, vengeance for past suffering, etc.). They perceive a high *ability* to deliver violence (by now with good reason).

To predict whether the Palestinians will continue to use violence, we must — at least for the purposes of evaluation — see the issues their way. The importance of seeing things from the perspective of the person whose behavior you are predicting cannot be overstated. A recent *60 Minutes* show gave a good example of most people's reluctance to do that. It profiled the mastermind terrorist known as the Engineer, a man who helped kamikaze martyrs strap explosives to their chests. His agents became walking bombs, carrying death into populated areas. Interviewer Steve Kroft asked one of the Engineer's terrorist followers to describe the man who could do such terrible things. The answer: "He's a very normal person, just like all of us."

Kroft took exception: "You said that he is just like all of the rest of us. I, I, I would say that, that no one would consider you and him normal."

The terrorist replied, "I believe your statement is incorrect. There are thousands and thousands in our country that believe what we believe — and not only our country, in the rest of the Arab world and even in your country." The terrorist was right.

JACA elements can be observed in governments just as with individuals. When America is preparing to go to war, justification is first: evil empire, mad dictator, international outlaw, protect our interests, "Cannot just stand by and watch," etc. Alternatives to violence shrink as we move from negotiations to demands, warnings to boycotts, and finally blockades to attacks. The perceived consequences of going to war move from intolerable to tolerable as public opinion comes into alignment with government opinion. Our appraisal of our ability rises as ships and troops are moved into proximity of an enemy.

At the end of the day, the American bomber who kills a hundred people in Iraq decides to use violence the same way as the Palestinian bomber who kills a hundred people in Israel.

This idea may bother some readers, but as was discussed in chapter 3, effective predictions require that we not make value judgments. Instead, we must see the battle — at least for a moment — from the deck of the enemy warship, because each person has his own perspective, his own reality, no matter how much it may differ from ours. As historian James Burke explains: "All that can accurately be said about a man who thinks he is a poached egg is that he is in the minority."

■ ■ ■

THE ELEMENTS OF PREDICTION

There is a way to evaluate the likelihood of success of any prediction, a way to predict the prediction, so to speak. It can be done by measuring eleven elements. These elements, which I am offering here as a glimpse into some of the strategies used by my firm, apply to every type of prediction, not just those involving violence. I know how universal they are, for many corporate clients whom we have advised on high-stakes predictions have asked us to assist on other types of predictions, such as what opposing litigants might do.

We start by answering the following questions:

1. Measurability

How measurable is the outcome you seek to predict? Will it be clear if it happens or does not happen? For example, imagine the predictive question is "Will a bomb explode in the auditorium during the pro-choice rally?" That outcome is measurable (i.e., it would be obvious if it happened).

If, however, the predictive question is "Will we have a good time on an upcoming trip to Hawaii?" we might not have a shared definition of "good time." My having a good time might not be obvious to you and might not be easily discoverable. Thus, the prediction is less likely to succeed than those with outcomes that are easily measurable.

2. Vantage

Is the person making the prediction in a position to observe the pre-incident indicators and context? For example, to predict what will happen between two quarreling people, it is valuable to have a vantage point from which you can see and hear them.

3. Imminence

Are you predicting an outcome that might occur soon, as opposed to some remote time in the future? Ideally, one predicts outcomes that might happen while they are still significant. "Will someone attempt to harm Senator Smith next week?" is an easier predictive question to answer successfully than "Will someone attempt to harm Senator Smith in thirty years?" Success is more likely for the first question because conditions next week will not be affected by as many intervening influences as conditions in thirty years will.

Our best predictive resources are applied when outcomes might occur while they are still meaningful to us. Though perhaps harsh to Senator Smith, it might not matter much to people today if he is harmed in thirty years.

There is a similar dynamic with more personal predictive questions, such as "Will smoking kill me?" Smokers can easily predict that it will likely kill them, but the outcome is so remote in time that it loses much of its significance.

4. Context

Is the context of the situation clear to the person making the prediction? Is it possible to evaluate the attendant conditions and circumstances, the relationship of parties and events to each other?

5. Pre-incident Indicators (PINs)

Are there detectable pre-incident indicators that will reliably occur before the outcome being predicted? This is the most valuable of the elements. If one were predicting whether a governor might be the object of an assassination attempt at a speech, pre-incident indicators could include the assassin's jumping on stage with a gun — but that is too recent a PIN to be very useful (as it provides little time for intervention). The birth of the assassin is also a PIN, but it is too dated to be valuable. Even though both of these events are critical intersections on the map of this particular prediction, one hopes to be somewhere between the two, between the earliest possible detectable factor and those that occur an instant before the act. Useful PINs for assassination might include the assassin's trying to learn the governor's schedule, developing a plan, purchasing a weapon, keeping a diary, or telling people "something big is coming."

Ideally, an outcome would be preceded by several reliable PINs, but they must also be detectable. Someone's getting the idea to kill and making the decision to kill are both extraordinarily valuable PINs, but since these occur in the mind, they might not be detectable on their own. Later I'll discuss the PINs for workplace violence, spousal killings, homicides by children, and public-figure attack. They are always there, though not always known to the people making the predictions.

6. Experience

Does the person making the prediction have experience with the specific topic involved? A lion tamer can predict whether or not a lion will attack more accurately than I can because he has experience. He can do an even better job if he has experience with both possible outcomes (lions that do not attack and lions that do).

7. Comparable Events

Can you study or consider outcomes that are comparable — though not necessarily identical — to the one being predicted? Ideally, one relies on events that are substantively comparable. Predicting whether a senator will be shot by a mentally ill member of the general public, one might study cases in which mayors were shot by deranged pursuers, as this is substantively the same situation, and the relationship between the players is similar. One can learn about the PINs in the mayor cases and consider whether they apply to the present prediction. On the other hand, studying cases of senators shot by their spouses or senators who shot themselves would not likely improve the success of a prediction about a stranger's shooting a senator.

8. Objectivity

Is the person making the prediction objective enough to believe that either outcome is possible? People who believe only one outcome is possible have already completed their prediction. With the simple decision to make a decision before the full range of predictive tests has been completed, they have hit the wall of their intuitive ability. Asked to predict whether a given employee will act violently, the person who believes that kind of thing never happens is not the right choice for the job. People only apply all their predictive resources when they believe either outcome is possible.

9. Investment

To what degree is the person making the prediction invested in the outcome? Simply put, how much does he or she care about avoiding or exploiting the outcome? Does he or she have reason to want the prediction to be correct? If I ask you right now to predict whether I will oversleep tomorrow, you won't bring your best predictive resources to the question because you don't care. If, however, you are relying on me to pick you up at the airport early tomorrow morning, your prediction will be far better.

10. Replicability

Is it practical to test the exact issue being predicted by trying it first elsewhere? Asked to predict if water in a pot will boil when heated, you need not heat *this* water to improve the prediction. You can test the issue, replicate it exactly, by heating other water first. It is a low-cost experiment for a low-stakes prediction. While replicability is the cornerstone of most scientific predictions, it is nearly useless in high-stakes predictions of human behavior. I cannot test whether an angry employee will shoot a supervisor by giving him a gun and watching him at work.

11. Knowledge

Does the person making the prediction have *accurate* knowledge about the topic? Unless it is relevant and accurate, knowledge can be the sinking ship the fool insists is seaworthy, because knowledge often masquerades as wisdom. If a corporate executive has knowledge that most perpetrators of workplace violence are white males between thirty-five and fifty years old, he might ignore someone's bizarre behavior because the employee does not "fit the profile."

(In my firm, we use a predictive instrument that assigns point values to each of these eleven elements. The scale and its ranges appear in appendix 6, along with some examples of popular predictions.)

▪ ▪ ▪

The most advanced concept of prediction has to do with deciding just when it is that a thing starts to happen. The prediction of earthquakes gives us an extreme example: There are, contrary to popular belief, reliable pre-incident indicators for earthquakes. The problem is that the PINs might be ten thousand years long, and for this reason earthquakes remain, in human terms, unpredictable. In geological terms, however, it is fair to say that the next earthquake in Los Angeles has already started. In geology, calling something a catastrophe means only that the event occurs in a time period short enough to be meaningful to man. The earth's moving is not the issue, because the ground you are on right now is moving. The suddenness is the issue.

In predicting violence, a pre-incident indicator that takes a long time begs the question of whether we need to wait until something becomes a catastrophe versus trying to detect it at a midway mark. Does an assassination attempt begin when the gun is fired at the victim, or when it is drawn, or when it is carried into the arena, or when it is loaded, or when it is purchased, or when assassination is first thought of? Prediction moves from a science to an art when you realize that *pre-incident indicators are actually part of the incident.*

When you apply this concept to human beings, you can see that behavior is like a chain. Too often, we look at just the individual links. When we ask why a man committed suicide, someone might say, "He was despondent over major financial losses," as if this could possibly explain it. Many people are despondent over financial losses and don't kill themselves. Though we want to believe that violence is a matter of cause and effect, it is actually a process, a chain in which the violent outcome is only one link. If you were predicting what a friend of yours might do if he lost his job, you wouldn't say, "Oh, he'll commit suicide" unless there were many other PINs of suicide present. You'd see the loss of his job as a single link, not the whole chain. *The process of suicide starts way before the act of suicide.*

The same is true for homicide. Though we might try to explain a murder using simple cause-and-effect logic (e.g., "He learned his wife was having an affair so he killed her"), it doesn't aid prediction to think this way. Like the earthquake, violence is one outcome of a process that started way before this man got married.

▪ ▪ ▪

By this point, you have read a lot about successful predictions, more perhaps than can easily be recalled. Still, there's no need for a memory test because the information is already in your mind. I know that because it came from your mind in the first place. These elements of prediction are the same ones our ancestors relied on to survive. If they seem new to you, it's because they have been largely ignored by modern Westerners. We perceive less need for them because we are at a point in our evolution where life is less about predicting risks and more about controlling them.

Endowed with great intellect with which to protect ourselves, we have developed extraordinary technologies for survival. Chief among them is modern medicine; though we are no less vulnerable to injury, we are far less likely to die from it. Technology has also provided the ability to call for help, so we rarely feel isolated in an emergency. We also have rapid transportation that can rush us to medical care, or rush it to us. Even with all this, we have more fear today than ever before, and most of it is fear of each other.

To be as free from it as possible, we need to recapture our inherent predictive skills. In the following chapters, the elements of prediction and intuition that I've discussed will come together in practice. You'll see that just as hearing intuition is no more than reading the signals we give ourselves, predicting human behavior is no more than reading the signals others give us.

■ 7 ■

PROMISES TO KILL

"Man is a coward, plain and simple. He loves life too much. He fears others too much."

— *Jack Henry Abbott*

"I am going to kill you." These six words may have triggered more high-stakes predictions than any other sentence ever spoken. They have certainly caused a great deal of fear and anxiety. But why?

Perhaps we believe only a deranged and dangerous person would even think of harming us, but that just isn't so. Plenty of people have thought of harming you: the driver of the car behind you who felt you were going too slowly, the person waiting to use the pay phone you were chatting on, the person you fired, the person you walked out on — they have all hosted a fleeting violent idea. Though thoughts of harming you may be terrible, they are also inevitable. The thought is not the problem; the expression of the thought is what causes us anxiety, and most of the time that's the whole idea. Understanding this will help reduce unwarranted fear.

That someone would intrude on our peace of mind, that they would speak words so difficult to take back, that they would exploit our fear, that they would care so little about us, that they would raise the stakes so high, that they would stoop so low — all of this alarms us, and by design.

Threatening words are dispatched like soldiers under strict orders: Cause anxiety that cannot be ignored. Surprisingly, their deployment isn't entirely bad news. It's bad, of course, that someone threatens violence, but the threat means that at least for now, he has considered violence and decided against doing it. The threat means that at least for now (and usually forever), he favors words that alarm over actions that harm.

For an instrument of communication used so frequently, the threat is little understood, until you think about it. The parent who threatens punishment, the lawyer who threatens unspecified "further action," the head of state who threatens war, the ex-husband who threatens murder, the child who threatens to make a scene — all are using words with the exact same intent: to cause uncertainty.

Our social world relies on our investing some threats with credibility while discounting others. Our belief that they really will tow the car if we leave it here encourages us to look for a parking space unencumbered by that particular threat. The disbelief that our joking spouse will really kill us if we are late to dinner allows us to stay in the marriage. Threats, you see, are not the issue — context is the issue.

For example, as you watch two people argue, an escalation of hostility that would otherwise cause alarm causes none if it is happening between actors on stage at the theater. Conversely, behavior that is normally not threatening, such as a man's walking up some stairs, becomes alarming when it is an uninvited audience member marching up onto that same stage. It is context that gives meaning to the few steps he takes.

A single word between intimates, perhaps meaningless to others, might carry a strong message of love or threat, depending on context. Context is the necessary link that gives meaning to everything we observe.

Imagine a man arriving for work one morning. He does not go in the unlocked front door where most people enter the building but instead goes around to a back entrance. When he sees someone ahead of him use a key to get in, he runs up and catches the door before it relocks. Once he is inside the building, he barely responds as a co-worker calls out, "The boss wants to see you." "Yeah, I want to see him too," the man says quietly. He is carrying a gym bag, but it appears too heavy to contain just clothes. Before going to his boss's office, he stops in the locker room, reaches into the bag, and pulls out a pistol. He takes a second handgun from the bag and conceals both of them beneath his coat. Now he looks for his boss.

If we stopped right here, and you had to predict this man's likely behavior on the basis of what you know, context would tell the tale, because to know just one thing changes every other thing: This man is a police detective. If he were a postal worker, your prediction would be different.

▪ ▪ ▪

Though knowing context is key to predicting which threats will be acted upon, people are often reluctant to put it ahead of content. Even some experts believe that threat assessments are aided by identifying and considering so-called key words. The assumption is that these words are significant by their presence alone, but the practice is rarely enlightening. As a person creates a communication, his selection of words is part of that creation, but they are instruments, not the final product.

Look at this list of words:

SKIN	RIP
PEEL	WARNING
BLOOD	KILL
MUTILATED	BOMB

A key-word enthusiast could enjoy plenty of alarm from a single paragraph containing *kill, blood,* and *bomb,* but you decide if the final product merits concern:

> The whole car trip I was cold right down to my skin. The wind would rip along so hard I thought it would peel the roof off. And here's a warning: Don't ever travel with relatives. Blood may be thicker than water, but trying to kill time listening to Uncle Harry's mutilated jokes bomb was just too much.

Conversely, look at this list of words and the context in which they appear:

TIDY
PRETTY
FLOWERS
BEAUTIFUL
WELCOME

> Tidy up your affairs and buy some pretty flowers, because God has ordered me to take you to his beautiful place, where he is anxious to welcome you.

Here is a letter I once assessed for a client:

> As I walked with you yesterday, the sheer grace of your body thrilled me. Your beauty gives me a starting point for appreciating all other beauty, in a flower or a stream. I sometimes cannot tell where you let off and the beauty of nature begins, and all I want is to feel your body and share my love with you.

It is context that makes the prose in this letter so alarming: It was written by a fifty-year-old man to the ten-year-old daughter of a neighbor. (The man moved soon after we interviewed him; he is now in prison for a predictable offense: repeatedly propositioning an underage girl to have sex with him.)

The phone message "Hi, honey, it's me" might, all by itself, communicate a terrible threat if it is the voice of an ex-husband whom a woman has tried to avoid by fleeing to another state and changing her name.

▪ ▪ ▪

As I said, context is much more important to predictions than content, and this truth relates to safety in some significant ways. For example, as I write this I am in Fiji, where from time to time a person is killed by something most of us don't consider dangerous: a coconut. Given that the trees are often very tall and the coconuts very large, if one falls on you, the impact is comparable to having a bowling ball dropped on your head from the roof of a five-story building.

Are there ways to see the coconut hazard coming? Absolutely, there are many, but to detect them would involve evaluating all the factors that influence a coconut's readiness to fall. I might have to climb the tree, test the stem strength, consider such things as the moistness and density of the fiber, the weight of the coconut, etc. I could measure the wind velocity and the rate at which similarly ripened coconuts have recently fallen from nearby trees. Ultimately, however, there's just one practical pre-incident indicator. It's the sound of a coconut falling through dried bark or leaves. Most of the time, this warning comes much too late to exploit. In other words, it could be the last sound one hears. So is there a way to avoid this lethal outcome?

Yes, there is, but I needn't sit at the base of a tree contemplating the question as a coconut rushes downward toward my skull. Since the outcome only happens in the very limited context of being under a coconut tree, I can avoid the hazard altogether . . . simply by sitting elsewhere. Similarly, we can avoid risks that are inherently present in certain situations. We need not walk defiantly through the territory of a violent gang, or wear our Rolex on a trip to Rio, or stay in a violent relationship. Context can be a useful predictor of hazard all by itself.

Context can also be a reliable guarantor of safety. Teaching a criminal-justice class at George Washington University, I asked five of the students to think up the most frightening, convincing death threats they could and then deliver them to me. I would assess and then accurately determine the seriousness of each one.

The first student I called on stood up and said matter-of-factly: "It's ironic that you would have this exercise tonight, and I can't believe you chose me to go first, because I actually have been planning to kill you. When I saw on the schedule that you were teaching tonight, I borrowed, well, *took* my brother's pistol. I have it here in my briefcase."

He held up the case and tilted it from side to side so we could hear that it did indeed contain something heavy. "I first planned to shoot you as you walked to your car, but I have decided to do it here in the classroom. Given the topic of the class and the fact that you are an expert on threats, this shooting will intrigue people and bring me attention for a long while."

He looked around at the other students, some of whom were a bit uncomfortable. "If anybody wants to avoid seeing this, you should leave right now." As he reached slowly into his briefcase, I called out, "Next threat," and he sat down. I had told the class I'd be able to predict the seriousness and outcome of each threat with perfect reliability, and I did. That's because it made no difference what they said or how they said it. Since I had asked the students to threaten me, context — not content — dictated the obvious: None of the threats would be acted upon.

Still, because most people have had little experience with death threats, and because they mistakenly believe that the death threat is inherently different from all other threats, the words usually cause undue fear. In fact, the death threat is among the threats least likely to be carried out.

The first step toward deciding which words actually portend danger is understanding what threats are and what they are not. A threat is a statement of an intention to do some harm, period. It offers no conditions, no alternatives, no ways out. It does not contain the words *if, or else, until, unless.* Sentences that do contain those words are not threats; they are intimidations, and there is an important distinction.

Intimidations are statements of conditions to be met in order to avert a harm. For example, "I will burn this building down *if* I don't get the promotion" is an intimidation, not a threat, because a condition is offered to avert the harm. With intimidations, the motive is always right in the statement, and the outcome the speaker desires is clear. "*Unless* you apologize, I'll kill you" (the speaker wants an apology). "*If* you fire me, you'll be sorry" (the speaker wants to keep his job).

These statements differ importantly from threats because they are brought into play as high-stakes manipulations. The speaker wants his conditions met — he does not want to inflict the harm. With threats, conversely, no conditions are offered, usually because the speaker sees few alternatives. Thus, threats carry more likelihood of violence than intimidations. Another tip: Threats that are end-game moves — those introduced late in a controversy — are more serious than those used early. That's because those used early likely represent an immediate emotional response as opposed to a decision to use violence.

As an instrument of communication, the threat is most similar to the promise (though promises are kept far more often). With a promise, if we judge that the speaker is sincere, we next assess the likelihood that he will retain his will over time. One may promise something today but feel different tomorrow. Because threats are often spoken from emotion, and because emotions are ephemeral, threateners often lose their will over time. Threats and promises alike are easy to speak, harder to honor.

Both promises and threats are made to convince us of an intention, but threats actually convince us of an emotion: frustration. Threats betray the speaker by proving that he has failed to influence events in any other way. Most often they represent desperation, not intention. Neither threats nor promises are guarantees, contracts, or even commitments; they are just words. (Guarantees offer to set things right if the promise isn't kept. With contracts there is some cost for breaches of the promise. People making commitments have a personal cost if they fail to keep them, but those who threaten have found the cheapest form of promise, and also the one that others actually hope they'll break.)

Though you wouldn't know it by the reaction they frequently earn, threats are rarely spoken from a position of power. Whatever power they have is derived from the fear instilled in the victim, for fear is the currency of the threatener. He gains advantage through your uncertainty, but once the words are spoken, he must retreat or advance and, like all people, he hopes to retain dignity through either course.

How one responds to a threat determines whether it will be a valuable instrument or mere words. Thus, it is the listener and not the speaker who decides how powerful a threat will be. If the listener turns pale, starts shaking, and begs for forgiveness, he has turned the threat or intimidation into gold. Conversely, if he seems unaffected, it is tin.

Even in cases in which threats are determined to be serious (and thus call for interventions or extensive precautions), we advise clients never to show the threatener a high appraisal of his words, never to show fear.

These days, bomb threats are a tactic popular with angry people. It's amazing how much fear can be caused by a single phone call; it might compel an organization to evacuate a building, close for the day, or enact restrictive security procedures. But to believe the caller who says, "I've planted a bomb, and it's going off in three hours," you have to believe that the person went to the extraordinary trouble and risk of obtaining the bomb components, then found a location where he could be sure nobody would ever see what he was doing, then assembled the bomb, then took the chance of losing his liberty and life while placing the device, and then undid it all by making the warning call.

What might be his motives for calling and telling you what he'd done? Does he make the call as a warning to help save lives? Wouldn't it be easier to save lives by planting a bomb in a place where there wouldn't be any people, or just not planting it at all?

Let's go one level deeper: Imagine a person built and planted a bomb but then changed his mind and called in a threat to be sure nobody was hurt. Wouldn't this unlikely on-again-off-again sociopath give you highly specific information, such as exactly where it was planted?

Another possible motive for a real bomber to call in a threat is to ensure that he gets credit for the explosion, because after it happens, several people or groups might say they did it. Only the person who called before the explosion is guaranteed the credit. Think about this, though: If a bomber is so egomaniacal that he wants to ensure he gets the attention for his mayhem, is he really going to self-sabotage by giving police time to find and defuse his pride and joy?

We give so much credence to the words "I've planted a bomb" that I often wonder if we'd react as gullibly to other unbelievable claims. If some anonymous caller said, "Listen, I've buried a million dollars cash in the planter in front of the building," would everybody from the CEO to the receptionist rush out and start digging through the dirt?

What about when the caller contradicts himself? First he says he planted a bomb in the lobby, then he calls ten minutes later and says he *didn't* plant a bomb in the lobby after all. Do we stop the search and just let everybody go back to work? What about when the same bomb threat we evacuated the building for on Monday comes again on Tuesday and again on Wednesday? At what point do we stop treating anonymous threateners as if they were the most credible people we'd ever heard from when in fact nearly 100 percent of these calls are bogus? The answer is, at the point where we have greater confidence in our predictions.

We get that confidence by understanding as much as possible about threats. For example, if the bomb threatener is angry and hostile, the call is probably designed to do what most threats are designed to do: cause fear and anxiety. A caller who wants to discharge anger over the telephone by using violent imagery ("You'll all be blown to bits"), or who is agitated and aggressive, is not behaving like a real bomber. Most real bombers are patient *I'll-get-you-in-time* type people who can mortgage their emotions for another day. They express anger by blowing things up, not by making hostile calls. Ironically, bombers do not have explosive personalities.

(Because bomb threats raise so many liability questions for employers — e.g., Should we evacuate? Should we tell employees about threats so they can make their own decisions? How should threats be assessed? Who should be notified? — our office assists organizations in establishing bomb-threat response policies. Most of the big questions can be answered ahead of time so one isn't searching for a light switch in the dark. Without this approach, critical decisions are made in the stress of some highly charged moment. As with all threats, context is the key issue. A threat made at an Olympic event, which is politically charged and the focus of world media attention, will be assessed differently than the same words aimed at a shopping center.)

▪ ▪ ▪

Some threateners are so unorganized that they modify their initial threats or spit out several alarming concepts in a row. Some say, "You'll all be blown up within the hour," then say, "You ought to be killed," then say, "Your day will come, I promise." We call these amendments "value reduction statements," and callers who use them reveal themselves to be more interested in venting anger than warning of danger.

The things people say when threatening others are intentionally shocking and alarming. Victims often describe a threat they received as "horrible" or "vicious" because it paints a gruesome picture. "I'll cut you up into little pieces" is a popular one. So is "I'll blow your brains out." Again and again, however, content is far less significant than context, and the choice of alarming words usually speaks more of someone's desire to frighten than of his intention to harm. "I'll blow your head off" or "I'll gun you down like a dog" may, depending upon context, portend less danger than does the simple statement "I can't take this any more."

Still, alarming words cause people to react by going into a defensive posture, psychologically speaking. Though shocking or bizarre things don't usually put us at any actual risk, uncertainty about risk causes us alarm, and this causes a problem: When we are stunned or distracted we raise the very drawbridge — perception — that we must cross in order to make successful predictions.

In the last thirty years, I've read, heard, and seen the world's most creative, gruesome, distasteful, and well-performed threats. I've learned that it's important to react calmly, because when in alarm we stop evaluating information mindfully and start doing it physically.

For example, a death threat communicated in a letter or phone call cannot possibly pose any immediate hazard, but the recipient might nonetheless start getting physically ready for danger, with increased blood flow to the arms and legs (for fighting or running), release of the chemical cortisol (which helps blood coagulate more quickly in case of injury), lactic acid heating up in the muscles (to prepare them for effort), focused vision, and increased breathing and heartbeat to support all these systems. These responses are valuable when facing present danger (such as when Kelly stood up and walked out of her apartment), but for evaluating *future* hazard, staying calm produces better results. A way to do this is to consciously ask and answer the question "Am I in immediate danger?" Your body wants you to get this question out of the way, and once you do, you'll be free to keep perceiving what's going on.

The great enemy of perception, and thus of accurate predictions, is judgment. People often learn just enough about something to judge it as belonging in this or that category. They observe bizarre conduct and say, "This guy is just crazy." Judgments are the automatic pigeonholing of a person or situation simply because some characteristic is familiar to the observer (so whatever that characteristic meant before it must mean again now). Familiarity is comfortable, but such judgments drop the curtain, effectively preventing the observer from seeing the rest of the play.

Another time people stop perceiving new information is when they prematurely judge someone as guilty or not guilty. Recall the story of the woman who was certain the threats she was getting were from the man she had sued. In telling me about it, she provided details that were not necessary to the story (details I call satellites). I could hear them for what they were — valuable information — but she couldn't hear them because she had already settled on one particular suspect, thus shutting down perception.

The opposite can also happen, as in cases in which people exclude one particular suspect. Find the satellite in Sally's story:

"Someone is terrorizing me, and I've got to find out who it is. A few weeks ago, a car drove up the hill to my house, and the driver just stared at the front door. I flipped the porch lights on and off, and he left. It happened again the next day. Then the calls started. A man's voice said, 'You should move; it's not safe there for a woman alone. You don't belong there.' I'm so lucky I met Richard Barnes a few days later — he's the guy I'm selling the house to. And you know what? My house really is too remote for a woman alone."

What is the satellite, the unneeded detail? The name of the man she is selling to.

"Tell me about Richard Barnes."

"Oh, he's got nothing to do with this. He's just the guy who is buying the house, and what a godsend he is. One day as I was getting my mail, he was jogging by, and we started talking. He mentioned how much he loved the bay windows at my house, and one thing led to another. He made an offer the next afternoon."

"What about the anonymous calls scared you?"

"I was worried whoever it was might want to hurt me, of course."

"But the caller said you should move. Your moving wouldn't serve someone who intended to hurt you. Who would be served by your moving?"

"Nobody. [A pause.] Someone who wanted to buy my house?"

You know where this is going. Further discussion revealed that Richard Barnes lived in a suburb more than an hour away, so why was he jogging in Sally's neighborhood? He knew details about her house (the bay windows) that a person could gain only by driving up the long driveway. Sally had made a judgment that excluded him as a suspect and accordingly she left him out of her thinking.

Since the motive for nearly all anonymous threats is to influence conduct, I suggest that clients ask who would be served if they took the actions that they'd take if they believed the threats would be carried out. This often leads to the identity of the threatener.

▪ ▪ ▪

One popular form of intimidation that is rarely done anonymously is extortion. In common extortion cases, a person threatens to disclose information he predicts will be damaging, and he offers to keep the secret if compensated. Since victims of threats — and not threateners — decide how valuable a threat will be, the way you react will set the price tag.

The proverbial extortion threat is actually an intimidation, because it contains the words *if, or else, unless,* or *until:* "If you don't give me ten thousand dollars, I'll tell your wife you are having an affair." Best response: "Hold on a moment, let me get my wife on the line and you can tell her right now." With that reaction, the threat is turned from gold to tin. If you can convince an extortionist that the harm he threatens does not worry you, you have at a minimum improved your negotiating position. In many cases, you may actually neutralize the whole matter.

Conversely, reacting with pleading and compliance increases the extortionist's appraisal of his threat. A threatened harm can be so intolerable to the victim that paying for silence seems worthwhile.

Often this paves the way to hear that threat another day, for the person who successfully extorts money once may come back to the reluctant bank.

Some people, of course, choose to pay extortionists, though I rarely recommend it. Aside from what I'd call legal extortion (letters from lawyers demanding payments for a client's unjustified claims), few extortionists can be relied upon to stick to the terms of agreements they might make. In other words, you are negotiating an agreement with someone who cannot be relied upon to honor it.

Public figures are probably the most frequent targets for extortion, and there are some lessons to learn from their experience. In a typical case, someone has potentially damaging information and now demands to be rewarded for keeping the confidence. I recall a young film star whose rise to fame brought a call from a sleazy ex-boyfriend she hadn't heard from in years. Unless my client gave him $50,000, he threatened, he would reveal that she had had an abortion. The thought of this becoming known caused her great anxiety and thus enhanced the value of the threat. By the time she met with me, she hadn't slept a full night in a week. My counsel for managing such cases is always to begin with an organized appraisal of the threat. I asked my client to make a list of the people she feared would react adversely if the information were made public.

"That's easy," she said. "My parents. I don't want them to know." I asked that she consider calling her parents and telling them the information in her way, rather than living with the dread that they would learn it his way (or a tabloid's way). I said she was the only person in the world who could determine the value of this threat.

Disclosing the harmful information oneself is so radical an idea that most victims of extortion never even consider it, but within ten minutes, my client made her difficult decision, called her parents, and killed the threat. She got off the phone visibly lighter and more powerful. "I came here willing to do anything to stop him from revealing that secret. Now, I am not willing to do anything at all, because I don't care what he says." (My client paid nothing, and the man never revealed the information anyway. I have a few cases a year just like this one.)

Extortion is a crime of opportunity, usually committed by amateurs who tend to first try the most roundabout approach: "You know, I saw you on the Emmys the other night, and you're doing so well and everything, making so much money, and I've had such a rough year financially, and I was thinking about how beautiful you looked in those pictures we took that time in Mexico . . ." Because extortion is a bit awkward for the neophyte, he wants his victim to jump in and make it easy by saying, "I'd be glad to help you out moneywise, but I wonder, could I get those photos back? I'd hate to see them become public."

Victims often try to appease the extortionist, but these efforts just allow him to retain the undeserved mantle of a decent person. I suggest that clients compel the extortionist to commit to his sleaziness, which puts him on the defensive. Don't let him simply flirt with his lowness — make him marry it by saying those ugly words. I ask victims to repeat "I don't understand what you're getting at" until the extortionist states it clearly. Many extortionists can't do it, and they either stumble around the issue or abandon their bad idea altogether. Making him explicitly state the extortion also helps clarify whether he is motivated by greed or malice, and this provides a road map to his desired outcome.

Though sometimes very difficult, it is important to be polite to the extortionist, because he may be looking for justification to do the hurtful thing he threatens. With the amateur, sinking so low is difficult, and believe it or not, it's a very vulnerable time for him. Don't misread this as sympathy on my part — it's just wise not to kick this guy around emotionally, because if he gets angry that empowers him.

Victims of extortion committed by someone they know are often reluctant to believe he'll actually go through with the threatened act. You can make your own predictions as to what he'll do, but to save time for any reader who ever faces the situation, extortionists who are motivated by malice are more likely to carry out the act than those motivated just by greed. Anyway, those motivated by malice are usually so hard to negotiate with that I usually suggest my clients not even try. Another tip: Those who say the shabby words explicitly right from the start are more likely to carry out the threatened act than those who stumble around.

When any type of threat includes indirect or veiled references to things they might do, such as "You'll be sorry," or "Don't mess with me," it is best to ask directly, "What do you mean by that?" Ask exactly what the person is threatening to do. His elaboration will almost always be weaker than his implied threat. If, on the other hand, his explanation of the comment is actually an explicit threat, better to learn it now than to be uncertain later.

■ ■ ■

One of the best examples of how powerful an influence context can be comes when evaluating threats to public figures. Assumptions that might be accurate in other situations are entirely inaccurate in this one. For example, in interpersonal situations (neighbor, friend, spouse) a threat tends to actually increase the likelihood of violence by eroding the quality of communication and increasing frustration, but the very same threat conveyed to a public figure does not portend violence at all.

Still, it is a tenacious myth that those who threaten public figures are the ones most likely to harm them. In fact, those who make direct threats to public figures are far less likely to harm them than those who communicate in other inappropriate ways (lovesickness, exaggerated adoration, themes of rejection, the belief that a relationship is "meant to be," plans to travel or meet, the belief that the media figure owes them something, etc.). Direct threats are not a reliable pre-incident indicator for assassination in America, as demonstrated by the fact that *not one successful public-figure attacker in the history of the media age directly threatened his victim first.*

While threats communicated directly to famous victims do not predict violence, those spoken to uninvolved second parties are more serious. The person who informs police that a disturbed cousin said he would shoot the governor is providing very valuable information. That's because threats spoken to people other than the victim are not as likely to be motivated by a desire to scare the victim. Though they too are rarely acted upon, threats delivered to second parties should always be reported to law enforcement.

The myth that those who will harm a famous person will directly threaten their victims first has led many to wrongly conclude that inappropriate communications that don't contain threats are not significant. The opposite is actually true. Public figures who ignore inappropriate letters simply because they don't contain threats will be missing the very communications most relevant to safety.

This idea that the presence of a threat lowers risk and the absence of a threat elevates risk is hard for people to grasp, perhaps because it feels counterintuitive, but it's true, and it's not the only fact about threats to public figures that surprises people.

For example, though anonymous death threats cause high concern, they actually portend less danger than accredited threats. People who send threats anonymously are far less likely to pursue an encounter than those who sign their names. There are some compelling reasons why this is so. The threatener who provides his true name is not trying to avoid attention, and is probably seeking it. Thus, he is most similar to assassins, most of whom stand at the scene of their crimes and say, "I did this."

Still, police have historically been intrigued by anonymous death threats and apathetic about accredited ones. Since police are usually faced with the challenge of apprehending suspects who seek to avoid detection, when they encounter one who self-identifies, a common response is "This guy would never do anything — he signed his name right here." The thinking is that if the sender were to carry out the threatened act, apprehension would be easy. This approach fails to recognize that actual public-figure attackers have rarely sought to avoid apprehension. The police misunderstanding about anonymous threats stems from how different the assassin is from almost all other criminals. Who else would actually design his offense to ensure that he gets caught? Who else would hope his act would be videotaped?

To the modern media criminal, most notably the assassin, that is the description of the perfect crime, and a few people will dedicate their lives to committing it. You aren't likely to ever face an assassin, of course, but you are likely to encounter people just as dedicated, people who refuse to let go.

▪ 8 ▪

PERSISTENCE, PERSISTENCE

"That's what happens when you're angry at people.
You make them part of your life."

— *Garrison Keillor*

In America, persistence is a bit like pizza: We didn't invent it, but we've certainly embraced it. We promise our children that persistence will pay off. We treat it as an attribute of success and we compliment the people who hang in there against all odds. However, when persistence is unwanted, those same people we praised can plague our lives. Few situations are more confounding than dealing with people who refuse to let go. We try to predict what they might do next, we worry that they might get angry or dangerous, and we agonize over what strategies will make them stop whatever it is they feel so compelled to continue doing.

Imagine that this happened to you instead of to a client of mine: You and your spouse attend a seminar, and an acquaintance there introduces you to Tommy, a preppy-looking, energetic young man. When told about the upcoming expansion of your travel agency business, the young man lights up with enthusiasm.

This chance meeting may not sound like the start of a nightmare, but that's exactly what it was for Mike Fedder and his wife, Jackie. Over the chatter of the seminar, Tommy told them some of his ideas about the travel business: "I've always been interested in unconventional travel packages, and it's clear that people are moving away from the big hotels kind of thing, more toward camping and rafting and hiking. I have some packaging ideas that I know will double any agency's sales. I just haven't found the right partners to kick it off." He told the Fedders about selling father-son vacations by marketing to lists gathered from Little League organizations.

"I work with some of these teams, and the parents put in a lot of time with their children, so they're obviously willing to invest money in enjoyable activities. The leagues are well organized, so the packages could be offered through their newsletters and meetings. Plus, you can get one father in a group and offer him incentives to sign up others."

Jackie told Tommy she liked the family aspect of the idea, Mike said it sounded interesting, "good nights" all around, and that was that.

Two days later, Tommy called Mike at his successful seventy-five-person travel agency. He'd gotten Mike's number from the woman who introduced them, and he was following up on the "business discussion we started." He wanted to have "just a brief meeting. I could stop by today. Ten minutes is all I need. I promise." Rather than hurt his feelings, Mike agreed. "Two o'clock?" Two o'clock.

Mike was on a long-distance call at two o'clock, so Tommy was kept waiting a few minutes. He seemed a bit put out by this: "I thought we agreed to two o'clock."

"Oh yeah, sorry, I've been working on a forty-person Africa excursion. . . ." *Why am I making excuses to this guy?* Mike wondered. It was a good question. The ten minutes Tommy requested turned to twenty. He had put together some material on his idea, and it was actually impressive — not so much the quality but the quantity; he had obviously put a good deal of effort into it.

Tommy said, "When we really clicked on this the other night, I got to thinking . . ." and then his drop-by visit became a formal proposal: He would take a leave of absence (from? Mike never did hear where Tommy worked) and he'd organize some father-son package tours to Yosemite. If it didn't succeed, Mike would pay him nothing, and if it did succeed, Tommy would get a percentage.

When Mike told him he didn't normally work with outside agents, Tommy said he understood: "I can join the team full time." When Mike told him there wasn't an opening, Tommy said, "Oh,

I can start anyway, and then we'll formalize it when something opens up."

Persistent, Mike thought. *Mark of those who succeed.* Indeed, it was the mark of something, but not success. It was refusing to hear "no," a clear signal of trouble in any context.

Forty minutes into the meeting: "Listen, Tommy, my best agent, Marlene, might be leaving in the next few months — she's getting married — and if that happens, I'll call you and we can revisit the matter."

Tommy was disappointed that there wasn't a more concrete result but said he'd be in touch to explore ways to move "into the next inning."

He called a week later and asked if Mike had made any decisions. (Decisions about what?) "Nothing's really changed, Tommy. Marlene and her fiancé haven't set a date yet," and brush off, brush off.

Tommy ended with "Well, say hi to Jackie." This call gave some clues to another feature of those who don't let go: projecting onto others commitments that were not expressed and are not present.

The next day Marlene asked Mike a bit hesitantly if he had a friend named Tommy. He had called and was wondering about her marriage plans! He had asked if she had "even a ballpark idea" of when she'd be leaving because "Mike and I are trying to get to the next inning."

Within five minutes, Mike had Tommy on the phone: "Listen, you're a nice kid, I know you're just excited about the business, but I have to be clear with you: *If* we ever want to pursue your idea, and *if* it fits into our plans, I will call you. There's no need to call me anymore, and I certainly don't think you should have called Marlene. Understand?"

Tommy didn't seem at all dejected. "Oh, I understand completely, sorry for the confusion. I just thought I should get a time frame from her so I'd be ready to come to work, that's all, no big deal. I won't bug her again." It sounded as if he had gotten it until he added: "She said about eight weeks, so I'll plan for that."

"Um, well, listen, Tommy, don't plan for anything. The travel business isn't like that; you never know what might happen. I hope our paths cross sometime, and I wish you all the luck in the world, and thanks again for your suggestions."

Finally, that was that. *What a persistent guy,* Mike thought, *but I'm sure he got the message.*

About three months later, Mike came back from lunch to find three messages from Tommy on his voice mail. *Mr. Persistent.* Before Mike got around to calling him back, Tommy was on the line again. He seemed agitated: "That was really kind of a surprise, Mike, and not a good surprise — more like a shock. When I called this morning to touch base, they told me Marlene had been gone for two weeks. Two weeks! We had an agreement, you know, so I was a little disappointed. I can't believe we lost two valuable weeks. I'm very committed to making this idea work, and I've put a lot more time into it, refining things. It's really come a long way. I sure hope you haven't hired anybody to replace Marlene."

Mike felt bad for the guy because it obviously meant a lot to him. How to let him down easy? "Well, first of all, Marlene's position is not filled yet (*Why'd I say that!?*), but, uh, that's not the point. We didn't have an agreement. We had a chat, really."

"Well, maybe that's what you think it was, but I've put my heart and soul into this thing. You know, I thought you'd have the kind of commitment it takes to stick with something, but maybe you don't."

An opening, Mike thought. "Maybe I don't, Tommy, so let's just agree to go our separate ways and chalk it up to experience. I'm sorry you went to so much trouble."

Mike hung up.

The next day, Tommy called again, twice, but Mike didn't return the calls. One of the messages said it was urgent, but what could be urgent with somebody you hardly know?

Tommy left five more messages that week, and Mike finally discussed it with his wife. "I don't feel like I led him on, but obviously I must have said something or done something that gave him all these hopes. I don't know what else to tell him and I can't just not return his calls. I don't want to get him angry."

"He's already angry," Jackie said wisely. "He was angry the moment we didn't become his best friends and go into business with him. I don't think anything you can say will be heard by him the way you mean it to be." Jackie, like most women, had much more experience than Mike in dealing with unwanted persistence. She knew that "maybe" is sometimes perceived as "definitely," that "like" can be taken as "love," and that people who don't hear you don't hear you. You get to the point that it doesn't help to keep trying, in fact, it makes matters worse, because it encourages attachment when you are seeking detachment.

If Tommy could read a lifelong partnership into almost nothing, then a response could be taken by him in who knows what way. Contact is fuel for the fire, and Tommy was someone who didn't need much fuel.

"I'll give it another week, and then if it doesn't stop, I'll call him back and lay it on the line."

"But Mike, you did that," Jackie reminded him. "You told him point-blank not to call you again. You said 'Let's go our separate ways.' That all seems pretty clear to me."

Jackie was right. If you tell someone ten times that you don't want to talk to him, you *are* talking to him — nine more times than you wanted to. If you call him back after he leaves twenty messages, you simply teach him that the cost of getting a call back is twenty messages.

For two weeks, there were no calls, and Mike was glad it was finally over. But then another message: "It's urgent I speak with you immediately." Mike felt that he really had to put a stop to this now. At each step, he was making predictions about how Tommy would respond, but he was doing it by applying his own standards for behavior. Mike reasoned that not calling back would be insulting but that somehow calling back and *being* insulting would make things better, and that's what he decided to do:

"What is it with you? You flake! We aren't going to be working together, period. Do you hear me? That should have been clear, but you don't listen. I don't want to talk to you about it anymore, okay?"

Tommy reacted in a way Mike hadn't predicted. He said he was just calling to apologize because he didn't want to burn his bridges behind him. "I still think we can hit a home run with this thing someday," he added.

"No, Tommy, you should move on to something else. If I hear of any interesting openings, I'll let you know. (*Oh, god, why'd I say that?*) But this will be our last call, okay? Can we just leave it at that?" Mike was asking, not telling.

Finally, finally, Mike thought he had gotten through to the guy. That night he told Jackie, "I called that guy back today, and it turns out all he wanted to do was apologize."

Jackie said, "Good, and I hope that's the last call you ever have with him."

"Of course it's the last call. He has apologized and it's over." Until a week later, when there was a Federal Express envelope from Tommy. It contained a note requesting that Mike sign an enclosed letter of reference, which Tommy said would help him at his bank.

Even though Mike had assured Jackie that he'd made his last call, he decided to respond to Tommy's request. To Mike's relief, he reached an answering machine and left this message: "I don't feel comfortable signing the reference letter you sent, but I wish you the best of luck."

People who refuse to let go often make small requests that appear reasonable, like Tommy's letter of reference, though the real purpose of such requests is to cement attachment or gain new reasons for contact. Within a few hours, Tommy left a message for Mike: "I'm not surprised you didn't have the courage to talk with me directly. You know, it would have taken less time to sign that letter than it did to leave me your condescending message. No wonder you're in the travel business; everybody wants to get away from you. Please mail the unsigned letter back to me." Unfortunately, Mike had thrown the letter away. Now Tommy had another issue to chew on.

The next day there was another message: "No need to call back, I just thought I'd let you know you are an asshole. I want that letter back!"

This was too much for Mike. He felt he had to take some real action now. It is at this point in these situations that a fascinating thing happens: The pursuer and the victim begin to actually have something in common — neither wants to let go. The pursuer is obsessed with getting a response and the victim becomes obsessed with making the harassment stop.

What the pursuer is really saying is "I will not allow you to ignore me." He'll push buttons until one provokes a reaction, and then as long as it works, he'll keep pushing it. Guilt is usually first, then harassment, then insult. Each works for a while, and then doesn't. When victims participate in this process, threats are not far behind.

But Mike wasn't going to just sit around and do nothing. He called the person who had introduced them, told her the whole story, and asked for her help. "Maybe you can get through to him and get him to leave me alone."

The next day Mike's voice mail had three messages from Tommy, one of them left at two A.M.: "Now you've ruined one of my best friendships, asshole! I don't know what lies you're spreading about me, but I demand an apology, a written apology. You are on notice."

Two days later, more messages, including one saying that Tommy was going to make a formal complaint, whatever that meant. Then a message saying, "I'm going to book twenty bogus trips with your agency every month. You won't know what's me and what isn't. Then you'll learn not to make promises you never intended to keep."

Jackie convinced Mike to keep the voice-mail messages but otherwise ignore them. The following week another message came in saying that if Mike would call and apologize, Tommy might accept that, "but we're getting to the point that an apology won't be good enough. I like Jackie, and I'm sorry for all the trouble your stubbornness is going to bring her."

Mike and Jackie finally ended up in my office, playing the tapes of the voice-mail messages. By this time, they had already been to the police twice. Officers had visited Tommy and warned him to stop, but he actually got worse after that. To understand the police inclination toward direct intervention, one must recognize that in all cultures of the world, the role of police is to control conduct. Police are the enforcement branch of our society, and when people misbehave, it is police we expect to make them stop. That's usually fine, except in cases in which police contact actually encourages the very behavior it is meant to deter. When nothing else worked, the police told Mike to get a restraining order, but Jackie convinced him to wait until after they had discussed it with me.

Sitting on a couch in my office, Mike made it clear that he was near the end of his rope. He wanted me to "send some people over" to convince Tommy to cut it out (even though that hadn't worked when their friend did it or when the police did it). He said he wanted me to "explain the facts of life to Tommy in no uncertain terms."

I told Mike that all terms were uncertain to Tommy.

"But if he knows he can get into trouble," Mike argued, "it's logical for him to stop."

"Tommy does not have a track record for being logical. He doesn't speak the same language we do, and we can't teach it to him with logic. If he were reasonable, he wouldn't have pursued this behavior in the first place. There is no straight talk for crooked people."

Mike argued more: "I don't want this guy thinking he can get away with harassment."

Jackie responded before I could: "If we can't control what he does, we certainly can't control what he thinks."

I suggested, with Jackie's quick agreement, that if Mike did not respond, Tommy would eventually turn his attention elsewhere. "That may take some time and some patience, and I know it isn't easy, but efforts to change his mind or to change him are the opposite of what you want. You don't want him improved — you want him removed. You want him out of your life. There is a rule we call 'engage and enrage.' The more attachment you have — whether favorable or unfavorable — the more this will escalate. You see, we know a secret, and that is that you are never going to work with him or be friends with him or want anything to do with him. Since anything less than that is not going to satisfy him, we already know that part of the outcome. He is going to be left disappointed and angry, and he is going to need to deal with that. If you talk to him, what you say becomes the issue. The only way you can have your desired outcome right now is to have no contact. Only then will he begin to find other solutions to his problems, which you can't help with anyway. As long as he gets a response from you, he is distracted from his life. If, however, you don't return the calls, then each time he leaves a message, he gets a message: that you can resist his pursuit."

"Yeah, but the guy never stops."

Jackie interjected: "You haven't tested 'never' yet, Mike. You haven't even tried two weeks."

She was right. I explained that every time Mike called Tommy back or showed any detectable reaction to his harassment, this engaged him. "With each contact, you buy another six weeks." I explained that the same concepts apply with romantic pursuers who don't let go, ex-boyfriends who don't let go, fired employees who don't let go, and all the other incarnations of don't-let-go. I wanted Mike to know that though Tommy was annoying, he wasn't unique.

I asked Mike what he thought Tommy might do next.

"I have no idea. That's why I came to you."

I waited.

"I guess he'll threaten some more." (An exactly accurate prediction from someone who a moment before had "no idea.")

Mike faced a type of situation that initially offers two widely different management plans: (1) change the pursuer, or (2) change the way the pursuer's conduct affects us. Under the first heading are such things as warnings, counterthreats, police interventions, and other strategies designed to control someone's conduct. Under the second heading are such things as insulating ourselves from hazard or annoyance, evaluating the likelihood of violence, and monitoring new communications. Under the second plan, we limit the impact the situation is allowed to have by limiting our fear and anxiety. We also limit impact on the pursuer by not responding.

In this case, we agreed that my office would conduct a general background inquiry on Tommy, evaluate all the messages and information available thus far, and institute the following management plan: Mike would get a new voice-mail extension. My office would check Mike's old voice mail every hour and forward to him all of his messages, except those from Tommy. We would review, evaluate, and keep each message left by Tommy. I assured Mike and Jackie: "Between where we are now and his becoming violent, there would be several detectable warning signs. If there is anything that gives us the slightest reason to believe he might escalate beyond phone calls, we will contact you immediately."

What impact a harasser has is one of the few things a victim can control, and from that day forward, Tommy's calls would have no impact whatsoever on Mike or Jackie.

In the end, Tommy continued to call for five more weeks. He left many messages, including threats that Mike would have found hard to resist responding to. Mike had predicted that Tommy would only stop if someone "made him stop," but in fact, the opposite was true. He would only stop if nobody tried to make him stop.

This case could have been very different. Mike and Jackie might have gotten a restraining order, which is really the process of suing someone in civil court to leave you alone and stay away from you. Would Tommy have advanced or retreated? Who had more to lose: Tommy, or Mike and Jackie? Had Tommy reacted favorably the other times Mike tried to put a cost on his conduct (enlisting Tommy's friend, sending the police)? What would a lawsuit have done to Tommy's perceived justification?

People in these very frequent situations, whether involving a former intimate partner, a former employee, or someone like Tommy, wrestle with their options, rarely seeing that doing nothing provocative is an option too. Everyone they know has a suggestion: "He'll stop if you just return his call; all he wants is to be recognized"; "Maybe you need to have someone else call and say you're out of town"; "Try changing your number, he'll get the message." There is an almost irresistible urge to do something dramatic in response to threats and harassment, but often, appearing to do nothing is the best plan. Of course, that isn't really doing nothing; it is a reasoned management plan and a communication to the pursuer every bit as clear as direct contact. This approach is a real test of patience and character for victims, but it is often the fastest way to end harassment.

The way a friend of mine describes his approach to work offers a valuable analogy for managing some interpersonal situations: "I have two drawers in my desk. One is for the things I must do something about, and the other is for the things time will take care of." Time will take care of most people who refuse to let go.

Some of these persistent people suffer from delusions, the very definition of which explains why they don't let go: a false belief that cannot be shaken even in the face of compelling contrary evidence. Most harassers, however, have something less than a delusion, something we might call an alternate perception or an unreasonable opinion. The resolution they seek is usually not attainable, and these people are so confounding because the original issue they cling to is seen from their unusual perspective. We may think Mike made no promises to Tommy, but Tommy can say he feels otherwise. He can even base his feelings on objective facts and statements that were actually made.

But it is the outcome he desires and his way of getting there that establish Tommy as an unreasonable person. Professor Mary Rowe of MIT is among the few academics who have studied these cases. She identifies as a warning sign the "extreme nature of a desire — for example, a desire for total physical and emotional control of another person, or total control of an office process, or the unwarranted firing of another person, or the total acceptance of a proposal." She also describes an "extraordinary sense of entitlement, such as 'She *must* talk with me!' . . . 'The department *must* let me work on that project!' or 'I refuse to vacate my office.'"

When a person requires something unattainable, such as total submission to an unreasonable demand, it is time to stop negotiating, because it's clear the person cannot be satisfied. Getting pulled into discussions about the original issue misses the point. It's as if one party has come to the table wanting a million dollars and the other party is prepared to give five dollars, or no dollars. In such situations there is nothing to negotiate.

In some cases a person's desired outcome can't even be determined, much less attained. What would Tommy have been satisfied with near the end of his harassment campaign? An apology? A successful partnership with Mike? I don't know, and I don't think Tommy knew either.

Professor Rowe brings into focus the great internal conflict for such people, explaining that they "certainly do not want to lose, but may also be unable to stand winning, in the conventional way, since that would mean the fight is over."

Of course, it isn't over until all participants are out of the ring, and as long as people try to change the pursuer or satisfy the pursuer, it goes on. Most often, the fear of violence lurks in the shadows and keeps people trying, but was Tommy likely to be violent? Let's look at him in terms of the four general elements of violence (JACA):

Perceived Justification

Tommy may have felt provoked when Mike called his friend, but he did not demonstrate that he felt violence was justified.

Perceived Alternatives

People likely to use violence perceive few or no alternatives, but Tommy's continuing calls proved that he saw many alternatives (interfering with Mike's business, harassing, threatening, etc.).

Perceived Consequences

Those likely to be violent perceive that it will bring them tolerable or even favorable consequences. Tommy showed no indication that he was willing to give up his freedom (an intolerable consequence to him) by escalating to violence. Interestingly, the consequences of threatening (including being visited by police) were clearly tolerable to him.

Perceived Ability

Those who use violence perceive that they have the ability to deliver it, but Tommy said nothing and did nothing that indicated he felt that ability.

▪ ▪ ▪

Though victims understandably find them confounding, most people who refuse to let go are highly predictable. It is perhaps too glib to say they continue until they stop, but that is basically what happens in the vast majority of cases — unless they are engaged. To accurately predict the little behaviors along the way, one must understand the languages of entitlement, attachment, and rejection. Above all, one must see the situation in the context of this culture, which teaches the myth that persistence pays. The earliest version most of us hear is "In America anyone can be president," when in fact only one person can be president, and 240 million others cannot. F. Scott Fitzgerald said something about persistence that all the Tommys could benefit from: "Vitality shows not only in the ability to persist, but in the ability to start over."

▪ ▪ ▪

No group knows more about being persistently pursued than famous people. From the local prom queen to the politician to the internationally famous media figure, all can teach us something about persistence. A very famous media figure might have hundreds of persistent pursuers, literally hundreds of Tommys.

People in Mike and Jackie's situation often wonder what it would be like to have unlimited resources to influence, control, and punish an unwanted pursuer. They even fantasize about how simple the situation would be if they had the police, the courts, the government on their side. But it is a fantasy, because no matter how famous the victim, no matter how powerful the advocates, it simply isn't always possible to control the conduct of other people.

Canadian singer Anne Murray experienced a case that proves this point decisively. She was stalked for years by a man who was given scores of court orders that he violated, arrested over and over again, and eventually put in prison for six years. Upon his release, a judge again ordered him to leave Murray alone, but within his first few months of freedom, the stalker violated the court order more than two hundred times.

John Searing, a thirty-six-year-old salesman of art supplies from New Jersey, was just as persistent in efforts to get what he wanted from Johnny Carson. In 1980 he wrote to *The Tonight Show* asking if they would let him do something he had wanted to do since he was a boy: yell "Here's Johnny!" on the air some night. In response, he got an eight-by-ten photo of Johnny Carson.

Though most people would have gotten the message, Searing wrote again and then again. After a while, he got a form letter from a staff person thanking him for his proposal and explaining that it would not be feasible. But Searing kept writing. He enclosed audiotapes of himself doing impressions of Jimmy Stewart and Richard Nixon. Their famous voices made the same request: "Let John Searing yell 'Here's Johnny.'"

This went on for a long while, long enough, in fact, for Searing to write more than eight hundred letters. *Tonight Show* staffers, tempered by decades of experience with persistent letter writers, did not become alarmed. They did not call the police to make it stop. They did, however, call John Searing to ask why it was so important to him.

"Because nothing in life means more to me," he told them. Soon after that call, an amazing thing happened: *The Tonight Show* said yes to the request they had ignored eight hundred times. Searing was flown to Los Angeles, given a dressing room with his name on the door, and like something out of a dream (his dream), he was walked into the studio. He watched from the side of the stage as Ed McMahon introduced Johnny Carson with the famous words "Here's Johnny." "But, what about me?" Searing wondered. He was told to be patient.

After the first commercial, Johnny Carson explained to the audience about John Searing and his hundreds of letters, and then Searing was introduced to America. He sat next to the famous man at the famous desk for about six minutes, explaining why he had been so persistent and what it meant to him. Carson directed Searing to a microphone and then went back behind the curtain. Searing was handed a script, from which he enthusiastically read: "From Hollywood, *The Tonight Show Starring Johnny Carson.* This is John Searing, along with Doc Severinsen and the NBC Orchestra, inviting you to join Johnny and his guests: Danny DeVito; from the San Diego Zoo, Joan Embery; letter writer John Searing, and adventures in the kitchen with Doc."

There was a drumroll. "And now, ladies and gentlemen . . .

heeere's Johnny!" Carson came through the curtain to great applause and gave Searing a simple instruction: "Now go and write no more."

And that is exactly what happened: Searing went back to work selling art supplies. Persistent though he had been, his letters never contained anything sinister or foreboding. He had always maintained a job, had other interests, and above all, he never escalated the nature of his communications. While giving pursuers exactly what they want is not often my recommended strategy, particularly recognizing the impracticality of applying it regularly, it is interesting to note that *The Tonight Show* made no effort to stop Searing from writing letters.

Johnny Carson and his staff knew that letters, no matter how frequent, can't hurt anyone, while starting a war can hurt everyone involved. Had Searing been left alone, he would likely have kept writing letters, maybe for years, maybe for his whole life, and that would have been fine. Our office has several cases of people who have written more than *ten thousand letters* to one media figure and never attempted an encounter. Those clients are entirely unaffected by the letters, which their staffs forward to us unopened and which we then review.

The issue, then, is not persistence but knowing the differences between communications and behaviors that portend escalation and those from which you can predict that a pursuer is likely to retreat or just fade away. In these situations, victims are understandably frustrated (to say the least), and they want something done to their pursuer to make him stop. The institutions of psychiatry, law enforcement, and government have proved that no matter what your resources, you cannot reliably control the conduct of all people. It is not fair, but it is so. My role is to increase safety and reduce fear, not to tell people what they want to hear. Still, there is always someone willing to do what a celebrity wants, whether or not it is the safest course.

I cannot recall how many times I have seen some private detective apply confrontational interventions and then feel these actions were justified by the fact that the pursuer's behavior ultimately got worse. Having guided the pursuer into a warlike stance, the detective will say, "Whew, it's a good thing we did all that stuff to him, because just look how serious a case this is. I told you something had to be done." Do they never wonder what might have happened if they had just left him alone?

By way of analogy, when you are driving on a slippery mountain road at night, you do not manage the hazard by getting out and drying off the pavement — you slow down through the dangerous curves. When dealing with people who won't let go, that means having strategies in place to lessen the likelihood of unwanted encounters. You change what you can and stop trying to change what you cannot.

A strategy of watch and wait is usually the wisest first step, but people frequently apply another management plan: engage and enrage. The option of engaging a pursuer will always be available to you, but once it is applied, you cannot simply go back to watching and waiting, even though you may find it wasn't so bad by comparison.

Though Johnny Carson knew it, the lesson that persistence on its own is not sinister would come too late for another media figure, Los Angeles radio personality Jim Hicklin. Best known to listeners as a pilot-commentator who advised on traffic conditions, he also reported on other newsworthy events from his helicopter. When he received some annoying letters from a fan, he quickly found people who told him what he wanted to hear: "We'll take care of it." They didn't.

The first letter had arrived at the Hicklin residence near the end of August 1971. The author was forty-five-year-old wimpy nebbish Edward Taylor, whose story is best told through his letters. The first one was intended to be friendly and supportive. It was addressed "Dear James" and signed "Respectfully Yours, Ed Taylor."

Though Hicklin didn't answer the letter, more came. They contained praise, remembrances, compliments, and one even suggested that Jim Hicklin run for governor. Another read, "You are a star."

Jim Hicklin was unaware that Taylor was a tireless letter writer who had been known to several prominent people in Los Angeles for years. Taylor's letters either amused or annoyed these people; mostly they were just ignored. But Hicklin did not ignore the letters. Instead he hired a pair of private detectives to resolve the matter. They made an unannounced visit to Taylor's home and gave him one clear order: Stop sending letters.

This intrusive intervention didn't stop the letters, but it did change them. The first letter following the visit from the detectives was six pages long. The penmanship was now erratic, there were many messy corrections, and all the friendliness and praise of the past was gone. "You have grievously offended me," wrote Taylor. "I have given much thought to your implied threat against me; your presumed paranoia . . . or your naiveté . . . or your innocent receipt of a Pack of rotten advice . . . or is it that you are just simply Insufferably Arrogant?"

This letter introduced a new theme that was to become the principal focus of Taylor's life for a year: litigation. It continued:

> I am both flattered and impressed to have been investigated. The Q is about what? That is precisely why there are lawyers . . . <u>and you need a good one badly</u>. . . . At Hicklin's earliest opportunity, it is <u>imperative</u> that he inform me, in writing, of the identity of his Attorney.

The next letter was to the general manager of the radio station Hicklin worked for:

> There appeared at my residence two private detectives in the name of Golden West Broadcasting [the owner of the radio station]. <u>They came unannounced to interrogate me</u> relating to some <u>very</u> personal and confidential memoranda I have in past months sent to Hicklin.
>
> Your people admitted they were instructed by Jim Hicklin to call on me . . . unannounced . . . with no regard to my Family, Guests, Responsibilities or even the State of my Health. It is harassment; it is a virulent invasion of one's privacy; it is threatening; it is intimidating & it is Wrong!
>
> Precisely of what reprehensible culpability does Jim Hicklin accuse me? Professionally & personally it is very important to me that I know. <u>And I shall</u>.

About a week later, Taylor sent the FAA the first of many letters calling into question Hicklin's competency to hold a pilot's license: "Until it has been established by your jurisdiction that Mr. Hicklin is of sound body & mind, I suggest he is a threat to life, property and himself."

Note that he had at this point introduced the concepts of threat and safety. Taylor next filed a civil complaint with the superior court, demanding an apology from Hicklin. He wrote to the judge:

> The referenced case has meant to scathingly denounce and repudiate the presumed right of one citizen to conspire to contravene the right of another's to free expression; to transmit mail; to be free from fear of retaliatory, psychological assault; emasculation at the door to one's own home.

This letter gives a good opportunity to see the situation from Taylor's perspective. He felt intruded upon, threatened, and, perhaps most importantly, emasculated. Recall the assumptions I said could be applied to most of us:

- We seek connection with others.
- We are saddened by loss and try to avoid it.
- We dislike rejection.
- We like recognition and attention.
- We will do more to avoid pain than we will do to seek pleasure.
- We dislike ridicule and embarrassment.
- We care what others think of us.
- We seek a degree of control over our lives.

The effort to deter Taylor by sending private detectives collided with most of these. He was seeking connection and then saddened by the loss of his chummy (albeit one-sided) relationship with Hicklin. He was rejected. He had reached the point where the situation could bring him no pleasure, and all he could do was try to stop the pain. He felt chastised and embarrassed. He felt that others would think less of him if he didn't reclaim his masculinity by getting an apology. Finally, he felt he had lost control over his life.

One day Hicklin made an on-air comment about people who

start brush fires: "They should be tied to a stake and left there." After hearing this, Taylor wrote that some teenager might "prod his group into acting out the sick fantasy as broadcast by Personality Pilot-Reporter-Folk-Hero Hicklin. Law enforcement finds enough skeletal remains in the hills. It is bestial to hear one condone murder-by-the-torch."

Note the sinister nature of his references. They continued in Taylor's next complaint to the FAA, which was that Hicklin had buzzed his home in what he called a "strafing mission": "Is there a more barbaric, mindless, obscene act than a pilot who would aim an aircraft at defenseless humans on the ground for the sole purpose of harassment; by a pilot whose sole sick mission is to establish his dominance over his victims?"

Needless to say, the FAA did not (and could not) take any action that would have satisfied Taylor. Likewise, the court dismissed his suit. With his alternatives shrinking, Taylor typed a seven-page memo recounting in detail each "incident" involving Hicklin. He stated that Hicklin used his helicopter as a weapon and that "aircraft in the hands of mentally unbalanced men constitute offensive weaponry."

Let's stop and look at the context of the situation. At the start, it was simple: A famous person was sent some overly praising letters by a member of his audience. Though perhaps not written in a style that appealed to Hicklin, the letters were appropriate for the context. At the start, the situation was not interpersonal, but after the admirer was visited by intimidating men who warned him to stop writing letters, it became interpersonal. Jim Hicklin got the last thing he wanted: a relationship with Edward Taylor. They had become enemies.

> Hicklin —
>
> I could've understood your conduct had you come to my door with a .38 in hand rather than having sent two private detectives — like a Strung-Out Queen.
>
> Now you've psyched up buddies to threaten my life. That's sad.
>
> Remember to call me "MR."

The day he sent this letter, Edward Taylor did more than just write about a .38. He went out and bought one.

Meanwhile, Hicklin decided to try his first strategy again. He asked the district attorney's office to send investigators and get Taylor to stop. They did visit him, but they did not get him to stop.

Taylor told the district attorney's investigators that he was the victim of Hicklin's harassment, not the other way around. He feared that Hicklin may have hovered above his house in order to draw a map. He explained that he was so apprehensive of Hicklin's bizarre behavior that he always carried with him a note of explanation addressed jointly to the Los Angeles Police Department and the D.A.'s office. Along with the note, he always carried the handgun.

After he was warned by the D.A.'s investigators, Taylor wrote to them:

> When a complainant perceives that established authority does not care and/or will not empathize with what it is like when one has his life threatened by a mindless, manipulative robopath; to experience the trauma of purchasing a .38 handgun in his 46th year in order to defend himself from a paid or emotionally-involved assassin; to see a handgun on his desk during working hours; to see it again first thing in the morning upon awakening and as the final objet-d'être upon retiring at night. Worst of all, is to consider the nature of complainant's alleged provocation against respondent (to hear the latter tell it): mail(!).

All the information needed was in this letter. What Taylor projected onto Hicklin, namely that he was "an emotionally-involved assassin," was actually at work inside him. As James Baldwin said, "In the face of one's victim, one sees oneself." Though Taylor never made a threat to harm Hicklin, the clear hazard can be gleaned from that letter nonetheless by applying the JACA elements: Taylor felt he had *justification* to use violence (defending himself); he had few *alternatives* left (established authority did not care about him); the *consequences* of violence had become favorable because violence would stop the "mindless robopath"; and finally, he had the *ability* to deliver violence — the gun.

The visit from the D.A. investigators, like the first visit from the private detectives, clearly had a major and unfavorable impact that Taylor had difficulty recovering from. The ultimate intrusion, the ultimate insult, was still to come, and from that one Taylor would be unable to recover.

One evening while his elderly mother was visiting him, Taylor answered a knock at his front door. It was the police, who, in front of his mother, arrested Edward Taylor. He was booked into Los Angeles County Jail for misdemeanor libel. Unable to contact anyone to bail him out over the weekend, he spent three days in jail.

Home from jail, shaken more than even he realized, Edward Taylor could not get relief from his indignation about all that had happened. Now that there was a cost on his writing letters, he stopped writing them. Instead, he stewed, tried to sleep, tried to eat, and stewed some more. He couldn't find the life he'd had before all this had started, such as it was, so he just sat at home listening to Jim Hicklin's radio show. In this sense, media figures are unavoidably adding some fuel to the fire just by being in the media. A person obsessed with a movie star, for example, might see her in magazines, on entertainment news programs and talk shows. Ironically, even if he wants to, an obsessed person might find it hard to get away from the object of his pursuit.

But soon Hicklin would be off the air. He and his wife were going on a vacation cruise. Just as he had planned, and *just as he had announced over the radio,* Jim Hicklin and his wife boarded the *Italia* cruise ship on April 2, 1973.

Before leaving port, the Hicklins entertained friends who'd come to see them off. But not everyone on board was a friend. In the presence of his wife, Jim Hicklin was shot to death by a man he'd never met and never spoken to. Edward Taylor had "defended" himself in the way he had obviously been thinking of for some time.

Believing that others will react as we would is the single most dangerous myth of intervention. When people wanted to stop Edward Taylor's letters, they were certain a strong warning would do it, then they were certain arrest would do it. But even his being arrested, tried, convicted, and incarcerated for life did not stop Edward Taylor's letters. He continued to write to the district attorney and others until the day he died in prison.

■ ■ ■

People who refuse to let go are becoming more common, and each case teaches us the same valuable lesson: Don't engage in a war. Wars rarely end well because by definition someone will have to lose.

In *Predicting Violent Behavior,* John Monahan explains that violence is *inter-actional:* "The reaction of a potential victim of violence may distinguish a verbal altercation from a murder." As you have now learned from cases of public-figure pursuers and other people who refuse to let go, the minute you get into it with someone, you are into it, and if you get angry, that all by itself is a kind of victory for him.

■ ■ ■

Remember Tommy? In the course of a follow-up investigation, my office learned that he got a job with a bank, enjoyed a three-month honeymoon there, and was fired for insubordination. He began a harassment campaign against the bank's personnel director that is still going on as I write this. The bank has threatened him with a lawsuit, and he has threatened them with everything he could think of. Tommy's former employers, like others concerned about violence from an angry employee, face situations that are highly predictable (second only, in fact, to those between intimates). This ease of predictability makes some employers uncomfortable, because with ability comes responsibility. After you finish the next chapter, you'll have both.

■ 9 ■

OCCUPATIONAL HAZARDS

"How much more grievous are the consequences of our anger than the acts which arouse it."

— *Marcus Aurelius*

Dear Laura,

It's time to remove the kid gloves. It's my option to make your life miserable if that is what you really want. I told you if I get fired or lose my clearance, I can force you to go out with me. You asked me what I could do, Kill you? The answer to that was + still is No. If I killed you, you would not be able to regret what you did. I have your parents' address, so what if you run, I'm ready to follow. I'm selling my houses, I have closed my retirement fund, sold my stock. I can go real quick. Let's say you don't back down + pretty soon I crack under the pressure + run amok, destroying everything in my path until the police catch me + kill me.

Take care,
Rick

As you read this letter, your intuition cries out for more details. Who is Rick? Who is Laura? What is their relationship? Did he get fired? Your intuition tells you to be curious because more information means a better prediction. You want to know the context, but knowing just what's in the letter, you can still use the JACA elements to see things the original readers did not see. It speaks of Rick's *justification* for violence (losing his job), his shrinking *alternatives* (taking off the kid gloves), the favorable *consequences* to violence (making

Laura regret what she did), and his high *ability* (he has her parents' address, has sold off his possessions and is ready to go).

The man who wrote the letter is named Richard Farley, and the woman he wrote to is Laura Black. They met while employed at a high-tech Silicon Valley company called ESL, a subsidiary of TRW. Farley had asked Laura Black to go out with him, and when she declined, he refused to accept her rejections. The company tried several interventions to make him stop bothering her, but with each one his harassment escalated. Eventually it included death threats. He also sent along an enclosure with one letter that chillingly communicated her vulnerability: It was a key to the front door of her home.

When supervisors at ESL told Farley that he'd be fired if he kept this up, his sinister reaction prompted one of them to ask him incredulously, "Are you saying that if you are fired you will kill me?"

"Not just you," Farley answered.

Around this time, Laura reluctantly sought a restraining order against Farley. Her intuition about him was right on the mark when she told the court, "I am afraid of what this man might do to me if I file this action."

Farley was fired from ESL and banned from the premises, but he came back one day with a vengeance. He passed through the access doors — literally through them — after blasting out the glass with one of the shotguns he'd brought along. He was also carrying a rifle and several handguns as he walked around the building furiously shooting at his former co-workers.

When he finally found Laura Black, he shot her once with a rifle and left her bleeding on the floor. He shot ten other people that day, seven of whom died. Laura, though losing blood and consciousness, was able to crawl out of the building.

Later she told me, "The restraining order was the catalyst that pushed him over the edge. I hesitated a long time before I went forward to get it, but the company urged me on. Ultimately, I was told that my reluctance might be impacting my advancement at work. That was when I finally said, 'Okay, it's worth taking a chance.' The shooting was the day before we were to appear in court with Farley to make the temporary restraining order permanent."

But Laura spent that day and many more in the hospital. Farley spent that day and many more in jail. Newspeople spent that day, and many more, reporting that Farley had "just snapped" and gone on a shooting spree. But that never, ever happens.

JACA has shown you that people don't just "snap." There is a process as observable, and often as predictable, as water coming to a boil. Though we call it workplace violence, it is really every type of violence, committed by every type of perpetrator. It is revenge killing, when an employee who feels humiliated or emasculated proves that he cannot be taken lightly. It is domestic violence, when a husband seeks out his wife at her work. It is date stalking, when the man who refuses to let go pursues his victim at her job. It is rage killing, when an employee primed to do something big and bad chooses to do it at work. The fear of violence at work is understandable because work is a place where many of us are forced to interact with people we did not choose to have in our lives.

Fortunately, violence in the workplace offers many predictive opportunities, and there are almost always several people in a position to observe the warning signs. Still, as the cases show, obvious warnings are frequently ignored. The cases also show that it doesn't have to be that way.

▪ ▪ ▪

Though you may not recognize the name Pat Sherill, he is one of the reasons that when you think of shooting sprees at work, you think of the U.S. Postal Service. The forty-four-year-old Oklahoma letter carrier was known to co-workers as Crazy Pat. In 1986, soon after his supervisors threatened to fire him, he came to work with something more than just his usual anger at his bosses: He brought along three pistols as well. Sherill shot twenty co-workers, fourteen of whom died, and then he killed himself.

Contrary to the public perception that Sherill helped cement, the statistics for violence by employees of the postal service are actually better than for most industries in America. It's just that with hundreds of thousands of full-time employees and nearly a million people affiliated with the service in some way, odds are they'll have more of everything — more failure, more medical problems, more creativity, more laziness, more kindness, more violence. There are shooting incidents at fast-food restaurants more often than at post offices, but they are not reported as if part of some trend. (This is not to say that postal service management style and strategies are everything they could be, but rather to debunk the myth that they are the worst in the nation.)

Though Sherill's attack was a bloodbath, within the year another angry employee would make it look like a minor incident by comparison. A USAir employee named David Burke was the man in the news this time. After the incident, reporters learned plenty of things about Burke that USAir could have benefited from knowing when they decided to hire him: He had a history that included drug trafficking, shoplifting, and auto theft, as well as violence toward his girlfriend. He had cut the wires in her car, beaten her, and threatened her with a gun. It had reached the point that she'd gotten a restraining order against him.

Burke's troubling behavior went with him to work, where he left a death threat on the answering machine of his supervisor, Ray Thompson, whom he blamed for many of his problems. Burke insisted he was being singled out for racial reasons, and he was indignant when USAir fired him for stealing sixty-nine dollars. Another USAir employee (with very poor judgment) lent Burke a .44 magnum revolver. It would never be returned.

When USAir fired Burke, they failed to take back his airport ID badge, and he wore it on his last day alive. Because of that badge, the woman operating the metal detector waved Burke around it and said, "Have a nice day." He replied, "I'll have a very nice day." He then walked into Thompson's office and demanded his job back. Thompson said no, then cut the discussion short because he was flying to San Francisco. Soon after, Burke stood in line and bought a ticket for the same flight. Unlike the other passengers taking their seats on Flight 1771 that afternoon, Burke did not care where the plane was scheduled to go, because he already knew where it would end up.

After take-off, he wrote a note on an air-sickness bag: "Hi Ray. I think it's sort of ironical that we end up like this. I asked for some leniency for my family, remember? And I got none. And you'll get none."

At twenty-two thousand feet, the flight crew heard two shots (Burke had just killed Ray Thompson). They immediately radioed air traffic controllers: "There's gunfire aboard!" Seconds later, the plane's black box recorded three more shots, then some commotion, then a final shot.

The tower tried to recontact the pilots, but the jet was no longer under their control. It was now under the firm control of gravity as it made a seven-hundred-miles-per-hour descent into the ground. Forty-three people died instantly, making Burke the perpetrator of the single worst workplace violence tragedy in American history. The worst, but far from the last.

We generally think of these shooting sprees as being committed by employees at large corporations or government agencies, but an increasing number are perpetrated by stalkers, patrons, and even college students. Several of our clients now are major universities. In years past, they would not have had these concerns, but violence finds its way into every institution of our culture, and people not expecting it are also not prepared for it.

Often, the signs are all there, but so is the denial. For example, after some terrible on-campus violence, school officials will describe a perpetrator as having been "a student in good standing." Such descriptions are meant to say, "Who could have known?" but further inquiry always answers that question.

The case of college student Wayne Lo is an informative example. On the morning of the day he became famous, Wayne received a package at the college. A receptionist was suspicious about its contents (suspicion is a signal of intuition) because of two words on the return address: "Classic Arms." She correctly notified resident directors, who took the package to a regularly scheduled meeting with the dean, Bernard Rodgers. Staff members wanted to open the package, which they thought might contain a weapon, but Dean Rodgers said it would be improper for the college to interfere with the delivery of a student's mail. He did agree that a member of the staff could approach Wayne Lo to discuss it.

Wayne was allowed to pick up the package and take it to his room. Soon after, Trinka Robinson, the resident director of his dormitory, came and asked Wayne what was in his heavy little package. He refused to open it. She asked again, and he again refused, so she left. When she returned later with her husband, Floyd, the box had been opened. Wayne told them that it didn't contain a weapon but rather three empty pistol clips and some other gun parts. There was also an empty ammunition box. He said he'd ordered some of the items as gifts and intended to use others himself.

Apparently electing to forget that Wayne had refused to open the package in Trinka's presence, Floyd Robinson was satisfied. He later described Wayne as "very open with me and not at all defensive." This observation was meant to communicate that same old "Who could have known?" even though by that point several people could have known.

At around nine P.M. that evening, an anonymous male caller told Trinka that Wayne had a gun and was going to kill her, her family, and others.

Trinka took the threat seriously enough to call several school officials. She also immediately took her children to the home of a school provost. Her husband joined them there at around 9:30. They decided they would go and search Wayne's room. If they found a weapon, or if he resisted, they would call the police. But since Dean Rodgers hadn't let them open Wayne's package, how would he react if they searched Wayne's room? Better call the dean, they decided, and that's what they were doing when they heard the first shots.

By the time the loud noises stopped, six people had been shot. Two of them were already dead. It had been less than twelve hours since Wayne had picked up the package that stimulated school officials to do everything except the obvious thing: call the police. Even the explicit warning call about Wayne's intentions hadn't convinced them to call the police.

It was ten more days before Dean Rodgers made any public explanation, and people were anxious to hear what he knew about the incident. Instead, he told them what he did not know: "I don't know anything about weapons. I don't know anything about guns." I am sure Dean Rodgers knew guns are dangerous, and I am sure he knew there were people he could call about the matter.

Given that so little about Wayne's feelings and perceptions was known to college officials, it would have been difficult to apply the JACA elements, but this is a perfect example of a case in which context alone is the dominant element of prediction: A student receives a package from a gun manufacturer; he refuses to open it or discuss its contents; he then opens it when he is alone; within hours, an anonymous caller warns that the student has a gun and plans to kill people. These things did not each happen independently; they *all* happened, and one could add another important factor: People felt intuitively that there was hazard.

When Wayne Lo appeared at his arraignment for murder, he wore a sweatshirt with the words "*Sick of It All*" across his chest. That speaks my feelings about the many, many cases in which denial was allowed to turn into negligence, and in which people in a position to know were the same ones later asking "Who could have known?"

▪ ▪ ▪

Having told several stories in which the warning signs were ignored and a tragedy occurred, I also want to acknowledge that the people involved — those who visited Edward Taylor to make him leave Jim Hicklin alone, those at Wayne Lo's school, at Laura Black's company, at USAir, even at the much-criticized U.S. Postal Service — were doing the best they could with the tools they had at the time. If they'd had the knowledge you now have, I believe they'd have made different choices, and thus, my observations are not about blame, but about education.

Park Dietz, the nation's leading forensic psychiatrist and an expert on violence, has noted that the case histories are "littered with reports, letters, memoranda, and recollections that show people felt uncomfortable, threatened, intimidated, violated and unsafe because of the very person who later committed atrocious acts of violence." One case Dietz studied tells a story of denial in its most undeniable form: A man killed one of his co-workers, served his prison time, was released, *and was rehired by the same company whose employee he had murdered.* While at the company the second time, he alienated people because he was always sullen and angry. He made threats that were known to supervisors and he stalked a female co-worker. After he resigned (on the verge of being fired), he continued to stalk the woman and then he killed her.

Who could have known?

▪ ▪ ▪

Destructive acts against co-workers and organizations are not rare or isolated incidents. In an age of takeovers, mergers, and downsizing, with people frequently laid off or fired, employee emotion is a force to be reckoned with. The loss of a job can be as traumatic as the loss of a loved one, but few fired employees receive a lot of condolence or support.

While the frequency of violent incidents has increased, most of the influencing factors have remained the same for a long while. Many American employers hire the wrong people and don't bother to find out a thing about them. Then employees are supervised in ways likely to bring out their worst characteristics. Finally, the way they are fired influences events as much as the fact that they were hired. Few people would knowingly light the fuse on a bomb, but many employers inadvertently do exactly that. Many come to me afterward, but only a few come wanting to learn about the topic before it's a crisis.

I tell those clients about the most common type of problem employee, the one I call the Scriptwriter. He has several characteristics that are detectable early in his employment. One is his inflexibility; he is not receptive to suggestions because he takes them as affronts or criticisms of his way of doing things. Another characteristic is that he invests others with the worst possible motives and character. Entering a discussion about a discrepancy on his paycheck, for example, he says or thinks, "You'd better not try to screw me out of any money." It is as if he expects people to slight him or harm him.

The Scriptwriter is the type of person who asks you a question, answers it himself, then walks away angry at what you said. In this regard, he *writes the script* for his interactions with co-workers and management. In his script, he is a reasonable and good worker who must be constantly on guard against the ambushes of co-workers and supervisors. The things that go wrong are never his fault, and even accidental, unintended events are the work of others who will try to blame him. People are out to get him, period. And the company does nothing about it and doesn't appreciate his contribution.

When you try to manage or reason with such a person, you find that he is not reacting to what you say but rather to what he expects you to say; he is reacting to his script. His is a personality that is self-defeating. The old "jack joke" demonstrates this dynamic at work.

> A man driving along a remote stretch of highway gets a flat tire. Preparing to put on the spare, he realizes he does not have a jack to raise the car. Far in the distance, he sees the lights of some small farmhouses and begins the long walk to borrow a jack. It is getting dark, and as he walks along, he worries that the people will be reluctant to help him.
>
> "They'll probably refuse to even answer the door, or worse still, pretend they're not home," he thinks. "I'll have to walk another mile to the next house, and they'll say they don't want to open the door and that they don't have a jack anyway. When I finally get somebody to talk to me, they'll want me to convince them I'm not some criminal, and if they agree to help me, which is doubtful, they'll want to keep my wallet so I don't run off with their stupid jack. What's wrong with these people? Are they so untrusting that they can't even help a fellow citizen? Would they have me freeze to death out here?"
>
> By this point he has reached the first house. Having worked himself into a virtual state of rage, he bangs loudly on the door, thinking to himself, "They better not try to pretend there's nobody home, because I can hear the TV."
>
> After a few seconds, a pleasant woman opens the door wide and asks with a smile, "Can I help you?"
>
> He yells back at her, "I don't want your help and I wouldn't take your lousy jack if you giftwrapped it for me!"

The Scriptwriter gives no credit when people are helpful, and this causes alienation from co-workers. His script actually begins to come true, and people treat him as he expects them to. By the time a given employer encounters him, he has likely been through these problems at other jobs and in other relationships.

The Scriptwriter issues warnings: "You'd better not try to blame me for what happened," or "I'd better get that promotion." Even when he gets his way, he believes it's only because he forced the company to give it to him. He still thinks management was trying to get out of promoting him, but couldn't.

When I review such an employee's personnel file, it's amazing how many serious performance or insubordination incidents are documented. Many are the kinds of things that companies could terminate for. He has made threats, he has bullied, he has intimidated. Sometimes the employee has even performed sabotage or already been violent at work, and yet he wasn't fired because everybody was afraid to fire him. Managers have generally shifted him around from department to department, or put him on a late shift, or done whatever it takes to make him somebody else's problem. Nobody wanted to sit down, look him in the eye, and fire him, because they knew he would react badly.

Since this dynamic feeds on itself and gets worse, and because the longer he is there, the more he feels entitled to be there, the key is to get rid of a Scriptwriter early. (I am not going into the quagmire of legally acceptable reasons for termination, but rather addressing those cases in which there is cause to fire someone and the decision to fire has been made.) When you first have cause to terminate this person, it should be done. Be sure, however, that the cause is sufficient and that your determination is unshakable, because if you try to fire him and fail, you are setting the stage for the TIME syndrome, which is the introduction of threats, intimidations, manipulations, and escalation.

Manipulations are statements intended to influence outcome without resorting to threat. Escalations are actions intended to cause fear, upset, or anxiety, such as showing up somewhere uninvited, sending something alarming, damaging something, or acting sinister.

When dealing with a difficult and violently inclined employee, it is important to understand that TIME is on his side unless you act quickly. Management may correctly intuit that he will not go quietly, but the sooner in the process he is fired, the easier it will be. If you believe it will be hard to fire him now, you can be certain it will be even harder later.

The Scriptwriter is often someone who has successfully used manipulations or intimidations in the past. His employer has, in effect, trained him that these strategies work and for this reason, he expects them to work again. When management does finally take the bold step of firing him, they are faced with a person who is shocked and who feels he is being treated unfairly. He may be partly right about the unfairness, because compared to all the things he has done that he didn't get fired for, the cited reason may appear petty. He is angry, threatening, and cannot be appeased.

When manipulations that have worked for him in the past appear not to work now, he escalates them. At this point, management must consider all the harms this person could do to the company or its personnel. When they saw this side of him before, they always retreated. This time, they've stood their ground, and he has upped the ante by saying or doing things that make clear the obvious: They should have fired him long ago.

▪ ▪ ▪

Before I provide some PINs that are a call for further scrutiny in the workplace, I want to explain that I generally avoid the use of checklists because they mislead people into believing that there are shortcuts for high-stakes predictions. I have waited until this point in the book, when you are familiar with predictive resources and philosophies, before providing a list of behaviors. In less prepared hands, it could be misused. In yours, it will inform intuition.

1. Inflexibility: The employee resists change, is rigid and unwilling to discuss ideas contrary to his own.

2. Weapons: He has obtained a weapon within the last ninety days, or he has a weapons collection, or he makes jokes or frequent comments about weapons, or he discusses weapons as instruments of power or revenge.

3. SAD: He is sullen, angry, or depressed. Chronic anger is an important predictor of more than just violence. People who experience strong feelings of anger are at increased risk of heart attack (in fact, anger supersedes even such risk factors as smoking, high blood pressure, and high cholesterol). Such people place others at risk and are at risk themselves. Accordingly, chronic anger should never be ignored. Signs of depression include changes in weight, irritability, suicidal thoughts and references, hopelessness, sadness, and loss of interest in previously enjoyable activities.

4. Hopelessness: He has made statements like "What's the use?" "Nothing ever changes anyway"; "I've got no future." He makes suicidal references or threats, or he makes or describes plans consistent with committing suicide (gets his affairs in order, sells off possessions, etc.). Pessimism is an important predictor of problems (just as optimism is an important predictor of success).

5. Identification: He identifies with or even praises other perpetrators of workplace violence. He refers to, jokes about, or is fascinated with news stories about major acts of violence. He is attracted to violent films, magazines like *Soldier of Fortune,* violent books, or gruesome news events.

6. Co-worker Fear: Co-workers are afraid of or apprehensive about him (whether or not they can articulate their reasons). This PIN seeks to capture the intuition of co-workers.

7. TIME: He has used threats, intimidations, manipulations, or escalations toward management or co-workers.

8. Paranoia: He feels others are "out to get" him, that unconnected events are related, that others conspire against him.

9. Criticism: He reacts adversely to criticism, shows suspicion of those who criticize him, and refuses to consider the merits of any critical observations about his performance or behavior.

10. Blame: He blames others for the results of his own actions, refuses to accept responsibility.

11. Crusades: He has undertaken or attached himself to crusades or missions at work. (This is particularly significant if he has waged what he might characterize as a "one-man war.")

12. Unreasonable Expectations: He expects elevation, long-term retention, an apology, being named "the winner" in some dispute, or being found "right."

13. Grievance: He has a grievance pending or he has a history of filing unreasonable grievances.

14. Police Encounters: He has had recent police encounters (including arrests) or he has a history that includes assaultive or behavioral offenses.

15. Media: There have recently been news stories about workplace violence or other major acts of violence. Press reports on these subjects often stimulate others who identify with the perpetrators and the attention they got for their acts. Like public-figure attacks, major incidents of workplace violence tend to come in clusters, with perpetrators often referring to those who preceded them in the news.

16. Focus: He has monitored the behavior, activities, performance, or comings and goings of other employees, though it is not his job to do so; he has maintained a file or dossier on another employee or he has recently stalked someone in or out of the workplace. (Since nearly half of all stalkers show up where their victims work, companies are wise to learn about this dynamic.)

17. Contact: If he was fired, he has instigated and maintained contact with current employees; he refuses to let go and appears more focused on the job he just lost than finding other employment.

While no single PIN can carry a prediction, and not all serious cases will contain the entire list, these are some warning signs to be alert to. Most of us know or have known people who have a few of these characteristics, but if you work with someone who has many, that is a matter for further attention.

When managers and supervisors and co-workers know these warning signs, they are far more likely to detect a serious situation before it becomes a critical situation. Park Dietz brought his brilliant thinking to a multiyear study of workplace violence incidents. After that, he and I produced and wrote a video training series used by many corporations and government agencies (see appendix 4). The comment we heard back most frequently from organizations using the program was that spotting these employees early was far easier than they expected. They also said that the most common resolution of these situations was counseling problem employees, not firing them. Counseling was possible because they recognized early the fact that a given employee needed help. After studying every major incident of multiple shooting in the workplace, Dr. Dietz concluded:

> If a company is going to be able to respond to the kinds of things that the employees felt were really predictive, they have to learn about them. It takes time to encourage employees to tell supervisors when someone makes them feel uncomfortable or apprehensive. It takes planning. But when the call comes that someone is shooting in Building 16, it's too late to do that planning.

His study also confirmed my beliefs about the relationship between media reporting and workplace violence:

> It is a pattern that has increased in frequency and is so dependent on media that we can anticipate after each nationally publicized story there will be several more in the weeks that follow. The reason for that is the people who commit these acts are searching for solutions to their dilemmas. When they see a news account of someone doing the things they feel like doing, who seems like them, they identify with such people, and this is part of what causes them to move from inaction to action.

Many situations that evolved into violence had been brewing for a long time, and senior executives had no idea what was going on. Why? Because nobody wanted to report it to a supervisor. Why? Because someone might say, "Hey, can't you handle your own people? Don't you know how to deal with these things?"

I had a meeting a couple of years ago with a client who is the CEO of a large national company. During a discussion about restaurants owned by the company, I said, "You must have had plenty of circumstances where female employees had to deal with unwanted pursuit or stalking." He replied, "I heard about one of those cases, but it really hasn't been a serious problem for us." A couple of hours later, I asked the human resources director, and he said, "Oh, sure, we've had about six or seven of those cases in the last year; they can sometimes be a problem." Then he called the executive in charge of the restaurant division, who said, "We probably have two of those a month. I can think of about twenty we've had in recent years. It's a very serious problem."

If managers never get an opportunity to comment on or to influence a situation that might be relevant to safety, then critical decisions are left in the hands of people who are only making them because they think their bosses want them to or because they are afraid to tell anybody they can't. Companies can stimulate reporting by communicating that they want to know and by welcoming information even when it is bad news. In some companies, if a manager makes a prediction that an employee's alarming or disturbing behavior might escalate, and he brings this to his seniors, he runs the risk of being perceived as wrong for overreacting and wrong for not being able to handle the matter himself. Most unfairly, he may be perceived as wrong every day that nothing happens. I propose that large organizations redefine the word *wrong* in this context to include just three criteria. A manager is wrong only if he or she:

1) Doesn't consider safety first
2) Doesn't ask the right questions
3) Doesn't communicate concerns clearly and early

I am fortunate to work with some forward-thinking companies that tell their managers, in effect, "We do not expect you to handle these behavioral-sciences issues. We do not expect you to know about how to manage people that are alarming or volatile. If you can manage 95 percent of the people you are dealing with, that's an accomplishment. The 5 percent that depart from normal behavior—

those that intimidate, threaten, or frighten — they should be reported to us."

▪ ▪ ▪

Difficult terminations and situations involving threatening employees are similar to other volatile social situations. These include divorce, disputes with neighbors, disputes with financial institutions, acrimonious lawsuits, and dissolving partnerships. What they all have in common is that the interests of one party are in direct conflict with the interests of another party. Accordingly, resolutions that are completely satisfactory to all parties are rare.

To complicate matters, the difficult employee often has similar problems away from work as well. The good things in his life are like dominos that have started to topple: Confidence has toppled into performance, which topples into identity, which knocks over self-esteem. The loss of his job may knock over the few remaining dominos, but the one that employers must be careful not to topple is the dignity domino, because when that falls, violence is most likely. Consider JACA:

Justification: The employee can feel justified in using violence when the employer has taken *everything* away.

Alternatives: He may perceive fewer and fewer alternatives to violence, particularly if he has exhausted all appeals processes.

Consequences: His evaluation of the consequences of violence changes as he sinks lower. If he feels angry enough, *particularly if he feels humiliated,* the consequences of violence may become favorable.

Ability: Often, angry current or former employees overestimate their ability to deliver violence. This is dangerous because they are more likely to try grandiose attacks intended to "kill everyone," or to "blow up everything." Though they rarely succeed at quite the level they envision, they still hurt plenty of people.

▪ ▪ ▪

What is it that employers who have had the worst outcomes did, or failed to do?

Of course hiring is where it starts. The hiring officer has made a prediction that the candidate will meet the needs of the company and will be a well-adjusted, capable, and productive employee. We know predictions are better with more information, so investigating candidates' backgrounds is key. I don't mean that background checks can be expected to reliably screen out employees who will later act violently, because violence is a process that evolves over time; it is not a condition or a state. But effective background checks do give an employer the opportunity to learn important information about a candidate the easy way.

I testified in a case involving a security firm called MacGuard, which employed a man named Rodney Garmanian. They gave him the uniform he used to lure an eighteen-year-old girl named Teak Dyer into his car. They gave him the car he used to drive her away. They gave him the keys to the locked building where he took her, the handcuffs he used to restrain her, the billy club he struck her with, and the gun he murdered her with. MacGuard had failed to conduct any pre-employment background check or even to review Garmanian's application. Had they taken those few minutes, they would have learned that he failed to fill out most of the form, and what he did fill out was not favorable. He had listed his term in the military as being three months. That kind of thing is an obvious area for inquiry: "Why were you in the military for only three months, Mr. Garmanian? Most people are in the military longer." He had listed his reason for leaving on two of the former jobs as "fired," yet MacGuard didn't ask him anything about that.

Perhaps the most chilling thing about this case is what I learned simply by calling two of his former employers. The first told me, "Oh, yes, I remember Rodney Garmanian. He once tried to have sex with a girl on the second floor when the building was closed." The second person said, "Oh, yes, I remember Rodney Garmanian. He drew sexually solicitous drawings and put them in the ladies' room." The murder Garmanian ultimately committed occurred in the ladies' room on the second floor of a closed building. For twenty-five cents I had learned information that, had Garmanian's employers bothered to get it, could have saved Teak Dyer's life. *Checking references and checking with former employers is an absolutely critical duty of every employer.*

Another case I testified in involved an employee who intentionally drove his truck at high speed through a line of picketers; several people were injured, and one was brain damaged. Here again, there was an ineffective pre-employment inquiry. References were not called, information offered on the application was not confirmed. In fact, just on the face of it, the application demonstrated a lack of full disclosure and a lack of honesty. For example, telephone numbers listed under references also appeared under relatives, and telephone numbers that when dialed went to people's homes were offered as being companies. Checking such things can tell you without much effort that the applicant is not honest. At a minimum, it tells you that there are some additional issues to be explored with him.

The failure to take the obvious step of calling references is an epidemic in America, and I have little patience for managers who complain about employees they didn't care enough to assess before hiring. A common excuse for this failure is that the references will say only good things since the candidate has prepared them for the call. In fact, there is a tremendous amount of information to be gained from references in terms of confirming facts on the application. "Did you know him when he worked for such and such a firm? When did he work for such and such a firm? Do you know roughly what salary he was making? Do you know what school he went to? You said you went to school with him." I suggest that questions asked of those listed as references be guided by information on the application.

The most important thing references can give you are other references. We call these "developed sources." These are people who know the applicant but whom he did not list as references. Accordingly, they are not prepared for your inquiry and will be more likely to provide valuable information. You get the names of developed sources by asking the references the applicant listed for the names of other people who know him.

The interview with the applicant is another opportunity to gain valuable background information. This may seem obvious, but many employers don't use this best resource. The first issue to explore is an applicant's truthfulness during the pre-employment process. When people lie on applications, they rarely recall exactly how they lied, so I suggest holding the application in your hand and asking questions right off it as you interview a candidate. The most common lie is about the duration of previous jobs. Eight months is reported as a year, eighteen months as two years, etc.

During pre-employment interviews (which can be videotaped), there are a series of questions we suggest asking. Though not an exhaustive list, here are some examples:

"Describe the best boss you ever had," and "Describe the worst boss you ever had."

This is a powerful inquiry that can reveal important attitudes about managers and management. If the applicant speaks for just a moment about his best boss, but can wax on enthusiastically about the worst bosses, this is telling. Does he use expressions like "personality conflict" to explain why things did not work out with previous employers? Does he ridicule former bosses? Does he take any responsibility for his part?

"Tell me about a failure in your life and tell me why it occurred."

Does the applicant say he cannot think of one? If he can describe something he perceives as a failure, does he take responsibility for it or does he blame others (e.g., "I never graduated high school because those damned teachers didn't know how to motivate me")?

"What are some of the things your last employer could have done to be more successful?"

Does the applicant offer a long list of items and appear to feel he could have run things better than management did? Are his comments constructive or angry? There is a follow-up:

"Did you ever tell your previous employer any of your thoughts on ways they could improve?"

If he says "Yes, but they never listened to anyone," or "Yeah, but they just said 'Mind your own business,'" this may tell more about the style of his approach than about managers at his last job. Most employers react well to suggestions that are offered in a constructive way, regardless of whether or not they follow them. Another unfavorable response is "What's the use of making suggestions? Nothing ever changes anyway." Some applicants will accuse former employers of stealing their ideas. Others will tell war stories about efforts to get a former employer to follow suggestions. If so, ask if this was a one-man undertaking or in concert with his co-workers. Sometimes an applicant will say his co-workers "didn't have the guts to confront management like I did."

"What are some of the things your last employer could have done to keep you?"

Some applicants will give a reasonable answer (slightly more pay, better schedule, etc.), but others will provide a list of demands that demonstrate unreasonable expectations (e.g., "They could have doubled my salary, promoted me to vice president, and given me Fridays off").

"How do you go about solving problems at work?"

Good answers are that he consults with others, weighs all points of view, discusses them with involved parties, etc. Unfavorable answers contain a theme of confrontation (e.g., "I tell the source of the problem he'd better straighten up," or "I go right to the man in charge and lay it on the line"). Another bad answer is that he does nothing to resolve problems, saying, "Nothing ever changes anyway."

"Describe a problem you had in your life where someone else's help was very important to you."

Is he able to recall such a situation? If so, does he give credit or express appreciation about the help?

"Who is your best friend and how would you describe your friendship?"

Believe it or not, there are plenty of people who cannot come up with a single name in response to this question. If they give a name that was not listed as a reference, ask why. Then ask if you can call that friend as a reference.

▪ ▪ ▪

Some statements in an interview that appear to be favorable may actually mask characteristics that are unfavorable. "I am *always* on time," or "I am very, very organized" are sometimes offered by applicants who will later be revealed as inflexible and territorial. Territorialism (*my* desk, *my* area, *my* assignment) is not necessarily an attribute. "If I say I'll give you eight hours, you can be sure that's what you'll get, not a minute less" might be said by an applicant who will also hold you to his expectations, treating understandings as commitments and unforeseen changes as unfairnesses.

We can all rationalize anything, and when an employer is too anxious to fill a position, intuition is ignored. As I mentioned earlier about hiring baby-sitters, the goal should be to disqualify poor applicants rather than qualify good applicants. *Those who are good will qualify themselves.*

▪ ▪ ▪

Another characteristic frequently seen in cases that ended badly is that the employee was not supervised appropriately.

The concept of appropriate supervision can be stated in six words: *praise for performance — correction for errors.* It is as important to catch employees doing something right — and tell them — as it is to catch them doing something wrong, but above all, noncompliance must not be ignored. With the problem employee, supervisors have often given up on correcting him. Many of the problems that arise could have been avoided by treating this employee appropriately at every step, but people treated him differently because it was easier than resolving the issues.

This type of employee is very sensitive and perceptive about being "handled," particularly if it's because of a concern that he will act violently. If he perceives that employers consider him dangerous, it can actually increase the likelihood of his acting out, because he has little to lose when he is already thought of as violent.

▪ ▪ ▪

In addition to hiring the wrong people and supervising them badly, employers who had the worst outcomes were also slow to fire people they knew had to go.

A problem employee is easier to terminate before he makes a substantial emotional investment in the job, before the minor issues become causes, before disappointments become disgruntlements. The longer that emotional investment is made, the stronger it becomes, and the more likely it is that the termination will be difficult.

Often employers are reluctant to fire someone who concerns them because they really don't know the best way to do it. Below, I list some strategies for difficult terminations, but many are also applicable to terminating other emotionally invested relationships, such as those involving unwanted suitors, business partners, and former spouses. Individual circumstances will always call for customized responses, but these philosophies will usually apply.

PROTECT THE DIGNITY DOMINO

Prop it up with courtesy and understanding. Never embarrass an employee. Keep secret from him any concerns you have about serious harms he might commit. Think the worst if the indicators are there, but treat the terminated employee as if he were what you hope him to be. Treat him as if he is reasonable, as if you are not afraid of how he might react. Terminate his employment in a manner that demonstrates that you expect him to accept the news maturely and appropriately. This does not mean ignore the hazard. Just the opposite is wise: Prepare for the worst, but not in ways detectable to the terminated employee. Do not lead him to believe that you are anticipating threats or hazard. If you do, you may be writing a script for him to follow. Further, you are letting him know your vulnerabilities.

MAKE THE TERMINATION COMPLETE

Often, employers are tempted to offer a gradual separation, thinking it will lessen the blow to the terminated employee. Though it may appear that this approach extends the term of employment, it really extends the firing, and the embarrassment and anxiety along with it. It is analogous to hooking someone up to life-support systems when he has no quality of life and no chance for survival. Though some may believe this extends the process of life, it actually extends the process of death.

DO NOT NEGOTIATE

This could be called the golden rule, and it applies to getting out of any kind of relationship with people who refuse to let go. Once the termination decision has been made, your meeting with the employee is to inform him of your decision, period. Other issues may come up, but do not negotiate, no matter how much he wants to. This is not a discussion of how to improve things, correct things, change the past, find blame, or start over. Revisiting the issues and contentions of his history with the company will only raise sore points and raise emotion. He cannot likely be convinced that terminating him is a good idea — it isn't in his nature to recognize that, no matter what the evidence — so keep the presentation brief. I suggest to clients that they actually write a script of the few points they want to make in informing the employee of the decision. I also suggest they come up with what my office calls a "boomerang line," a sentence that can be repeated each time he tries to derail the conversation: "Bill, if you had made this decision instead of us, we'd respect it," or "This is not the time to rehash the past; we have to work on the future."

KEEP THE DISCUSSION FUTURE BASED

Avoid rehashing the past. Establish some issues about the future to be resolved during the meeting. For example, "What would you like us to tell callers about where to reach you?" "Would you like us to forward mail or advise the sender of your new address?" "How can we best describe your job here to future employers who may contact us?" Make the employee feel that his input has bearing. Uncertainty about what a former employer will tell callers causes high anxiety, so address it directly and show that it is resolvable. This way it is not left simmering beneath the surface. These points may seem minor, but they direct focus to the future, to his starting over again rather than dwelling on the past.

BE DIRECT

Instead of simply informing an employee that the decision to fire him has been made, some employers sidle up to the issue so delicately that the person doesn't fully realize he has just been fired. After listening, he might say he understands he has to improve his performance, to which the employer responds, "No, you don't understand; we're firing you." This can make the fired employee feel foolish on top of all the other feelings that go with being fired. Trying to be delicate often results in being vague. There is a joke that seems at first to endorse delivering bad news in a roundabout way, but it shows that directness actually makes more sense:

> A woman calls the friend who is house-sitting for her and asks how things are going. "Well, your cat fell off the roof and died," the friend reports. "My God," the woman replies. "How could you tell me like that? You should have said, 'Fluffy was playing on the roof having a wonderful time, and she began to slip. She regained her footing and seemed okay, but then she slipped again and fell off the roof. She was rushed to the vet, and the injuries seemed serious, but then Fluffy rallied, and everyone thought she'd make it, but . . . well . . . finally she passed away.' That's how you should have told me."
>
> The house-sitter apologizes for being so unfeeling. A week later the woman calls again to see how things are going. The house-sitter hesitates and then says, "Well, your mother was playing on the roof . . ."

People benefit most from hearing bad news forthrightly.

The whole theme of the termination meeting should be that you are confident he will succeed in the future, find work he will enjoy, and do well. (You may actually feel he has emotional problems, is self-defeating, and will always fail, but there is nothing to be gained from letting these messages surface.) The tone of the meeting should be matter-of-fact, not solemn and depressing: "These changes are part of professional life that we all experience at one time or another. I've been through it myself. We know you'll do well and that this needn't be a setback for you."

CITE GENERAL RATHER THAN SPECIFIC ISSUES

Many employers want to justify to the terminated employee why they are taking this action, as if they could possibly convince him that his being fired is a good idea. Others use the termination meeting for more efforts to correct the employee's attitude or improve him, turning the termination meeting into a lecture. Many employers give more frank and constructive criticism at the moment of firing someone than they ever gave that employee while he was employed. Forget about that — it's too late. A wiser course is to describe the decision in general terms, saying it is best for all parties. Say employment is a two-way street and the present situation isn't serving either side. Say he is obviously a capable person but this job is not providing the best environment for him to excel in. Do not get dragged into a discussion about who will replace him. Use a boomerang line or say those decisions haven't been made.

REMEMBER THE ELEMENT OF SURPRISE

In consideration of the security and safety of those handling the firing, the employee should not be aware of the termination meeting ahead of time. Believe it or not, many employees are summoned to their firing meeting with the words "They're going to fire you."

TIME IT RIGHT

A firing should take place at the end of the day, while other employees are departing. This way, when the meeting is over, the fired employee cannot immediately seek out those he feels are responsible. Further, he will then be going home at the same time as usual as opposed to finding himself home on a weekday morning, for example. I suggest firing at the end of the work week. If fired on a Friday, he has the weekend off as usual and won't feel the impact of having no place to go the next morning. Unlike on a weekday, he will not awaken with the knowledge that his former co-workers are at the job (and possibly discussing him). He won't have the experience of everything being different from usual, different shows on TV, familiar people not at home, etc. Though some believe that firing earlier in the week is advisable, I find it makes possible targets of aggression available to him at work while he is still at a point of high emotion.

CHOOSE YOUR SETTING

A firing should take place in a room out of the view of other employees. It should not be in the office of the person doing the firing, because then there's no way to end the meeting if the terminated employee wants to keep talking. The person doing the firing needs to have the ability to stand up and leave if it is no longer productive to stay. One experienced executive I know avoids using his office because he feels that a person will always vividly remember where he was fired and might return there if angry.

CHOOSE YOUR CAST

Who should be present? I suggest that a higher level manager than the employee usually worked with should make the termination presentation. It should be someone distant from the day-to-day controversies that surrounded the terminated employee. It should be someone who is calm and can retain that demeanor in the face of anger or even threats. When workable, a second participant can be someone in management the fired employee is known to admire, or someone with whom he has a good relationship. The reason for this second person is that the employee will act his best self in front of someone he feels likes or respects him.

Who should *not* be present? Armed security guards, local police, or Big Ed from the loading dock should not be part of the termination meeting. Though some employers believe that this presence puts them in a position of strength, it does exactly the opposite. It sets all your vulnerabilities on the table for the potentially dangerous employee to exploit. No equal co-worker or direct supervisor should be present either. They increase the likelihood of embarrassment, along with the likelihood of getting into a heated discussion about the past. The manager running the termination meeting shows his strength by not appearing to need any reinforcements.

■ ■ ■

Many employers view firing as something done from a position of power, but it is not so. There was a day when Richard Farley was the most powerful man at ESL. There was a day when David Burke was the most powerful man at USAir. They had anger and righteous indignation, and as Emerson said, "A good indignation brings out all one's powers." Righteous indignation can be the engine for behaviors that an employee might never have even considered before. Remember, this man is not a monster. He is someone they hired who might have worked at a company for years. But now he is in shock. This firing has shaken his world. Either he didn't expect it or it confirms his view of the world because he always expected it. In any case, it is an unwelcome and belittling change that is being forced on him.

He could stand not being liked in the company, but being ignored, rejected, *erased* — that is quite a different matter. The firing is much bigger to him because of what he links to it: loss of status, loss of income, loss of security, loss of purpose, loss of identity, and above all loss in a fight. His opponents have won and he has lost.

Because of all this, an important power shift takes place at the instant of firing. Everything changes as a wide range of options and alternatives opens up to the fired employee that he could never have applied when he was trying to keep his job. The primary leverage of employers is the ability to fire, but once they do it, once that power is exercised, their one shot has been fired, and the gun is empty. After that, the power is in the hands of the employee. Many companies have learned that the cost of underestimating this power is far greater than the cost of respecting it.

Given the industriousness of lawyers and the prevalence of wrongful termination suits, some companies have been more concerned about litigation than hazard. When a fired employee threatens a lawsuit, he may get more attention than for other threats, but this is ironic, because in the context of the kind of employee we are discussing here, the threatening of a lawsuit is actually good news. As long as he is focused on a lawsuit, he sees alternatives to violence. The problem with lawsuits comes not when they start, but when they end. We know that eventually, particularly when claims are unreasonable or outrageous, the employee will lose the legal battle. Then the company may have to face that person's anger again. When employers avoid provoking or engaging a fired employee, however, time itself will heal most wounds, hopefully including those to his dignity and identity.

What is the best way to respond to threats in a termination meeting? In chapter 7, I provided many concepts about threats that apply to this question. Remember that the value of threats is determined by our reaction. Accordingly, if an employee makes threats when he is fired, the best theme for the reaction is "I understand you are upset, but the things you are talking about are not your style. I know you are far too reasonable and have too good a future to even consider such things." This reaction is not intended to convince the threatener that he isn't angry but rather to convince him that you are not afraid.

It is also important to let the threatener know that he has not embarked on a course from which he cannot retreat. A good theme is "We all say things when we react emotionally; I've done it myself. Let's just forget it. I know you'll feel different tomorrow."

Even in the cases in which the threats are determined to be serious (and thus call for interventions or extensive preparations), we advise clients never to show the threatener a high appraisal of his words and never to show fear. This doesn't mean they shouldn't take precautions. In fact, when clients are firing difficult employees, we guide them through many precautions, including monitoring the meeting by video from nearby rooms, having security intervention teams at the ready, installation of emergency call buttons, and improved access-control procedures after the firing.

All termination meetings, whether they go well or poorly, provide valuable insights into how the fired employee is going to behave later. As important, this meeting also shows the fired employee how management will react to his behavior. Immediately after a termination meeting, the person who conducted the firing should make a report of the attitude, behavior, responses and statements of the fired employee. The information can then be assessed by professionals whose opinions can help inform decisions about security and other relevant matters.

Among the issues to be decided after a difficult termination is whether anyone needs to be notified about possible risk. The failure to warn people who might be the targets of violence can be negligent, as can be the failure to take back access credentials, monitor an angry employee's departure from the building, notify security personnel and receptionists, or take any other steps appropriate when someone is believed to be dangerous to others.

The worst possible reaction to a threat is a counterthreat. When threats work for the employee, it's because, having little to lose, he might actually do a reckless thing — and management knows that. Conversely, the employee intuitively knows that management will not do a reckless thing. Also, counterthreats make things worse. Think of violence as interactional. The way you respond to a threat might up the ante and turn this situation into a contest of threats, escalations, and counterthreats. It is a contest employers rarely win, for they have far more at risk than the terminated employee and far more ways to lose. Examples of counterthreats include management's saying, "Oh, yeah? Well I'll have the cops on you the minute you try it!" Counterthreats engage the threatener and put you on his playing field. You want exactly the opposite, which is to disengage and to play by your rules.

Having said this, I should add that there is also a time to let go of rules altogether. My office consulted on a case in which our client, a midsized city, put rules above safety. An employee who was retiring on a mental disability rejected the $11,000 the city offered because it didn't include a $400 reimbursement he felt entitled to. The rules prohibited reimbursement for expenditures that were not approved ahead of time, so the city refused to pay it. One afternoon the ex-employee arrived without an appointment and demanded to see the administrator who had made that decision. The two argued, but the administrator held firm to the rules. The employee stood up and said, "Let me see if I can put this another way." He then placed two .38 caliber bullets on the administrator's desk and left.

Our office was asked to assess the situation. We learned that this employee had shown a handgun to his therapist and commented on the principle of the financial dispute: "Right is right, and right always wins." In our report, we suggested that the city pay the $400, since winning that point had become a matter of pride and identity to the former employee. Acceding to people's demands isn't always possible or practical, but in this case the entire consequence was the $400.

By the city's reaction to our suggestion, you would think we had asked them to give up their firstborn sons. The administrator told me, "We have rules, and if we buckle under to everybody who makes a demand, those rules will be meaningless." He could have benefited from the wisdom of Oliver Wendell Holmes: "The young man knows the rules, but the old man knows the exceptions."

Like the threatener, this administrator was committed to the principle of the matter. In such cases, we say both parties are "in the ring," meaning they are willing or even anxious to stay in the fight. I said, "We aren't suggesting that you give four hundred dollars to everyone who asks for it, but rather that you give four hundred dollars just to the desperate, emotionally disturbed ex-employees who, after showing a gun to their therapists, plop bullets down on your desk to make a point. I don't expect the city will be paying out on that policy too often." But the administrator was clinging to some higher ideal than just the money — in fact, he was spending more than $400 just arguing his opinion with me. After he finished his second, more spirited lecture on the sanctity of rules, I wanted to bring us back to the high-stakes context: "I have a suggestion: Since rules are so powerful, let's make a new rule that says employees cannot shoot administrators. Won't that solve the problem?"

He actually appeared to be thinking over my rhetorical suggestion when I asked, "Which rule would you rather see broken?" Wars have been fought over easier issues, but the administrator finally agreed to the $400 payment, the ex-employee moved to Arizona, and the city survived its brief affair with flexibility. Such resolutions may seem obvious, but when participants are in the ring, it's hard for them to see past their fists.

▪ ▪ ▪

Not a week passes without an organization's seeking my advice on an employee who scares his co-workers. Reviewing so many situations with near identical features and seeing how they harm productivity, cause anxiety, and put people at risk, I have come to respect the value of avoidance and prevention. The corporations and agencies that have dedicated the time and resources to addressing these hazards before they occur have, in effect, elected to learn lessons secondhand rather than have their employees learn them firsthand.

No matter how well managers manage, however, there may still be some violence in the workplace that doesn't reveal itself early. That's because it starts closer to home.

▪ 10 ▪

INTIMATE ENEMIES

"You never do anything about him.
You talk to him and then you leave."
— *Nicole Brown Simpson to police*

I don't see how anyone could have had doubts after hearing the eloquent prosecutor describe the case. We all know the story: The murdered woman had reportedly suffered violence at the hands of the defendant for a long while, virtually since the start of their relationship. A few times, she had called the police, and once she even brought battery charges against him (he was acquitted), but the violence continued. The day of the murder, she hadn't invited him to come along to a social event, and not long after ten P.M., she was stabbed to death. The defendant told a friend that he'd had a dream in which he killed her, but later his lawyers said she was probably murdered by drug dealers.

These facts became famous during the O. J. Simpson case, but the story I just told occurred thousands of miles from Brentwood, when Nicole Brown Simpson still had six months left to live. The murdered woman in this case was named Meredith Coppola. If I told of all the other women killed in America this year by a husband or boyfriend, the book you are holding would be four thousand pages long — and the stories would be stunningly similar. Only the names and a few details would change.

I worked with the prosecution on the stalking aspects of the Simpson criminal trial, and later on the civil suit brought by the Goldman family, but I don't discuss the case here as an advocate. In one sense, it is nothing more than an example of this common crime. In another sense, however, it is much, much more. For American children who are under ten in 1997, this one case dominated the news for at least 30 percent of their lives. It was all that was on daytime TV, all they saw on tabloid covers at their eye level at the supermarket, and all that the adults seemed to be discussing at the dinner table. It is, ultimately, an American myth about Daddy killing Mommy — and getting away with it. Whatever your opinion of the case, that myth is part of its legacy. So are the many myths that were widely promoted by the Scheme Team, Simpson's criminal defense lawyers.

They told us, "Just because a man beats his wife doesn't mean he killed her," and that's true. But what's that got to do with O. J. Simpson, who beat his wife, broke into her home, threatened her (at least once with a gun), terrorized her, and stalked her? That behavior puts him very near the center of the predictive circle for wife murder.

The Scheme Team's observation is a little like saying, "Just because someone buys dough doesn't mean he's going to make pizza," and that's true, but if he buys dough, spreads it around on a tin tray, adds tomato sauce, adds cheese, and puts it in the oven, then, even if Simpson lawyer Alan Dershowitz tells you differently, you can be comfortable predicting that pizza is being made.

Why do I call the Simpson lawyers the Scheme Team? Because it reminds me that wife murderers and their lawyers frequently scheme to design defenses for an indefensible crime. Every murder discussed in this chapter, except those in which the perpetrators committed suicide after killing their spouses, was followed by some creative legal excuse making.

What was clear in the Simpson case is that while Ron Goldman may have been in the wrong place at the wrong time, Nicole had been in the wrong place for a long time. As prosecutor Scott Gordon, now the chairman of L.A.'s forward-thinking Domestic Violence Council, said, "Simpson was killing Nicole for years — she finally died on June twelfth." This concept of a long, slow crime is what I want to focus on as we discuss predicting and preventing these tragedies.

Despite the misinformation offered to the American public by paid advocates in service of just one man, there are many reliable pre-incident indicators associated with spousal violence and murder. They won't all be present in every case, but if a situation has several of these signals, there is reason for concern:

1) *The woman has intuitive feelings that she is at risk.*
2) At the inception of the relationship, the man accelerated the pace, prematurely placing on the agenda such things as commitment, living together, and marriage.
3) He resolves conflict with intimidation, bullying, and violence.
4) He is verbally abusive.
5) He uses threats and intimidation as instruments of control or abuse. This includes threats to harm physically, to defame, to embarrass, to restrict freedom, to disclose secrets, to cut off support, to abandon, and to commit suicide.
6) He breaks or strikes things in anger. He uses symbolic violence (tearing a wedding photo, marring a face in a photo, etc.).
7) He has battered in prior relationships.
8) He uses alcohol or drugs with adverse affects (memory loss, hostility, cruelty).
9) He cites alcohol or drugs as an excuse or explanation for hostile or violent conduct ("That was the booze talking, not me; I got so drunk I was crazy").
10) His history includes police encounters for behavioral offenses (threats, stalking, assault, battery).
11) There has been more than one incident of violent behavior (including vandalism, breaking things, throwing things).
12) He uses money to control the activities, purchases, and behavior of his wife/partner.
13) He becomes jealous of anyone or anything that takes her time away from the relationship; he keeps her on a "tight leash," requires her to account for her time.
14) He refuses to accept rejection.
15) He expects the relationship to go on forever, perhaps using phrases like "together for life," "always," "no matter what."

16) He projects extreme emotions onto others (hate, love, jealousy, commitment) even when there is no evidence that would lead a reasonable person to perceive them.
17) He minimizes incidents of abuse.
18) He spends a disproportionate amount of time talking about his wife/partner and derives much of his identity from being her husband, lover, etc.
19) He tries to enlist his wife's friends or relatives in a campaign to keep or recover the relationship.
20) He has inappropriately surveilled or followed his wife/partner.
21) He believes others are out to get him. He believes that those around his wife/partner dislike him and encourage her to leave.
22) He resists change and is described as inflexible, unwilling to compromise.
23) He identifies with or compares himself to violent people in films, news stories, fiction, or history. He characterizes the violence of others as justified.
24) He suffers mood swings or is sullen, angry, or depressed.
25) He consistently blames others for problems of his own making; he refuses to take responsibility for the results of his actions.
26) He refers to weapons as instruments of power, control, or revenge.
27) Weapons are a substantial part of his persona; he has a gun or he talks about, jokes about, reads about, or collects weapons.
28) He uses "male privilege" as a justification for his conduct (treats her like a servant, makes all the big decisions, acts like the "master of the house").
29) He experienced or witnessed violence as a child.
30) His wife/partner fears he will injure or kill her. She has discussed this with others or has made plans to be carried out in the event of her death (e.g., designating someone to care for children).

With this list and all you know about intuition and prediction, you can now help prevent America's most predictable murders. Literally. Refer the woman to a battered women's shelter, if for nothing else than to speak to someone who knows about what she is facing, in her life and in herself. Refer the man to a battered women's shelter; they will be able to suggest programs for him. When there is violence, report it to the police.

This list reminds us that before our next breakfast, another twelve women will be killed — mothers, sisters, daughters. In almost every case, the violence that preceded the final violence was a secret kept by several people. This list can say to women who are in that situation that they must get out. It can say to police officers who might not arrest that they must arrest, to doctors who might not notify that they must notify. It can say to prosecutors that they must file charges. It can say to neighbors who might ignore violence that they must not.

It can also speak to men who might recognize themselves, and that is meaningful. After Christopher Darden's closing argument in the Simpson trial, co-prosecutor Scott Gordon and I joined him in his office. We read faxes from around the country sent by victims of domestic violence, but we were equally moved by messages from abusive men, one of which read, "You may have just saved my wife's life, for as I listened to you describing Simpson's abuse, I recognized myself." Unlike some murders, spousal homicide is a crime that can strike *with* conscience.

▪ ▪ ▪

Before any discussion on how a woman can get out of an unwanted relationship, we must first recognize that many women choose not to get out. Right now, as you are reading these words, at least one woman in America is being beaten by her husband — and now another, for it happens once every few seconds. So while it's old news that many men are violent, we must also accept that a nearly equal number of women choose to stay with them. This means that many accurate predictions of danger are being ignored. Why?

I can share part of the answer from my personal experience as a boy. I vividly recall the night when my sister and I ran out the door at two A.M. after hours of violence. Afraid to go back home, we called the police from a pay phone and reported two kids loitering so that we'd get picked up and taken to jail, where we'd be safe. That experience and the years that led up to it helped me to understand that many women stay for the same reason I stayed: Until that night, no other possibility ever occurred to me. Before that night, you could no more have gotten me to voluntarily leave my family than I could get you to leave yours right now.

Like the battered child, the battered woman gets a powerful feeling of overwhelming relief when an incident ends. She becomes addicted to that feeling. The abuser is the only person who can deliver moments of peace, by being his better self for a while. Thus, the abuser holds the key to the abused person's feeling of well-being. The abuser delivers the high highs that bookend the low lows, and the worse the bad times get, the better the good times are in contrast. All of this is in addition to the fact that a battered woman is shell-shocked enough to believe that each horrible incident may be the last.

Understanding how people evaluate personal risk has helped me better understand why so many women in danger stay there. As I learned from my experiences with violence as a child, many of these women have been beaten so much that their fear mechanism is dulled to the point that they take in stride risks that others would consider extraordinary. The relationship between violence and death is no longer apparent to them. One woman who'd been at a shelter and then returned to her abuser gives us a good example: She called the shelter late one night to ask if she could come back. As always, the first question the counselor asked was "Are you in danger now?" The woman said no. Later in the call the woman added, almost as an aside, that her husband was outside the room with a gun. Hadn't she just a moment earlier said she wasn't in danger? To her, if he was in the same room with the gun or the gun was being held to her head, *then* she would be in danger.

How could someone feel that being beaten does not justify leaving? Being struck and forced not to resist is a particularly damaging form of abuse because it trains out of the victim the instinctive reaction to protect the self. To override that most natural and central instinct, a person must come to believe that he or she is not worth protecting. Being beaten by a "loved one" sets up a conflict between two instincts that should never compete: the instinct to stay in a secure environment (the family) and the instinct to flee a dangerous environment. As if on a seesaw, the instinct to stay prevails in the absence of concrete options on the other side. Getting that lopsided seesaw off the ground takes more energy than many victims have.

No amount of logic can usually move a battered woman, so persuasion requires emotional leverage, not statistics or moral arguments. In my many efforts to convince women to leave violent relationships, I have seen their fear and resistance firsthand. I recall a long talk with Janine, a thirty-three-year-old mother of two who showed me photos the police had taken of her injuries after one of the frequent beatings she received. She was eager to tell me about her husband's abuse but just as eager to make excuses for him. Though the most recent beating had left her with three broken ribs, she was going back to him again. I asked her what she would do if her teenage daughter was beaten up by a boyfriend. "Well, I'd probably kill the guy, but one thing's for sure: I'd tell her she could never see him again."

"What is the difference between you and your daughter?" I asked. Janine, who had a fast explanation for every aspect of her husband's behavior, had no answer for her own, so I offered her one: "*The difference is that your daughter has you — and you don't have you. If you don't get out soon, your daughter won't have you either.*" This was resonant to Janine because of its truth: She really didn't have a part of herself, the self-protective part. She had come out of her own childhood with it already shaken, and her husband had beaten it out completely. She did, however, retain the instinct to protect her children, and it was for them that she was finally able to leave.

Though leaving is not an option that seems available to many battered women, I believe that *the first time a woman is hit, she is a victim and the second time, she is a volunteer.* Invariably, after a television interview or speech in which I say this, I hear from people who feel I don't understand the dynamic of battery, that I don't understand the "syndrome." In fact, I have a deep and personal understanding of the syndrome, but I never pass up an opportunity to make clear that *staying is a choice.* Of those who argue that it isn't, I ask: Is it a choice when a woman finally does leave, or is there some syndrome to explain leaving as if it too is involuntary? I believe it is critical for a woman to view staying as a choice, for only then can leaving be viewed as a choice and an option.

Also, if we dismiss the woman's participation as being beyond choice, then what about the man? Couldn't we point to his childhood, his insecurities, his shaky identity, his addiction to control, and say that his behavior too is determined by a syndrome and is thus beyond his choice? Every human behavior can be explained by what precedes it, but that does not excuse it, and we must hold abusive men accountable.

Whoever we may blame, there is some responsibility on both sides of the gender line, particularly if there are children involved. Both parents who participate are hurting their children terribly (the man more than the woman, but both parents). Children learn most from modeling, and as a mother accepts the blows, so likely will her daughter. As a father delivers the blows, so likely will his son.

Though I know that dedicated, constructive people want to educate the public as to why so many women stay, I want to focus on how so many women leave. Helen Keller, a woman in another type of trap, said, "Although the world is full of suffering, it is also full of the overcoming of it."

▪ ▪ ▪

Many batterers control the money, allowing little access to bank accounts or even financial information. Some control the schedule, the car keys, the major purchases, the choice in clothes, the choice in friends. The batterer may be a benevolent control freak at the start of an intimate relationship, but he becomes a malevolent control freak later. And there's another wrinkle: He gives punishment and reward unpredictably, so that any day now, any moment now, he'll be his great old self, his honeymoon self, and this provides an ingredient that is essential to keeping the woman from leaving: hope. Does he do all this with evil design? No, it is part of his concept of how to retain love. Children who do not learn to expect and accept love in natural ways become adults who find other ways to get it.

Controlling may work for a while, even a long while, but then it begins not to work, and so he escalates. He will do anything to stay in control, but his wife is changing, and that causes him to suffer. In fact, the Buddhist definition of human suffering applies perfectly: "Clinging to that which changes." When men in these situations do not find out what is going on inside them, when they do not get counseling or therapy, it is a choice to continue using violence. Such men are taking the risk that violence will escalate to homicide, for as Carl Jung said, "When an inner situation is not made conscious, it appears outside as fate."

Working closely with the Domestic Violence Council, I've learned that for every battered woman who makes the choice to leave, we as a society must provide a place for her to go. In Los Angeles County, where eleven million people live, there are only *420* battered women's shelter beds! On any given night, 75 percent of those beds are occupied by children.

In Los Angeles we have a hotline that automatically connects callers to the nearest shelter. Through that number, established by Los Angeles District Attorney Gil Garcetti, battered women are taught how to get out safely. They learn to make duplicates of car keys and identification papers, how to hide these items from their husbands, how to choose the best time to run, and how not to be tracked when they escape into the modern-day underground railroad that shelters have become. I believe so strongly in the value of this hotline that my company funds it. I mention it here because every city in America needs such a number, and needs to get it prominently displayed in phone booths, phone books, gas stations, schools, and hospital emergency rooms.

An 800 number like ours, answered by people who have been there and understand the dilemma, is often more likely to be used than the alternative number (which I also recommend): 911. The reason for some women's reluctance to call the police is eloquently expressed by the case of Nicole Brown Simpson.

In one episode not revealed during the criminal trial, Simpson pushed Nicole out of a moving car in a parking lot. A police officer who happened on the scene told Simpson, "Take your wife home."

In another incident (well after they were divorced) Simpson broke down the door into Nicole's home. A responding police officer told Nicole his conclusion about what had happened: "No blows were thrown, he didn't throw anything at you; we don't have anything other than a verbal altercation." Nicole responded correctly: "Breaking and entering, I'd call it." "Well," the officer countered, "it's a little different when the two of you have a relationship; it's not like he's a burglar." Absolutely wrong, officer. It's very much like he's a burglar, and it *was* breaking and entering, and trespassing. After assuring O. J. Simpson that they'd keep the incident as quiet "as legally possible," the officers left. (By the way, the LAPD and the L.A. Sheriff's Department are now leading the nation in new ways to manage domestic violence cases.)

Earlier I noted that America has tens of thousands of suicide prevention centers but no homicide prevention centers. Battered women's shelters are the closest thing we have to homicide prevention centers. There are women and children in your community whose lives are in danger, who need to know how to get out, and who need a place to escape to. Los Angeles, the home city of the nation's most notorious wife abuser, is, I am proud to say, also the city with an escape plan for battered families that other cities can use as a model.

▪ ▪ ▪

Just as there are batterers who will victimize partner after partner, so are there serial victims, women who will select more than one violent man. Given that violence is often the result of an inability to influence events in any other way, and that this is often the result of an inability or unwillingness to effectively communicate, it is interesting to consider the wide appeal of the so-called strong and silent type. The reason often cited by women for the attraction is that the silent man is mysterious, and it may be that physical strength, which in evolutionary terms brought security, now adds an element of danger. The combination means that one cannot be completely certain what this man is feeling or thinking (because he is silent), and there might be fairly high stakes (because he is strong and potentially dangerous).

I asked a friend who has often followed her attraction to the strong and silent type how long she likes men to remain silent. "About two or three weeks," she answered. "Just long enough to get me interested. I like to be intrigued, not tricked. The tough part is finding someone who is mysterious but not secretive, strong but not scary."

One of the most common errors in selecting a boyfriend or spouse is basing the prediction on potential. This is actually predicting what certain elements might add up to in some different context: *He isn't working now, but he could be really successful. He's going to be a great artist — of course he can't paint under present circumstances. He's a little edgy and aggressive these days, but that's just until he gets settled.*

Listen to the words: *isn't* working; *can't* paint; *is* aggressive. What a person is doing now is the context for successful predictions, and marrying a man on the basis of potential, or for that matter hiring an employee solely on the basis of potential, is a sure way to interfere with intuition. That's because the focus on potential carries our imagination to how things might be or could be and away from how they are now.

Spousal abuse is committed by people who are with remarkable frequency described by their victims as having been "the sweetest, the gentlest, the kindest, the most attentive," etc. Indeed, many were all of these things during the selection process and often still are — between violent incidents.

But even though these men are frequently kind and gentle in the beginning, there are always warning signs. Victims, however, may not always choose to detect them. I made these points on a recent television interview, and a woman called in and said, "You're wrong, there's no way you can tell when a man will turn out to be violent. It just happens out of nowhere." She went on to describe how her ex-husband, an avid collector of weapons, became possessive immediately after their marriage, made her account for all of her time, didn't allow her to have a car, and frequently displayed jealousy.

Could these things have been warning signs?

In continuing her description of this awful man, she said, "His first wife died as a result of beatings he gave her."

Could *that* have been a warning sign? But people don't see the signs, maybe because our process of falling in love is in large measure the process of choosing not to see faults, and that requires some denial. This denial is doubtless necessary in a culture that glorifies the kind of romance that leads young couples to rush to get married in spite of all the reasons they shouldn't, and fifty-year-old men to follow what is euphemistically called their hearts into relationships with their young secretaries and out of relationships with their middle-aged wives. This is, frankly, the kind of romance that leads to more failed relationships than successful ones.

The way our culture pursues romance and mating is not the way of the whole world. Even here within our nation is another nation, of Native Americans, whose culture historically involved arranged marriages. The man and the woman were selected by tribal elders, told to live together, and quite possibly without a scintilla of attraction, told to build a life together. For such relationships to succeed, the partners had to look for favorable attributes in each other. This is the exact opposite of the process most Americans use, that of *not* looking at the unfavorable attributes.

The issue of selection and choice brings to mind the important work of psychologist Nathaniel Branden, author of *Honoring the Self.* He tells of the woman who says: "I have the worst luck with men. Over and over again, I find myself in these relationships with men who are abusive. I just have the worst luck." Luck has very little to do with it, because the glaringly common characteristic of each of this woman's relationships is her. My observations about selection are offered to enlighten victims, not to blame them, for I don't believe that violence is a fair penalty for bad choices. But I do believe they are choices.

Though leaving is the best response to violence, it is in trying to leave that most women get killed. This dispels a dangerous myth about spousal killings: that they happen in the heat of argument. In fact, the majority of husbands who kill their wives stalk them first, and far from the "crime of passion" that it's so often called, killing a wife is usually a decision, not a loss of control. Those men who are the most violent are not at all carried away by fury. In fact, their heart rates actually drop and they become physiologically calmer as they become more violent.

Even the phrase "crime of passion" has contributed to our widespread misunderstanding of this violence. That phrase is not the description of a crime — *it is the description of an excuse,* a defense. Since 75 percent of spousal murders happen after the woman leaves, it is estrangement, not argument, that begets the worst violence. In the end, stalking is not just about cases of "fatal attraction" — far more often, it is about cases of fatal inaction, in which the woman stayed too long.

Of all the violence discussed in this book, spousal homicide is the most predictable, yet people are reluctant to predict it. A man in Los Angeles was recently accused of killing his wife, three of his children, and three other family members. News reporters questioning neighbors about the accused murderer were told, "He always seemed normal." Another said, "He must be crazy," and another said, "I can't imagine that a father would kill his own children." As you know, if you cannot imagine it, you cannot predict it. When will we have seen this story often enough to realize that if several members of a family are killed, it was probably done by another member of that family? In this case, the man neighbors couldn't imagine was responsible for the murders had already tried to kill his wife three other times. He had also been arrested twice on domestic violence charges. Sounds predictable to me.

So how does the system usually respond to society's most predictable murder risk? It tells the woman to go to court, to civil court, and sue her abuser to stay away. In many states this is called a temporary restraining order, because it is expected to restrain the aggressor. In some states it's called a protection order, expected to protect the victim. In fact, on its own, it doesn't achieve either goal.

Lawyers, police, TV newspeople, counselors, psychologists, and even some victims' advocates recommend restraining orders wholesale. They are a growth industry in this country. We should, perhaps, consider putting them on the New York Stock Exchange, but we should *stop* telling people that a piece of paper will automatically protect them, because when applied to certain types of cases, it may do the opposite. It is dangerous to promote a specific treatment without first diagnosing the problem in the individual case.

It is perhaps obvious to say that a restraining order will not restrain a murderer, but there is substantial controversy on the topic. While I warn that they should not be universally recommended because they aren't right for every kind of case or every stage of a case, most police departments encourage them all the time. Restraining orders (often called TROs) have long been homework assignments police give women to prove they're really committed to getting away from their pursuers. The orders do get the troubled women out of the police station and headed for court, perhaps to have continuing problems, perhaps not, and they do make arrests simpler if the man continues his unwanted pursuit. Thus, TROs clearly serve police and prosecutors. But they do not always serve victims. In California, for example, TROs are valid for only fourteen days, after which the woman must return to court for a trial to determine if the order will be extended.

Even with all the failures of the present system, there are those who aggressively defend it, including one psychiatrist who has been a loyal apologist for the status quo. At a large police conference he trumpeted, "TROs work, and we have proven it." He based his reckless statement on a woefully biased study of a small sample of stalking cases that didn't even include spousal stalkers, the very type most likely to kill.

In fact, if you work back from the murders, you'll find restraining orders and other confrontational interventions alarmingly often. The personal effects of a woman murdered by her estranged husband frequently include the piece of paper that that psychiatrist assured us has been "proven" effective. How does he explain that?

"Look at it this way," he says. "Some people die on chemotherapy. Some people die when they get restraining orders. But that doesn't mean that you don't do chemo — or that you don't get restraining orders." The doctor's comparison of cancer (which the afflicted patient cannot get away from) with the risks posed by an estranged husband (which the woman *can* get away from) is not only callous, but dangerously flawed.

Since so many women die as a result of this type of careless thinking, and because most of those deaths are preventable, I am going to go several layers deeper into the topic. I hope you never need this information for yourself, but I know that someone in your life will need it sometime.

■ ■ ■

Many homicides have occurred at the courthouse where the women were seeking protection orders, or just prior to the hearings. Why? Because the murderers were allergic to rejection. They found it hard enough in private but intolerable in public. For men like this, rejection is a threat to the identity, the persona, to the entire self, and in this sense their crimes could be called *murder in defense of the self.* In *To Have or To Harm,* the first major book on stalking, author Linden Gross details case after case in which court orders did not prevent homicides. Here are just a few:

Shirley Lowery was waiting outside the courtroom for the TRO hearing when she was stabbed nineteen times by her husband. Tammy Marie Davis's husband beat and terrorized her and their twenty-one-month-old child, sending them both to the hospital. Right after he was served with the restraining order Tammy obtained, he shot and killed her. She was nineteen years old.

Donna Montgomery's husband had held a gun to her head and stalked her, so she obtained a restraining order. He came to the bank where she worked and killed her, then himself.

Theresa Bender obtained a restraining order that her husband quickly violated. Even though he was arrested, she remained so committed to her safety that she arranged for two male co-workers to accompany her to and from work. Her husband was equally committed: He shot all three to death before turning the gun on himself.

Maria Navarro called 911 and reported that her estranged husband had just threatened to kill her and was on the way to her house. Despite the fact that he'd been arrested more than once for battery, police declined to dispatch officers to her home because her restraining order had expired. Maria and three others were dead within fifteen minutes, murdered by the man who kept his promise to kill.

Hilda Rivera's husband had violated two restraining orders and had six arrest warrants when he killed her in the presence of their seven-year-old son. Betsy Murray's husband violated his TRO *thirteen* times. He reacted to her divorce petition by telling her, "Marriage is for life and the only way out is death." When nothing else worked, Betsy went into hiding, and even after police assured her that her husband had fled the country to avoid being arrested again, she still kept her new address a secret. When she stopped by her old apartment one day to collect mail a neighbor had been holding, her estranged husband killed her and then himself. He had been stalking her for more than six months.

The fact that so many of these murderers also commit suicide tells us that refusing to accept rejection is more important to them than life itself. By the time they reach this point, are they really going to be deterred by a court order?

The last case I want to cite is that of Connie Chaney. She had already obtained four protective orders when her husband raped her at gunpoint and attempted to kill her. The solution recommended by police? Get a restraining order; so she did. Before gunning her down, her husband wrote in his diary: "I couldn't live with myself knowing she won, or she got me. No! *This is war.*" Those three words speak it all, because the restraining order is like a strategy of war, and the stakes are life and death, just as in war.

In a study of 179 stalking cases sponsored by the San Diego District Attorney's Office, about half of the victims who had sought restraining orders felt their cases were worsened by them. In a study done for the U.S. Department of Justice, researchers concluded that restraining orders were "ineffective in stopping physical violence." They did find that restraining orders were helpful in cases in which there was no history of violent abuse. The report wisely concluded that "given the prevalence of women with children who utilize restraining orders, their general ineffectiveness in curbing subsequent violence may leave a good number of children at risk of either witnessing violence or becoming victims themselves."

A more recent study done for the U.S. Department of Justice found that more than a third of women had continuing problems after getting restraining orders. That means, favorably, that almost two thirds did *not* have continuing problems — but read on. While only 2.6 percent of respondents were physically abused right after getting the orders, when they were recontacted six months later, that percentage had more than tripled. Reports of continued stalking and psychological abuse also increased dramatically after six months. This indicates that the short-term benefits of restraining orders are greater than the long-term benefits.

I want to make clear that I am not saying TROs never work, because in fact, most times that court orders are introduced, the cases do improve. It is often for the very reason one would hope: The men are deterred by the threat of arrest. Other times, TROs demonstrate the woman's resolve to end the relationship, and that convinces the man to stay away. Whatever the reasons they work, there is no argument that they don't work in some cases. The question is: Which cases?

Restraining orders are most effective on the reasonable person who has a limited emotional investment. In other words, they work best on the person least likely to be violent anyway. Also, there is a substantial difference between using a restraining order on an abusive husband and using one on a man you dated a couple of times. That difference is the amount of emotional investment and entitlement the man feels. With a date-stalker (discussed in the next chapter), a TRO orders him to leave the woman alone and go about his life as it was before he met her. The same court order used on an estranged husband asks him to abandon, at the stroke of a judge's signature, the central features of his life: his intimate relationship, his control and ownership of another human being, his identity as a powerful man, his identity as a husband, and on and on. Thus, a TRO might ask one man to do something he can easily do, while it asks another to do something far more difficult. This distinction has been largely ignored by the criminal-justice system.

There is a glib response to all this: When men are very violent and dangerous, they are going to kill no matter what, so the TRO can't make things worse. But here's the rub: The TRO does hurt by convincing the woman that she is safe. One prominent family-court judge has said, "Women must realize that this paper won't stop the next fist or the next bullet." But it isn't only women who must realize it — it is the whole criminal-justice system. A woman can be expected to learn from her own experience, but the system should learn from all the experiences.

Carol Arnett has had experience running a battered women's shelter and, years before that, running *to* a battered women's shelter. Now the executive director of the Los Angeles County Domestic Violence Council, Arnett says:

> We shelter workers have watched the criminal justice system fail to protect, and often even endanger women for so many years that we are very cautious about recommending restraining orders. We rely upon the woman herself to plan a course of action. Anyone, in or out of the system, who tells a woman she must follow a particular course that goes against her own judgment and intuition is not only failing to use the philosophy of empowerment, but may well be endangering the woman.

Above all, I want to encourage people to ask this simple question: Will a restraining order help or hurt in my particular case? At least then, whatever choice is made can be called a choice and not an automatic reaction. Think of restraining orders as *an* option, not the only option.

Among those options, I certainly favor law enforcement interventions such as arrests for battery, assault, breaking and entering, or other violations of the law. You might wonder how this differs from being arrested for violating a TRO. Charges for breaking the law involve the system versus the lawbreaker, whereas restraining orders involve an abuser versus his wife. Many batterers find intolerable the idea of being under the control of their victims, and with a court order, a woman seeks to control her husband's conduct, thus turning the tables of their relationship. Conversely, when the system pursues charges for a crime like battery, it is the man's actions – not those of his wife — that bring him a predictable consequence. Abusers should be fully prosecuted for every offense, and I believe prosecutions are an important deterrent to further abuse, but even then, the women must be prepared for the possibility of escalation.

The bottom line is that there is really only one good reason to get a restraining order in a case of wife abuse: The woman believes the man will honor it and leave her alone. If a victim or a professional in the system gets a restraining order to stop someone from committing murder, they have probably applied the wrong strategy.

▪ ▪ ▪

So what can we tell a woman who thinks she might be killed? *Seek and apply strategies that make you unavailable to your pursuer. If you really believe you are at risk, battered women's shelters provide the best way to be safe.* Shelter locations are secret, and the professionals there understand what the legal system often doesn't: that the issue is safety — not justice. The distinction between safety and justice is often blurred, but it becomes clear when you are walking down a crowded city sidewalk, and an athletic young man grabs your purse or briefcase. As he runs off into fast-moving traffic, justice requires that you chase the youth down to catch and arrest him. But as he zigzags through traffic, cars barely missing him, safety requires that you break off the chase. It is unfair that he gets away unpunished, but it is more important that you come away unhurt. (To remind clients that my job is to help them be safer, I have a small sign on my desk that reads, "Do not come here for justice.")

Shelters are where safety is, where guidance is, and where wisdom is. Admittedly, going to a shelter is a major and inconvenient undertaking, and it's easy to see why so many victims are lured by the good news that a restraining order will solve the whole problem. But imagine that your doctor said you needed immediate surgery to save your life. Would you ask, "Isn't there a piece of paper I can carry instead?"

Los Angeles city attorney John Wilson, a thoughtful and experienced man who pioneered the nation's first stalking prosecutions, knows of too many cases in which the victim remained available to her victimizer after the man was arrested and released. Wilson attended a talk I gave to police executives, and he later wrote to me. I am comfortable sharing this part of his moving letter:

> Your theme really hit home. Unfortunately for one young wife, I failed to heed your advice in mid-April. I filed a battery on her husband, and when he got out of jail, he killed her. This was my sixth death since joining the office, and each of them fit right into your profile.

Having read all of this, you may wonder how there is any disagreement whatsoever about the indiscriminate use of restraining orders and other confrontational interventions, but there is. I've heard all sides of the issue, and I must tell you, I don't get it. Perhaps since TROs are issued in America at the rate of more than one thousand every day, and women aren't killed at that same rate, it may look, statistically speaking, as if they are successful. I don't know, but in any case and in every case, police must urge extreme caution in the period following issuance of a TRO. That time is emotionally charged and hazardous, and I hope that when police recommend restraining orders they will also put great effort into ensuring that the woman takes every practical step to make herself unavailable to her pursuer.

Psychologist Lenore Walker, who coined the term "battered wife syndrome" (and who later surprised the domestic violence community by joining O. J. Simpson's defense team) has said of spousal homicide, "There's no way to predict it." She is wrong. Spousal homicide is the single most predictable serious crime in America. Walker's error does make clear, however, that there is an urgent need to help police, prosecutors, and victims systematically evaluate cases to identify those with the ingredients of true danger. Toward this goal, my firm designed MOSAIC-20, an artificial intuition system that assesses the details of a woman's situation as she reports it to police. This computer program flags those cases in which the danger of homicide is highest. Part of the proceeds from this book go to its continued development, and I am proud to be working with the Los Angeles County District Attorney's Office, the Los Angeles County Sheriff's Department, and the Los Angeles Police Department on the nation's first use of MOSAIC-20. (See appendix 5 for more information.) This system brings to regular citizens the same technologies and strategies used to protect high government officials. That's only fair considering that battered women are at far greater risk of murder than most public figures.

In the meantime, restraining orders continue to be what author Linden Gross calls law enforcement's "knee-jerk response." I can't ask rhetorically if somebody has to die before things change, because so many people already have.

▪ ▪ ▪

Thousands of cases have made it clear to me that getting away safely is wiser than trying to change the abusive husband or engaging in a war, even if the police and the courts are on your side. As with other aspects of safety, government cannot fix violent relationships. Many people in law enforcement, motivated by a strong desire to help, are understandably reluctant to accept that some forms of criminality are beyond their reach. Thankfully, there are also those in law enforcement tempered by experience who know all about these cases and become heroes. That brings me to Lisa's story.

Lisa did not know that this police sergeant had looked across the counter into plenty of bruised faces before that night. She thought her situation was unique and special, and she was certain the department would act on it right away, particularly when she explained that her husband had held a gun to her head.

An hour earlier, after climbing out the window and running down several darkened streets, she had looked around and realized she was lost. But in a more important sense, she was found. She had rediscovered herself — the young woman she'd been fifteen years before — before he'd slapped her, before he escalated to choking her, and before the incident with the gun. The children had seen that one, but now they would see her stronger, supported by the police. They would see him apologize, and then it would be okay. The police would talk some sense into her husband and force him to treat her right, and then it would be okay.

She proudly told the sergeant, "I'm not going back to him unless he promises never to hit me again." The sergeant nodded and passed some forms across the counter. "You fill these out — fill them out completely — and then I'm going to put them over there." He pointed to a messy stack of forms and reports piled on a cabinet.

The sergeant looked at the young woman, the woman planning to go back to her abuser, back to the man with the gun he claimed he bought for self-defense but was really for defense of the self.

The sergeant then said the words that changed Lisa's life, the words that a decade later she would thank him for speaking, the words that allowed her to leave her violent abuser: "You fill out these forms and go back home, and the next time I look for them, it will be because you have been murdered."

▪ 11 ▪

"I WAS TRYING TO LET HIM DOWN EASY"

With these words begins a story my office hears several times each month. Before meeting with me, the intelligent young woman may have told it to friends, a psychologist, a private detective, a lawyer, a police officer, maybe even a judge, but the problem persisted. It is the story of a situation that once seemed innocent, or at least manageable, but is now frightening. It is the story of someone who started as a seemingly normal suitor but was soon revealed to be something else.

There are two broad categories of stalking: unwanted pursuit by a stranger, and unwanted pursuit by someone the victim knows. The cases of total strangers fixating on private citizens are, by comparison to other types of stalking, very rare, and they are also the cases least likely to end in violence. Accordingly, I'll be exploring those cases that affect the largest population of victims: stalking by someone who has romantic aspirations, often someone a woman has met or dated.

Though it is fashionable for the news media to report on stalkers as if they are some unique type of criminal, those who choose regular citizens are not. They're not from Mars — they are from Miami and Boston, San Diego and Brentwood. They are the man our sister dated, the man our company hired, the man our friend married.

Against this background, we men must see in them a part of ourselves in order to better understand the issue. Giving talks around the country, I sometimes ask the audience, "How many of the men here ever found out where a girl lived or worked by means other than asking her? How many have driven by a girl's house to see what cars were there, or called just to see who answered the phone and then hung up?"

By the overwhelming show of hands, I've learned that the acceptability of these behaviors is a matter of degree. After one speech, a policeman who'd been in the audience asked to talk with me alone. He told me how he realized just then that he had relentlessly pursued a female student at the police academy when he was on the staff there. She said no to him for eighteen months, all the while concerned that the rejection would have an impact on her career. "She gave me no indication that she wanted a relationship with me, but I never let up, not for a moment," he said. "It paid off, though. We got married."

I suppose you could say it paid off, but the story tells more about how complicated the issue of romantic pursuit is. It is clear that for women in recent decades, the stakes of resisting romantic attention have risen sharply. Some invisible line exists between what is all right and what is too far — and men and women don't always agree on where to place that line. Victims and their unwanted pursuers never agree, and sometimes victims and the police don't either.

Everyone agrees, however, at the point where one of these situations includes violence, but why can we not reach consensus before that? To answer this, I have to recall the images of Dustin Hoffman storming into a church, and Demi Moore showing up uninvited at a business meeting. I have to talk about regular, everyday guys, and about the dictionary. It may seem that these things aren't related to stalking and unwanted pursuit, but — as I'm sure your intuition has already told you — they are.

In the sixties, a movie came out that painted a welcome and lasting picture of how a young man could court a woman. It was *The Graduate.* In it, Dustin Hoffman dates a girl (played by Katherine Ross) and then asks her to marry him. She says no, but he doesn't hear it. He waits outside her classes at school and asks again, and then again. Eventually she writes him a letter saying she's thought it over carefully and decided not to marry him. In fact, she is leaving town and marrying another man. That would seem a pretty clear message — but not in the movies.

Hoffman uses stalking techniques to find her. He pretends to be a friend of the groom, then a family member, then a priest. Ultimately, he finds the church and breaks into it just seconds after Katherine Ross is pronounced the wife of another man. He then beats up the bride's father, hits some other people, and wields a large wooden cross against the wedding guests who try to help the family.

And what happens? He gets the girl. She runs off with Dustin Hoffman, leaving her family and new husband behind. Also left behind is the notion that a woman should be heard, the notion that no means no, and the notion that a woman has a right to decide who will be in her life.

My generation saw in *The Graduate* that there is one romantic strategy to use above all others: *persistence.* This same strategy is at the core of every stalking case. Men pursuing unlikely or inappropriate relationships with women and getting them is a common theme promoted in our culture. Just recall *Flashdance, Tootsie, The Heartbreak Kid, 10, Blame It on Rio, Honeymoon in Vegas, Indecent Proposal.*

This Hollywood formula could be called Boy Wants Girl, Girl Doesn't Want Boy, Boy Harasses Girl, Boy Gets Girl. Many movies teach that if you just stay with it, even if you offend her, even if she says she wants nothing to do with you, even if you've treated her like trash (and sometimes because you've treated her like trash), you'll get the girl. Even if she's in another relationship, even if you look like Dustin Hoffman, you'll eventually get Katherine Ross or Jessica Lange. Persistence will win the war *Against All Odds* (another of these movies, by the way). Even the seemingly innocuous TV show *Cheers* touches the topic. Sam's persistent and inappropriate sexual harassment of two female co-workers — eight years of it — doesn't get him fired or sued. It does, however, get him both women.

There's a lesson in real-life stalking cases that young women can benefit from learning: Persistence only proves persistence — it does not prove love. The fact that a romantic pursuer is relentless doesn't mean you are special — it means he is troubled.

It isn't news that men and women often speak different languages, but when the stakes are the highest, it's important to remember that men are nice when they pursue, and women are nice when they reject. Naturally this leads to confusion, and it brings us to the popular practice of letting him down easy.

True to what they are taught, rejecting women often say less than they mean. True to what they are taught, men often hear less than what is said. Nowhere is this problem more alarmingly expressed than by the hundreds of thousands of fathers (and mothers), older brothers (and sisters), movies and television shows that teach most men that when she says no, that's not what she means. Add to this all the women taught to "play hard to get," when that's not what they are really feeling. The result is that "no" can mean many things in this culture. Here's just a small sample:

Maybe
Hmm . . .
Not sure
I've found my man!
Not yet
Give me time
Keep trying

There is one book in which the meaning of *no* is always clear. It is the dictionary, but since Hollywood writers don't seem to use that book very often, we have to. We have to teach young people that "No" is a complete sentence. This is not as simple as it may appear, given the deep cultural roots of the no/maybe hybrid. It has become part of the contract between men and women and was even explored by the classic contract theorists, Rousseau and Locke. Rousseau asked: "Why do you consult their words when it is not their mouths that speak?" Locke spoke of a man's winning "silent consent" by reading it in a woman's eyes "in spite of the mouth's denial." Locke even asserted that a man is protecting a woman's honor when he ignores her refusal: "If he then completes his happiness, he is not brutal, he is decent." In Locke's world, date rape wouldn't be a crime at all — it would be a gentleman's act of courtesy.

Even if men and women in America spoke the same language, they would still live by much different standards. For example, if a man in a movie researches a woman's schedule, finds out where she lives and works, even goes to her work uninvited, it shows his commitment, proves his love. When Robert Redford does this to Demi Moore in *Indecent Proposal,* it's adorable. But when she shows up at *his* work unannounced, interrupting a business lunch, it's alarming and disruptive.

If a man in the movies wants a sexual encounter or applies persistence, he's a regular, everyday guy, but if a woman does the same thing, she's a maniac or a killer. Just recall *Fatal Attraction, The King of Comedy, Single White Female, Play Misty for Me, The Hand That Rocks the Cradle,* and *Basic Instinct.* When the men pursue, they usually get the girl. When the women pursue, they usually get killed.

Popular movies may be reflections of society or designers of society depending on whom you ask, but either way, they model behavior for us. During the early stages of pursuit situations in movies — and too often in life — the woman is watching and waiting, fitting in to the expectations of an overly invested man. She isn't heard or recognized; she is the screen upon which the man projects his needs and his idea of what she should be.

Stalking is how some men raise the stakes when women don't play along. It is a crime of power, control, and intimidation very similar to date rape. In fact, many cases of date stalking could be described as extended rapes; they take away freedom, and they honor the desires of the man and disregard the wishes of the woman. Whether he is an estranged husband, an ex-boyfriend, a onetime date, or an unwanted suitor, the stalker enforces our culture's cruelest rule, which is that women are not allowed to decide who will be in their lives. It quickly becomes clear that we have something worse than just a double standard — we have a dangerous standard.

I've successfully lobbied and testified for stalking laws in several states, but I would trade them all for a high school class that would teach young men how to hear "no," and teach young women that it's all right to explicitly reject. The curriculum would also include strategies for getting away. Perhaps needless to say, the class would not be called "Letting Him Down Easy." If the culture taught and then allowed women to explicitly reject and to say no, or if more women took that power early in every relationship, stalking cases would decline dramatically.

Looking for Mr. Right has taken on far greater significance than getting rid of Mr. Wrong, so women are not taught how to get out of relationships. That high school class would stress the one rule that applies to all types of unwanted pursuit: *Do not negotiate.* Once a woman has made the decision that she doesn't want a relationship with a particular man, it needs to be said one time, explicitly. Almost any contact after that rejection will be seen as negotiation. If a woman tells a man over and over again that she doesn't want to talk to him, that is talking to him, and every time she does it, she betrays her resolve in the matter.

If you tell someone ten times that you don't want to talk to him, you *are* talking to him — nine more times than you wanted to.

When a woman gets thirty messages from a pursuer and doesn't call him back, but then finally gives in and returns his calls, no matter what she says, he learns that the cost of reaching her is leaving thirty messages. For this type of man, any contact will be seen as progress. Of course, some victims are worried that by not responding they'll provoke him, so they try letting him down easy. Often, the result is that he believes she is conflicted, uncertain, really likes him but just doesn't know it yet.

When a woman rejects someone who has a crush on her, and she says, "It's just that I don't want to be in a relationship right now," he hears only the words "right now." To him, this means she will want to be in a relationship later. The rejection should be "I don't want to be in a relationship *with you.*" Unless it's just that clear, and sometimes even when it is, he doesn't hear it.

If she says, "You're a great guy and you have a lot to offer, but I'm not the one for you; my head's just not in the right place these days," he thinks: "She really likes me; it's just that she's confused. I've got to prove to her that she's the one for me."

When a woman explains why she is rejecting, this type of man will challenge each reason she offers. I suggest that women never explain why they don't want a relationship but simply make clear that they have thought it over, that this is their decision, and that they expect the man to respect it. Why would a woman explain intimate aspects of her life, plans, and romantic choices to someone she doesn't want a relationship with? A rejection based on any condition, say, that she wants to move to another city, just gives him something to challenge. Conditional rejections are not rejections — they are discussions.

The astute opening scene of the film *Tootsie* illustrates well why conditional rejections don't work. Dustin Hoffman plays an actor reading lines at an audition. A voice from offstage tells him he isn't getting the part.

Voice: The reading was fine, you're just the wrong height.

Hoffman: Oh, I can be taller.

Voice: No, you don't understand. We're looking for somebody shorter.

Hoffman: Oh, well look, I don't have to be this tall. See, I'm wearing lifts. I can be shorter.

Voice: I know, but really . . . we're looking for somebody different.

Hoffman: I can be different.

Voice: We're looking for somebody *else,* okay?

This last line offers no reasons and begs no negotiations, but women in this culture are virtually prohibited from speaking it. They are taught that speaking it clearly and early may lead to unpopularity, banishment, anger, and even violence.

Let's imagine a woman has let pass several opportunities to pursue a relationship with a suitor. Every hint, response, action, and inaction has communicated that she is not interested. If the man still pursues at this point, though it will doubtless appear harsh to some, it is time for an unconditional and explicit rejection. Because I know that few American men have heard it, and few women have spoken it, here is what an unconditional and explicit rejection sounds like:

> No matter what you may have assumed till now, and no matter for what reason you assumed it, I have no romantic interest in you whatsoever. I am certain I never will. I expect that knowing

this, you'll put your attention elsewhere, which I understand, because that's what I intend to do.

There is only one appropriate reaction to this: acceptance. However the man communicates it, the basic concept would ideally be: "I hear you, I understand, and while I am disappointed, I will certainly respect your decision."

I said there's only one appropriate reaction. Unfortunately, there are hundreds of inappropriate reactions, and while they take many forms, their basic message is "I do not accept your decision." If a man aggressively debates, doubts, negotiates, or attempts to change her mind, it should be recognized for what it is. It should be clear that:

1) She made the right decision about this man. Instead of her resolve being challenged by his response, it should be strengthened.
2) She obviously would not want a relationship with someone who does not hear what she says and who does not recognize her feelings.
3) If he failed to understand a message this clear and explicit, his reaction to anything ambiguous, or to being let down easy, can only be imagined.

Unwanted pursuers may escalate their behavior to include such things as persistent phone calls and messages; showing up uninvited at a woman's work, school, or home; following her; and trying to enlist her friends or family in his campaign. If any of these things happens, assuming that the woman has communicated one explicit rejection, it is very important that no further detectable response be given. When a woman communicates again with someone she has explicitly rejected, her actions don't match her words. The man is able to choose which communications (actions versus words) actually represent the woman's feelings. Not surprisingly, he usually chooses the ones that serve him. Often, such a man will leave phone messages that ostensibly offer closure but that are actually crudely concealed efforts to get a response — and remember, he views any response as progress.

Message: Hi, it's Bryan. Listen, I'm moving back to Houston, but I can't leave town without an opportunity to see you again. All I'm asking for is a chance to say good-bye; that's all. Just a fast meeting, and then I'm gone.

Best response: No response.

Message: Listen, it's Bryan, this is the last call you'll ever get from me. [This line, though spoken often by stalkers, is rarely true.] It's urgent I speak with you.

Best response: No response.

When a woman is stalked by a person she dated, she may have to endure some judgment from people who learn about her situation: "You must have encouraged the guy in some way," "You must be the kind of woman who enjoys being pursued," etc. Someone will also doubtless give her the conventional wisdom on stalking, which should be called conventional *un*wisdom. It will include (as if it is some creative plan): Change your phone number. In fact, our office does not recommend this strategy, because as any victim will tell you, the stalker always manages to get the new number. A better plan is for the woman to get a second phone line, give the new number to the people she wants to hear from, and leave the old number with an answering machine or voice mail so that the stalker is not even aware she has another number. She can check her messages, and when she receives calls from people she wants to speak with, she can call them back and give them her new number. Eventually, the only person leaving messages on the old number is the unwanted pursuer. In this way, his calls are documented (keep the messages), and more importantly, each time he leaves a message, he *gets* a message: that she can avoid the temptation to respond to his manipulations.

We also suggest that the outgoing message be recorded by a female friend, because he may be calling just to hear his object's voice. While people believe that an outgoing message with a male voice will lead the pursuer to believe his victim is in a new relationship, more commonly it leads him to investigate further.

Stalkers are by definition people who don't give up easily — they are people who don't let go. More accurately, the vast majority of them are people who don't let go at the point most of us would, but who ultimately do let go — if their victims avoid engaging them. Usually, they have to attach a tentacle to someone else before detaching all the tentacles from their current object.

▪ ▪ ▪

An axiom of the stalking dynamic: *Men who cannot let go choose women who cannot say no.*

Most victims will concede that even though they wanted to, they were initially reluctant to explicitly reject. Often, the niceness or delicacy of a woman's rejection is taken as affection. Demonstrating this, and proving that nobody is exempt from these situations, is Kathleen Krueger, the wife of United States Senator Bob Krueger. She could not shake the unwanted pursuer who had once piloted her husband's campaign plane. When Mrs. Krueger described her case to me, she eloquently explained it from the stalker's perspective: "We were nice to him, not unusually so, but it was obviously a big deal to him. He took it as love. *I guess when you are starving, even a morsel seems like a feast.*"

In cases in which the pursuer has initially gotten what he perceived as favorable attention, or in which he has actually dated or had a relationship with his victim, he may be so desperate to hold on that he'll settle for any kind of contact. Though he'd rather be her boyfriend, he'll accept being just a friend. Eventually, though he'd rather be a friend, he'll accept being an enemy if that's the only position available. As a stalking ex-boyfriend wrote to a young client of ours: "You'll be thinking of me. You may not be thinking good thoughts, but you'll be thinking of me."

Another rule to be taught in the "Getting Rid of Mr. Wrong" class would be: *The way to stop contact is to stop contact.* As I noted above, I suggest one explicit rejection and after that absolutely no contact. If you call the pursuer back, or agree to meet, or send him a note, or have somebody warn him off, you buy another six weeks of his unwanted pursuit. Some victims think it will help to have a male friend, new boyfriend, or a male family member tell the stalker to stop. Most who try this learn that the stalker takes it as evidence that his love object must be conflicted. Otherwise she'd have told him herself.

Sending the police to warn off a pursuer may seem the obvious thing to do, but it rarely has the desired effect. Though the behavior of pursuers may be alarming, most have not broken the law, so the police have few options. When police visit him and say, in effect, "Cut this out or you'll get into trouble," the pursuer intuitively knows that if they could have arrested him they would have arrested him. So what's the result of the visit? Well, the greatest possible weapon in his victim's arsenal — sending the police after him — came and went without a problem. The cops stopped by, they talked to him, and they left. Who got stronger, the victim or the pursuer?

To be clear, I feel that police should be involved when there is an actionable crime that if prosecuted would result in improving the victim's safety or putting a high cost on the stalker's behavior. But the first time a stalker should see police is when they show up to arrest him, not when they stop by to chat.

Pursuers are, in a very real sense, detoxing from an addiction to the relationship. It is similar to the dynamic in many domestic violence situations in which both partners are addicted to the relationship. In date-stalking cases, however, it is usually one-sided; the stalker is the addict and his object is the drug. Small doses of that drug do not wean him, they engage him. The way to force him out of this addiction, as with most addictions, is abstinence, cold turkey — no contact from her, no contact from her designates, and no contact about her.

As with domestic violence situations, victims will often be advised that they must do something (police intervention, warning) to their stalkers. From the larger social point of view, such advice might be correct. If one thinks of a stalker as a danger to society — a virtual tiger lurking around the corner waiting to victimize someone — then it may be true that somebody should do something about it, but nobody is obligated to volunteer for that fight, particularly if it's avoidable. If one could know and warn a stalking victim that as she rounds the next corner, she'll be attacked, which option makes more sense: Go around the corner, or take another route? If the fight is avoidable, and it's my wife, my daughter, my friend, or my client, I would recommend avoidance first. That's because fighting will always be available, but it isn't always possible to go back to avoidance once a war is under way.

Victims of stalking will also hear the same conventional wisdom that is offered to battered women: Get a restraining order. Here, as with battered wives, it is important to evaluate which cases might be improved by court intervention and which might be worsened. Much depends upon how escalated the case is and how much emotional investment has been made by the stalker. If he has been actively pursuing the same victim for years and has already ignored warnings and interventions, then a restraining order isn't likely to help. Generally speaking, court orders that are introduced early carry less risk than those introduced after the stalker has made a significant emotional investment or introduced threats and other sinister behavior. Restraining orders obtained soon after a pursuer has ignored a single explicit rejection will carry more clout and less risk than those obtained after many months or years of stalking.

There is a category of stalker for which court orders frequently help (or at least aren't dangerous). It is the one we call the naive pursuer. He is a person who simply does not realize the inappropriateness of his behavior. He might think, "I am in love with this person. Accordingly, this is a love relationship, and I am acting the way people in love act."

This type of unwanted pursuer is generally rational, though perhaps a bit thick and unsophisticated. Not all naive pursuers are seeking romantic relationships. Some are persistently seeking to be hired for a job or to learn why they were not hired for a job, why their idea was not accepted, why their manuscript was rejected, etc. The naive pursuer is usually distinguishable from conventional stalkers by his lack of machismo and his lack of anger at being rejected. He just seems to go along, happily believing he is courting someone. He stays with it until someone makes completely clear to him that his approach is inappropriate, unacceptable, and counterproductive. This isn't always easy, but it's usually safe to try.

Because victims are understandably frustrated and angry, they may look to a court order to do any of the following things:

*D*estroy
*E*xpose
*T*hreaten
*A*venge
*C*hange
*H*umiliate

Note that the acronym for this list is also the only goal that makes sense from a safety point of view, and that is to DETACH, to have the guy out of your life. As with battered women, the restraining order may move you closer to that goal, or it may move you farther away. It is one management plan, but not the only one.

■ ■ ■

The type of stalker whom a woman has briefly dated (as opposed to a stranger she's never met) is quite similar to the controlling or battering husband, though he is far less likely to introduce violence. His strategies include acting pathetic to exploit a victim's sympathy or guilt, calling on supposed promises or commitments, annoying a victim so much that she gives in and continues seeing him, and finally the use of fear through intimidating statements and actions (threats, vandalism, slashing tires, etc.).

Recall Katherine, who asked me if there was a list of warning signs about men who might later become a problem. I'll repeat her story, this time pointing out the warning signs:

> I dated this guy named Bryan. We met at a party of a friend of mine, and he must have asked somebody there for my number [researching the victim]. Before I even got home, he'd left me three messages [overly invested]. I told him I didn't want to go out with him, but he was so enthusiastic about it that I really didn't have any choice [*Men who cannot let go choose women who cannot say no*]. In the beginning, he was superattentive, always seemed to know what I wanted. He remembered everything I ever said [hyperattentiveness]. It was flattering, but it also made

> me uncomfortable [victim intuitively feels uncomfortable]. Like when he remembered that I once mentioned needing more space for my books, he just showed up one day with shelves and all the stuff and just put them up [offering unsolicited help; loan sharking]. I couldn't say no. And he read so much into whatever I said. Once he asked if I'd go to a basketball game with him, and I said maybe. He later said, 'You promised' [projecting onto others emotions or commitments that are not present]. Also, he talked about serious things so early, like living together and marriage and children [whirlwind pace; placing issues on the agenda prematurely]. He started with jokes about that stuff the first time we went out, and later he wasn't joking. Or when he suggested that I have a phone in my car. I wasn't sure I even wanted a car phone, but he borrowed my car and just had one installed [loan sharking]. It was a gift, so what could I say? And, of course, he called me whenever I was in the car [monitoring activity and whereabouts]. And he was so adamant that I never speak to my ex-boyfriend on that car phone. Later, he got angry if I spoke to my ex at all [jealousy]. There were also a couple of my friends he didn't like me to see [isolating her from friends], and he stopped spending time with any of his own friends [making another person responsible to be one's whole social world]. Finally, when I told him I didn't want to be his girlfriend, he refused to hear it [refusing to hear "no"].

All this is done on autopilot by the stalker, who seeks to control the other person so she can't leave him. Being in control is an alternative to being loved, and since his identity is so precariously dependent on a relationship, he carefully shores up every possible leak. In so doing, he also strangles the life out of the relationship, ensuring that it could never be what he says (and maybe even believes) he wants.

Bryan would not pursue a woman who could really say and mean no, though he is very interested in one who initially says no and then gives in. I assure you that Bryan tested Katherine on this point within minutes of meeting her:

> Bryan: Can I get you something to drink?
> Katherine: No, but thank you.

Bryan: Oh, come on, what'll you have?
Katherine: Well, I could have a soft drink, I guess.

This may appear to be a minor exchange, but it is actually a very significant test. Bryan found something she said no to, tried a light persuasion, and Katherine gave in, perhaps just because she wanted to be nice. He will next try one a notch more significant, then another, then another, and finally he's found someone he can control. The exchange about the drink is the same as the exchange they will later have about dating, and later about breaking up. It becomes an unspoken agreement that he will drive and she will be the passenger. The trouble comes when she tries to renegotiate that agreement.

■ ■ ■

Popular news stories would have us believe that stalking is like a virus that strikes its victims without warning, but Katherine, like most victims, got a signal of discomfort from the beginning — and ignored it. Nearly every victim I've ever spoken with stayed in even after she wanted out. It doesn't have to be that way. Women can follow those early signals of intuition right from the start.

Dating carries several risks: the risk of disappointment, the risk of boredom, the risk of rejection, and the risk of letting some troubled, scary man into your life. The whole process is most similar to an audition, except that the stakes are higher. A date might look like the audition in *Tootsie,* in which the man wants the part so badly that he'll do anything to get it, or it can be an opportunity for the woman to evaluate important pre-incident indicators. Doesn't sound romantic? Well, daters are doing an evaluation anyway; they're just doing it badly. I am suggesting only that the evaluation be conscious and informed.

The woman can steer the conversation to the man's last breakup and evaluate how he describes it. Does he accept responsibility for his part? Is he still invested? Was he slow to let go, slow to hear what the woman communicated? Has he let go yet? *Who broke up with whom?* This last question is an important one, because stalkers are rarely the ones who initiate breakups. Has he had several "love-at-first-sight" relationships? Falling for people in a big way based on just a little exposure to them, particularly if this is a pattern, is a valuable PIN. A woman can explore a new date's perception of male and female roles as well as his ideas about commitment, obsession, and freedom. A woman can observe if and how the man tries to change her mind, even on little things. I am not proposing a checklist of blunt questions, but I am suggesting that all the information is there to be mined through artful conversation.

The final lesson in that ideal class for young men and women would center on the fact that contrary to the scary and alarming stories shown on the local news, very few date-stalking situations end in violence. The newspeople would have you believe that if you're being stalked, you'd better get your will in order, but this level of alarm is usually inappropriate. Date-stalkers do not jump from nonviolent harassment to homicide without escalations along the way, escalations that are almost always apparent or at least detectable.

To avoid these situations, listen to yourself right from the start. To avoid escalation if you are already in a stalking situation, listen to yourself at every step along the way. When it comes to date-stalkers, your intuition is now loaded, so listen.

▪ ▪ ▪

The families of those date-stalkers who physically harmed their victims, like the families of the other criminals discussed in this book, have had to face a question no parent ever wants to ask: Why did our child grow up to be violent? The answers can help parents and others see the warning signs and patterns years before they get that tragic phone call or visit from the police.

I've learned a lot about this from young people who killed others, some who killed themselves, and as you'll see in the next chapter, one who did a little of both.

▪ 12 ▪

FEAR OF CHILDREN

"My father did not tell me how to live.
He lived, and let me watch him do it."
— *Clarence Budinton Kelland*

The staff at Saint Augustine Church was busy preparing for its biggest day of the year. Those who'd been around for a while correctly predicted a full chapel, but their prediction of a congregation gathered in happy anticipation of Christmas was very wrong. This year it would be more like a funeral, though different in one important respect: Mourners in a church are usually far from where their loved ones died, but those gathered at Saint Augustine's that Christmas Eve would be just a few feet from where the bodies were found, one dead, one near dead.

Everyone at the mass knew about the grisly discovery, but not one person could claim to understand why two eighteen-year-old boys would stand in the shadow of their church and each shoot himself in the mouth with a sawed-off shotgun.

After every violent tragedy, loved ones are forced to take a hard look at everything in their lives. They begin an awful and usually unrewarding search for responsibility. Family members cluster at the two far ends of the spectrum: those who blame themselves and those who blame others. The kids their children spent time with, the other parent, the jilting girlfriend — someone will invariably be doused with the family's shame and rage and guilt.

Often, a parent will blame the person who sold a child drugs, but James Vance's mother went much farther from home. She blamed a heavy-metal rock band named Judas Priest, and she blamed the mom-and-pop record store that sold their records. She insisted the proprietors should have predicted that the album *Stained Class* would compel her son to enter into a suicide pact with his friend Ray. She felt the store should have warned the boys about the lethality of that album.

When I was asked to testify in the case on behalf of the owners of the record store, I anticipated an interesting study into the media's impact on violence. I did not expect it to be the only case of my career I would later wish I hadn't taken. I had volunteered for many unpleasant explorations and performed with fairly unhesitating professionalism, but when the time came, I did not want to go into that churchyard, I did not want to feel the quiet depression and grief of Ray's mother, nor challenge Mrs. Vance's strong denial. I did not want to study the autopsy reports, nor see the photos, nor come to learn the details of this sad story.

But I did it all, and James Vance ended up as my unwitting and unlikely guide into the lives and experiences of many young Americans. From him, I learned how they feel about drugs, alcohol, television, ambition, intimacy, and crime. He would help me answer the question of so many parents: What are the warning signs that my child might be prone to violence? From the vantage point of that churchyard, I saw young people as I'd never seen them before. Much of what James taught me applies to gang violence, but it also helps explain the sometimes more frightening behavior of middle-class young men whose brutality takes everyone by surprise.

James Vance was obsessed with Judas Priest, attracted to the sinister and violent nature of their music and public persona. He liked the demonic themes of the artwork on their album covers, the monsters and gore, so at the instant he saw Ray shoot himself in the head, the sheer gruesomeness of it did not impress him. Like too many other young Americans, he had been getting comfortable with graphic violence for a long while, and images of gory skulls were fairly mundane to him.

Standing in the churchyard, he looked at his friend's body and for a moment considered breaking the suicide pact they'd made. But then he figured that if he didn't shoot himself, he'd get blamed for Ray's death anyway, so he reached down into the blood, picked up the shotgun, put it in his mouth, and pulled the trigger. But he did not die.

In his less than enthusiastic positioning of that shotgun in his mouth, he failed to kill himself but succeeded at creating an unsettling irony: He became as frightening to behold as anything that ever appeared on the cover of a Judas Priest album. In his hesitation to murder himself, James shot off the bottom of his face. His chin, jaw, tongue, and teeth were all gone, blown around that churchyard. I cannot describe how he looked, and I also cannot forget it. I've seen my share of alarming autopsy photos, of people so injured that death was the only possible result, people so injured that death was probably a relief, but something about James Vance living in a body damaged more than enough to be dead was profoundly disturbing.

Even lawyers who thought they'd seen it all were shaken when he arrived at depositions, a towel wrapped around his neck to catch saliva that ran freely from where the bottom of his face had been. His appearance had become a metaphor for what had been going on inside him. He had wanted to be menacing and frightening. He had aspired to the specialness he thought violence could bring him, and he got there . . . completely.

Aided by his mother, who helped interpret his unusual speech during the days he was questioned, James told lawyers about his case, and also about his time. I listened carefully. I learned that he and Ray had wanted to do something big and bad, though not necessarily commit suicide. It was the violence they wanted, not the end of life. They had considered going on a shooting spree at a nearby shopping center. Unlike thousands of teens who commit suicide, they were not despondent that night — they were wild. High on drugs and alcohol, their choice of music blaring, they destroyed everything in Ray's room, then jumped out the window with the shotgun and ran through the streets toward the church.

They were not unique among young people who commit terrible violences, and neither were their families. Mrs. Vance was not the only parent to bring a lawsuit against a rock band; in fact, such suits are becoming fairly frequent.

During the Vance case, there were plenty of other teenagers around the country who did horrible things. Three boys in a small Missouri town, one of them the student-body president, invited their friend Steven Newberry to go out in the woods with them to "kill something." Steven wasn't told that he was the something, though that became apparent when they began beating him with baseball bats. He asked them why, and they explained to the near-dead boy, "Because it's fun, Steve."

Within hours, they were caught and confessed matter-of-factly to murder. Like James Vance, they were fans of heavy metal, but these teenagers did not blame a musical group. They jumped right over Judas Priest and went directly to blaming Satan. Just like Michael Pacewitz, who said the devil instructed him to stab a three-year-old to death. Just like Suzan and Michael Carson, who blamed Allah for telling them to kill people. But families can't sue Satan or Allah, so record stores and musical groups are sometimes all they've got.

James Vance referred to the members of the band as "metal gods." He said they were his bible and that he was "the defender of the Judas Priest faith." Of his relationship with these people he'd never met, he said, "It was like a marriage — intimacy that developed over a period of time, and it was until death do us part."

Can specific media products compel people to violence that they would otherwise not have committed? This is perhaps a reasonable question.

Could that record store have predicted that the *Stained Class* album was dangerous and would lead to the shootings? This is a less reasonable question, but great controversies are often tested at the outside edges of an issue.

When researchers in my office studied hazards that were supposedly associated with music albums, they found one man who had gotten sick after ingesting a vinyl record, another who had a heart attack while dancing to some jaunty polka music, another who made a weapon out of shards from a broken record. (The range of things people might do with any product makes it next to impossible to foresee all risks.) Researchers also found an article with a headline that at first seemed relevant: "*Man Killed While Listening to Heavy-Metal Music.*" The victim, it turned out, was walking along listening to an Ozzy Osbourne tape on headphones when he was struck by a train. On the news clipping, a dark-humored associate of mine had written the words "Killed by heavy metal, literally." The heavy metal in trains surely has resulted in many more deaths than the heavy metal in music, even so-called death-metal music.

The group Judas Priest did not create James Vance, of course, but in a sense, he created them. When he was asked about a particular lyric, "They bathed him and clothed him and fed him by hand," he recited it as "They bathed him and clothed him and fed him *a* hand." So he had done more than just react to the songs; he had actually rewritten them, taken a lyric about someone being cared for and turned it into something about cannibalism. Even his admiration was expressed in violent terms. James said he was so enamored of the band that he would do anything for them, "kill many people or shoot the president through the head." He told lawyers that if the band had said, "Let's see who can kill the most people," he would have gone out and done something terrible. In fact, the band said no such thing, and he did something terrible anyway.

As part of my work on the case, I studied fifty-six other cases involving young people who involved a music star in their violent acts, suicides, attempted suicides, or suicide threats. This sampling provides a window through which to view the topic:

- A teenager asked a famous singer to send him a gun he could use to commit suicide.
- A young man threatened to commit suicide unless a female recording artist visited him. He wrote to her, "I even tried to put myself into a coma in hopes that my mom would get ahold of you and you would come see me."
- A man took an overdose of pills in order to "travel through time" and reach a recording artist.
- A man wrote to a female recording artist, "If you don't marry me, I'll take an overdose." (In a turning of the legal liability ta-

bles, he sent along the lyrics to a song he had written for her entitled "Suicide Is on My Mind.")

- A young man who believed that a female recording artist was his wife and that she was hiding from him attempted suicide by cutting his wrists.
- A young man wrote to a media star in terms reminiscent of James Vance: "I smoke pot and listen to rock music; basically, my story is in the vinyl. Life as I live it really isn't worth it. I'll tell you this, when I attempt suicide it won't be an attempt."

Could the parents of all these people and the thousands like them reasonably blame some distant media star for the challenges their families faced, or would the answers be found closer to home?

To explore that, I started a hypothetical list of the hundred most significant influences, the PINs that might precede teen violence. An addiction to media products is somewhere on that list, but alcohol and drugs are closer to the top. They, unlike media products, are proven and intended to affect the perceptions and behavior of all people who ingest them. James Vance offered support for this position when he described an acquaintance who had attempted suicide a number of times. Asked if that individual had a drug problem, he replied, "Yes, that goes hand in hand." He also stated, "An alcoholic is a very violent individual, and when you drink excessively, you become violent, and that has been my life experience." (I wonder with whom he gained that experience.)

The list of PINs includes a fascination with violence and guns, which was a central part of James's personality — to the point of his planning to become a gunsmith. Both he and Ray regularly went target shooting and played games involving guns. As part of what James called his "training to be a mercenary," he often played "war," pretending to be in gunfights. "There would be two cops and one criminal. The criminal would be behind you and would have to flush you out, you know, how cops check a house out. Ninety-nine percent of the time I always got both of the cops." About his less violent friend Ray, he said: "I would usually get him because, you know, just watching TV, you learn. TV is a really good teacher." James said he watched the news and saw "a lot of violence and killing and fighting go on." He summarized all this succinctly: "*Violence excited me.*"

Finally, he unknowingly described one of the leading PINs for attention-getting violent acts: He said he felt "ignored for twenty years." Explaining how Judas Priest motivated the shootings, he said that he perceived the song "Hero's End" to be about how one has to die to be recognized.

When James was asked if anything other than the lyrics might have caused the shootings, he responded, "A bad relationship? The stars being right? The tide being out? No." Though he was being sarcastic, any of these is probably as reasonable as blaming the lyrics on an album for what happened, for once he excluded family life and parenting from the inquiry, he might as well have cited anything. By pointing his trigger finger at a rock band, James washed away all of the scrutiny that might reasonably have been focused on himself, his family, or even his society.

After all, James was not the only young man who spent more time consuming media products than he spent on any other activity in his waking life. He was an avid patron of the violence division of the entertainment industry. In his book *Selling Out America's Children,* David Walsh likens it to "a guest in our families that advocates violence, but we don't throw him out." He notes that since children learn by modeling and imitation, the 200,000 acts of violence they will witness in the media by age eighteen pose a serious problem. Park Dietz has said that "the symbolic violence in an hour-long episode of a violent television show does more harm, when summed up over the millions of participants, than a single murder of the usual variety." Finally, writer (and mother) Carrie Fisher says that "television exposes children to behavior that man spent centuries protecting them from."

The content of media products matters, but the amount may matter more, whether it is watching television too much, playing video games too much, listening to too much rock music, or for that matter listening to too much classical music. It isn't only the behavior this consumption promotes that concerns me. It's the behavior it prevents, most notably human interaction. I would admittedly be happier if my children chose Tina Turner or Elton John or k. d. lang over Judas Priest, but the bigger issue arises when media consumption replaces the rest of life.

No matter what their choice of music, in the lives of too many teenagers, recognition is more meaningful than accomplishment, and, as it was for James, recognition is available through violence. With the pull of a trigger, a young person whose upbringing has not invested him with self-worth can become significant and "unignorable."

If you took away James's obsession with Judas Priest, you would have just another young man with goals and ambitions that changed day to day, with unrealistic expectations of the world, and without the perseverance or self-discipline to succeed at any endeavor. At various times, James planned to write a book, be a gunsmith, be a member of a band, even be a postal worker, but in the end he will be most remembered for just a few seconds in his life — a few seconds of barbarism in a churchyard.

The court eventually decided that the proprietors of the record store could not have predicted the shootings, but James Vance did not get to finish his search for someone to blame. He died, finally, from that single shotgun blast to the head, though the complications took a long time to kill him, longer than anyone could have expected. I never got to ask James about his early years and never learned about the childhood that the lawsuit had so effectively eclipsed.

▪ ▪ ▪

Some parents are unable to blame anyone for the violence their children commit because they are themselves the victims. Children kill their parents far less frequently than parents kill their children, but the cases so fascinate the public that it might seem they happen frequently. In fact, any kind of murder by a young person is relatively rare. Though Americans under eighteen make up almost 25 percent of the population, they commit less than 10 percent of the murders. Even so, people are afraid of teenagers, and at times with good reason.

So you'll know which times those are, I want to inform your intuition accurately: Most people killed by teenagers are known to them, but about one in five is a stranger killed during a robbery, either because the teenager panicked or because of peer pressure. Murder is most likely to occur when two or more juveniles jointly commit a crime, so fear in that context is appropriate. A recent study shows that an astonishing 75 percent of homicides by young people occur when they are high or drunk, so encountering criminal teenagers under the influence is most dangerous.

Though teenagers are generally not as dangerous to you as adults are, some juvenile offenders, like Willie Bosket, acquire remarkable criminal credentials early in life. By the time he was fifteen, he had stabbed twenty-five people and been in and out of detention facilities for an estimated two thousand other crimes. When authorities finally released him, a jailer made the prediction that "One day, Willie Bosket is going to kill somebody." That prediction was doubly accurate: Willie killed two people, saying he did it "for the experience." (Being a minor, he was incarcerated for only five years, but is now back in prison for other crimes. Even there, his violence continues: He has reportedly set fire to his cell seven times and attacked guards nine times. "I'm a monster the system created," he says. The statute that allows the state of New York to try juveniles as adults is now called the Willie Bosket law.)

Steven Pfiel is another young person who was relentless in his efforts to hurt others. At age eight, he dropped bricks onto traffic from a freeway overpass. At nine, he assaulted another boy with an ax. School officials designated a separate bus stop for him because he regularly threatened to kill other children. By fourteen, he was abusing drugs and reportedly drank entire bottles of hard liquor in single sittings. At seventeen, he committed his first known murder, that of a young girl. (A court ruled that his parents could be sued for negligence because even knowing about his past behavior, they gave him the knife he used to kill the girl.) While awaiting trial, he killed his older brother.

In the brilliant book *Emotional Intelligence,* Daniel Goleman describes seven key abilities most beneficial for human beings: the ability to motivate ourselves, to persist against frustration, to delay gratification, to regulate moods, to hope, to empathize, and to control impulse. Many of those who commit violence never learned these skills. If you know a young person who lacks them all, that's an important pre-incident indicator, and he needs help. Another predictor of violence is chronic anger in childhood. If you know a child who is frequently or extremely angry, he too needs help.

There are usually plenty of warning signs for teen violence, as with eighteen-year-old Jason Massey, who killed his thirteen-year-old stepsister and a fourteen-year-old boy. He was missing all the abilities Goleman cites, but it was the lack of an ability to control impulses that probably explains the gruesome things Massey did, like cutting off the girl's hands and head. The warning signs were obvious: He idolized serial killers Ted Bundy and Henry Lee Lucas, studied everything he could find on Charles Manson, and avidly followed his favorite music group, Slayer. In the years before he killed people, Massey slaughtered cows, cats, and dogs. He kept the skulls. He often spoke of wanting to kill girls. He robbed a fast-food restaurant. He stalked and terrorized a teenage girl for five years, sending her letters about slitting her throat and drinking her blood. People knew all these details, and yet denial prevailed.

Unlike James Vance, Massey was forthcoming about his goals: "All I want is the murdering of countless young women. I wish to reap sorrow for the families." This kind of anger at family does not come out of nowhere.

Many young murderers kill within the family, often shooting abusive fathers or stepfathers, which is no surprise. You will, however, be surprised at how young they can be. A boy I'll call Robbie shot and killed his father after watching his mother being beaten. The drunk father had left a gun on the table and though Robbie confessed to the killing, few people initially believed that he could have done it. That's because he was only three years old. After gunpowder tests confirmed him as the killer, he explained to authorities: "I killed him. Now he's dead. If he would have hit my mother again, I would have shot him again."

In his compelling and disturbing book *When a Child Kills,* lawyer Paul Mones unflinchingly explores parricide. He observes that unlike with most murders, events that occur twelve years before a parricide are as important as those that occur twelve hours before it. *The single most reliable pre-incident indicator of parricide is child abuse.* It is recognized that most runaway children in America leave their families to escape abuse or to call attention to it, but some of those who stay at home, Mones explains, "lay family secrets bare with the report of a gun."

Children who kill their parents are usually found to have been beaten, degraded, sodomized, tied up, or tortured in other ways. Mones tells of one sixteen-year-old, Mike, whom prosecutors described as "just one of those violent, rebellious, degenerate teenagers who are coldhearted killers." But there was much more to the story than that.

Mike had been beaten by his father from kindergarten on. Though he was an athletic and coordinated boy, he had constant injuries from "falling off his bike," "tripping," or "cutting himself." During the trial, he was asked to strip to a bathing suit so the jury could see the scars his father had given him over the years.

The abuse ended abruptly one night. Mike had returned home late, and his father was waiting for him with a pistol. "You got two choices," he explained to the boy. "You kill me or I kill you." The ultimatum had been offered before, but this time Mike's father actually held the gun out to him, and this time Mike took it and shot his father in the head.

Another young boy who killed a parent told Mones that living in prison was better than living with the abuse at home. He described himself as "locked up but free."

Some people believe that children who kill shouldn't have been so docile during their abuse; they should have at least reported the abuse long before it reached the point that murder seemed their only way out. Proponents of these ideas may have forgotten that adult victims of rape or hijacking are often just as docile as children, and we don't later blame them for failing to do something.

The warning signs of parricide and other awful violence are shown to parents, teachers, policemen, neighbors, and relatives. It is they (often we), not children, who must report these cases.

Of all the violence discussed in this book, being killed by one's own daughter or son is the easiest to avoid. A precaution that is virtually guaranteed starts years before the child is big enough to hurt anyone: Be a loving parent.

▪ ▪ ▪

Unlike teens, preteens who kill within the family are more likely to kill a sibling than a parent. As with other violence, it doesn't happen without warning. Most of these cases have involved an abused or severely disturbed child whose prior attempts to kill a sibling were not taken seriously. That's because many people believe that violence by children against children is a natural part of growing up. It may be, but when a child does something that places another child in serious hazard, it should not be ignored. I recently testified in a case where it was, and after reading what follows, few parents should ever feel blind confidence when sending their children off to school.

The offender was a grammar school student I'll call Joey. He sodomized a seven-year-old boy in the school bathroom. Though he acted alone, he was aided by some astonishing negligence on the part of the school system, and the principal in particular. Though the school district claimed Joey's rape couldn't have been predicted, there had been a striking pre-incident indicator a month earlier: Joey had actually been arrested for victimizing *another* boy the same way in the same bathroom!

Because this was not my only case involving disturbing negligence by schools, and because school policies and personnel are not what you think they are, I want to take a moment and give some background.

First of all, though they claim otherwise, schools are in the business of high-stakes predictions. Schoolteachers and administrators regularly face these predictive questions:

> Will this visitor seek to kidnap a child?
> Will this teacher molest a child?
> Is this child being abused at home?
> Will this child bring a lethal weapon to school?

Though most people cannot imagine that young boys can rape anyone, the school district in Joey's case knew better. For years they'd had a specific written policy entitled "Child-On-Child Sexual Abuse." Since the existence of that policy makes clear that such things happen, it in effect raises a predictive question for every principal.

Imagine that all the students are gathered in the auditorium, and the principal surveys the group with this question in mind: Who among these students might sexually abuse another child? Through his behavior, Joey stands up in this imaginary assembly and calls out, "It might be me," but the principal chooses to ignore the boy.

The administrators at Joey's previous school had made the whole matter simpler for the principal: They actually predicted — in writing — that Joey would act out in sexually inappropriate ways, and they sent his records to the school where the rapes ultimately occurred. It is hard to imagine that anyone could have ignored the warning signs he wore like a banner: carrying a knife, threatening homicide, threatening and attempting suicide, lighting a building on fire, pouring gasoline on his mother and trying to light a match, displaying fascination with sex and sexual organs, inappropriate sexual conduct toward other children, exposing himself, aggression, violence. As if all these warning signs were not enough, the principal took no effective action when he learned of Joey's sexual assault of another student. Is this kind of negligence really possible? This and more.

After the first rape accusation, the principal chose not to take the obvious step that might have increased supervision of Joey at the school: He did not tell the boy's teachers anything about what had happened. It gets worse. When one teacher found Joey to be unmanageable, he was sent to another class of younger, smaller boys! By this action, the school provided him a virtual "beauty contest" of victims, and he chose one.

The presence of security guards at a school may add comfort for some parents, but understand that at this school, part of one of the nation's largest school districts, security guards received absolutely no training on any aspect of student safety. They received no written guidelines, no post instructions, no policies on the topic whatsoever. Even if they'd known what their jobs were supposed to be, they weren't informed about the rape accusation, not even told anything as simple and easy as "Be extra alert," or "Keep an eye out." When organizations of any kind are pressured to improve security, a typical response is to hire guards. Everyone sighs and feels the matter has been addressed, but if guards are not trained or supervised or properly equipped, if there is no intelligent plan for them to follow, their presence can hurt more than help. That's because, having taken this expensive step, everyone stops looking at safety and security.

I've noted the precautions the principal failed to take, but there is one precaution he did take. After the first rape accusation, he arranged to have the dangerous boy escorted whenever he went to that bathroom. This may sound like a reasonable precaution until I tell you that the principal had Joey escorted not by a teacher or security guard, but by another student! I do not imagine that any parent would have volunteered his or her son for the job of escorting a violent criminal, particularly one that even experienced teachers could not handle.

If an adult employee at the school, say the janitor, for example, had Joey's background and was arrested for raping a student, would the principal have let him come back to work? I can't answer even this obvious question with any certainty. I know only that Joey leaped on the stage of that imaginary assembly and yelled, "It is me, I am the child-on-child sexual offender," and the principal turned away.

Joey was finally taken out of school and placed in a treatment facility (where he sexually attacked two people in one day). The investment of abuse and neglect in Joey's own childhood will continue to pay dividends of pain and violence for others, including those he will likely kill one day. As I write this sad but accurate prediction, Joey is only nine years old.

As I did after describing other cases in which blindingly obvious warning signs went unheeded, I want to acknowledge that the principal at Joey's school was probably doing the best he could with the skills and knowledge he had at the time. This is not some legal disclaimer — it is what I believe, but I also believe that cases like these involve organizational and individual laziness, as well as the hope that something will just "go away" if it is ignored.

Advising on another case in which a young child was sexually assaulted at school (this time by a nonstudent), I reviewed the school district's entire policy book. It will not be reassuring to parents to learn that the topic of safety wasn't even raised until page 10, and that reference was about *faculty* safety when breaking up fights. The policy contained three full pages and twenty-one separate items about the protection of keys, but didn't even mention the topic of danger to students until page 91.

Children require the protection of adults, usually from adults. Their fear of people is not yet developed, their intuition not yet loaded with enough information and experience to keep them from harm. The lesson for parents in the cases I've cited is to take nothing for granted when it comes to the safety of your children. I suggest that you request a copy of the school's safety policies and then settle in for a very discouraging read. Go to the school and ask them every obvious question you can think of and see if the answers make you feel better or worse. Just the fact that you ask puts safety on the agenda and forces the school to focus on it. Ask about the school's background screening process for employees. If they have security personnel, ask to meet them and see how they respond to probing questions. Ask about previous crimes at the school. This last question is particularly important. Federal law requires that colleges maintain campus crime statistics and make them available upon request. This is so college students and their parents selecting a school can evaluate security and safety. There is no law requiring grammar schools or high schools to keep such statistics, but I wish there were.

Rather than relying on government, you can make at least as vigorous an inquiry of your child's school as you should of your child's baby-sitter, because if you assume that the school is addressing the matter of your child's safety as seriously as you would, you may be very disappointed. (See appendix 7 for a list of suggested questions.)

Though Joey was only nine, he already had the widely established risk factors for future criminality. They are: poverty, child abuse (in the form of violence, witnessing violence, humiliation, or neglect), drug addiction in a parent, drug or alcohol abuse by the child, and a single-parent childhood. Joey had another hugely significant risk factor, one that is often overlooked: the absence of a father in his life. David Blankenhorn, author of *Fatherless America,* notes that 80 percent of the young men in juvenile detention facilities were raised without fully participating fathers. Fathers are so important because they teach boys various ways to be men. Sadly, too many boys learn from the media or from each other what scholars call "protest masculinity," characterized by toughness and the use of force. That is not the only way to be a man, of course, but it's the only way they know.

Some people seriously ponder the question of whether males are even necessary for raising children, and we do little to encourage the role of fathers. In fact, as Blankenhorn points out, prison is our number one social program for young men.

Recently, I met with a group of men graduating from that social program. As a court-ordered part of their recovery from heroin addiction, I was asked to discuss with them the experience of growing up with violence and drugs.

Joined by some graduates of a women's prison, we sat in what looked like a schoolroom. In a sense it was, for here each person learned the benefits and blessings of twelve-step programs (the founding of which M. Scott Peck, author of *The Road Less Traveled,* calls "the greatest positive event of the twentieth century"). Ideally, such programs would teach these prisoners to accept their pasts, for only then could they learn responsibility for their present.

One after another, they gave their three-minute life stories. Each told of violence, fear, abandonment, and neglect. All of the men had been physically abused as children, and all but one of the ten women had been sexually abused by family members. A few told of the regret and horror they felt at having grown up to be violent to their own children.

I wept as I heard about the progress they had made, for though this locked halfway house was a long way from the mainstream of our society, it was also a long way from the hell these people had all occupied, and caused others to occupy. I wept because the stories were moving, they were personal, they were mine, and also because my mother had not found the routes out of addiction that these people were finding.

When it was time for me to give a forty-five-minute talk, I related some of my experiences as a child and a teenager. The similarity of our stories was immediately apparent to everyone there.

When I finished, several people had questions. The first hand to go up was that of a man about my age, but I'd have thought we had little else in common. He was tattooed, scarred, overly muscular, and weathered. He was the kind of man most people would fear on a dark street, and during much of his life they'd have been right to fear him. His most recent long stay in prison had been for arson. He'd broken into an apartment to steal anything he could sell. ("I didn't need money just for drugs. I also had to pay my lawyer because I had a court appearance coming up on another burglary charge.") To cover up any evidence of the burglary, he had set a fire that destroyed several apartments and sent one person to the hospital badly burned.

He looked me up and down and asked, "Why are you sitting over there and I'm over here?" I didn't understand the question, and he explained, "You and me had the same childhood, but you're in that nice suit and probably drive a nice car. You get to leave today. You're sitting over there — how'd that happen?"

This question had often presented itself in my work and my life, first as a curiosity, later as more than that. I could have been a likely and welcome resident of the world of violence (as opposed to the tourist I became), but somehow I followed a different route. Some people come through awful childhoods and become productive, contributing adults, while others do antisocial or even monstrous things. Why?

It is similar to one brother asking another, "Why did you grow up to be a drunk?" The answer is "Because Dad was a drunk." The second brother then asks, "Why *didn't* you grow up to be a drunk?" The answer is "Because Dad was a drunk."

Some more complete answers are found in *Whoever Fights Monsters . . .*, Robert Ressler's classic book. He speaks of the tremendous importance of the early puberty period for boys. Before then, the anger of these boys might have been submerged and without focus, perhaps turned inward in the form of depression, perhaps (as in most cases) just denied, to emerge later. But during puberty, this anger collides with another powerful force, one of the most powerful in nature: sexuality. Even at this point, say Ressler and others, these potential hosts of monsters can be turned around through the (often unintentional) intervention of people who show kindness, support, or even just interest.

I can say from experience that it doesn't take much.

Ressler's theories on the childhoods of the worst killers in America have an unlikely ideological supporter, psychiatrist and child advocate Alice Miller. Her emotionally evocative books (including *The Drama of the Gifted Child* and *The Untouched Key*) make clear that if a child has some effective human contact at particularly significant periods, some recognition of his worth and value, some "witness" to his experience, this can make an extraordinary difference.

I have learned that the kindness of a teacher, a coach, a police officer, a neighbor, the parent of a friend, is never wasted. These moments are likely to pass with neither the child nor the adult fully knowing the significance of the contribution. No ceremony attaches to the moment that a child sees his own worth reflected in the eyes of an encouraging adult. Though nothing apparent marks the occasion, inside that child a new view of self might take hold. He is not just a person deserving of neglect or violence, not just a person who is a burden to the sad adults in his life, not just a child who fails to solve his family's problems, who fails to rescue them from pain or madness or addiction or poverty or unhappiness. No, this child might be someone else, someone whose appearance before this one adult revealed specialness or lovability, or value.

This value might be shown through appreciation of a child's artistic talent, physical ability, humor, courage, patience, curiosity, scholarly skills, creativity, resourcefulness, responsibility, energy, or any of the many attributes that children bring us in such abundance.

I had a fifth-grade teacher, Mr. Conway, who fought monsters in me. He showed kindness and recognized some talent in me at just the period when violence was consuming my family. He gave me some alternative designs for self-image, not just the one children logically deduce from mistreatment ("If this is how I am treated, then this is the treatment I am worthy of").

It might literally be a matter of a few hours with a person whose kindness reconnects the child to an earlier experience of self, a self that was loved and valued and encouraged. Sadly, for children who didn't have nurturing even in infancy, there isn't any frame of reference, no file in the mind in which to place kindness and recognition so that they might be seen as part of life. (All of this shows the great value of mentoring and of programs like Big Brothers and Big Sisters. See appendix 2.)

When a child's primary caregiver delivers both praise and brutality, it is a virtual coin toss as to which will attach itself to the child's identity. Terribly unhealthy families damage children in many ways, but one of the saddest is the destruction of the child's belief that he has purpose and value. Without that belief, it is difficult to succeed, difficult to take risks. Perhaps more to the point, it may seem foolish to take risks, "knowing," as such people do, that they are not up to the task.

The way circus elephants are trained demonstrates this dynamic well: When young, they are attached by heavy chains to large stakes driven deep into the ground. They pull and yank and strain and struggle, but the chain is too strong, the stake too rooted. One day they give up, having learned that they cannot pull free, and from that day forward they can be "chained" with a slender rope. When this enormous animal feels any resistance, though it has the strength to pull the whole circus tent over, it stops trying. Because it believes it cannot, it cannot.

"You'll never amount to anything"; "You can't sing"; "You're not smart enough"; "Without money, you're nothing"; "Who'd want you?"; "You're just a loser"; "You should have more realistic goals"; "You're the reason our marriage broke up"; "Without you kids I'd have had a chance"; "You're worthless" — this opera is being sung in homes all over America right now, the stakes driven into the ground, the heavy chains attached, the children reaching the point they believe they cannot pull free. And at that point, they cannot.

Unless and until something changes their view, unless they grasp the striking fact that they are tied with a thread, that the chain is an illusion, that they were fooled, and ultimately, that whoever so fooled them was wrong about them and that they were wrong about themselves — unless all this happens, these children are not likely to show society their positive attributes as adults.

There's more involved, of course, than just parenting. Some of the factors are so small they cannot be seen and yet so important they cannot be ignored: They are human genes. The one known as D4DR may influence the thrill-seeking behavior displayed by many violent criminals. Along with the influences of environment and upbringing, an elongated D4DR gene will likely be present in someone who grows up to be an assassin or a bank robber (or a daredevil). Behavioral geneticist Irving Gottesman: "Under a different scenario and in a different environment, that same person could become a hero in Bosnia."

In the future, genetics will play a much greater role in behavioral predictions. We'll probably be able to genetically map personality traits as precisely as physical characteristics like height and weight. Though it will generate much controversy, parents may someday be able to use prenatal testing to identify children with unwanted personality genes, including those that make violence more likely. Until then, however, we'll have to settle for a simpler, low-tech strategy for reducing violence: treating children lovingly and humanely.

■ ■ ■

Frank Sulloway, author of *Born to Rebel,* says that "life's miseries fall disproportionately on children," and this is certainly true. Throughout history, half of all children have failed to reach adulthood. Considering this and all that we know about violence against young people, they have much more reason to be afraid of us than we have to be afraid of them. Even so, the mistreatment we invest in children does come back to us, and is already costing us our safety and our peace.

A federal research project selected 1,600 children who had been abused or neglected and followed them for nearly twenty years. As of last year, fully half of them had been arrested for some crime. Still, even though it is so expensive for us, mistreatment will probably continue until we take an entirely different view of children, not as temporary visitors who will someday grow into citizens, but as full-fledged, fully contributing, fully entitled members of our society just as they are right now. Children are often seen as burdens to society, no more than hapless victims of their circumstance, but nothing could be further from the truth. Recognize that children are the primary child-care providers in America. Siblings caring for siblings and children caring for themselves represent an important part of our economy. They also care for the elderly, cook meals, take cigarettes out of the hands of sleeping parents, and contribute in countless other ways.

If only more abused children could know that they are the residents of their homes, not the architects, then they might believe that where they are will not limit where they might go. Until America focuses shame on perpetrators instead of victims, these children will have children, and the war they thought was over won't be over, for them or for us.

We can, of course, continue ignoring these children, but a few of them will grow up and commit the one crime that is impossible to ignore: assassination. While that may feel distant from your life, I raise the topic here for a very practical reason. Just as the members of a troubled family are forced to look inward when their teenage son gets into serious trouble — after years of signaling that he would — the assassin makes us look at ourselves as a nation. The assassin makes us look at the media, at attention-seeking crimes, at our huge harvest of handguns, at violence, and at child rearing. Understanding the assassin, who may seem the most remote of criminals, can help you understand and be safer from the least remote of criminals.

13

BETTER TO BE WANTED BY THE POLICE THAN NOT TO BE WANTED AT ALL

The intercom in Rebecca Schaeffer's apartment was broken, so when the buzzer rang on Sunday morning, she had to go down to the front door of the building to see who it was. It turned out to be a fan who'd first seen the young actress on her weekly TV show, *My Sister Sam*. She spoke to him briefly, and he left. A while later, the buzzer sounded again, and again she went down to see who was there. It was the same young man, but this time he was not her admirer — he was her murderer. He fired one shot into her chest. She screamed out "Why? Why?" and fell to the floor. She was still alive as he stood there looking down at her. He could have asked someone in the building to call an ambulance, or he could have called one himself, but that would have defeated the whole purpose.

■ ■ ■

Among individual crimes, assassination has the greatest impact on the American psyche. Bullets have demonstrably influenced most presidential elections in the past forty years. A nation based on the concept that the majority chooses its leaders is entirely undermined when a minority (usually of one) undoes that choice with a gun. Whether the assassin's target is the mayor of La Porte, Indiana (killed in his bed by an angry citizen), or the president of the United States, the system we live by also falls victim. Because of their disproportionate impact on our culture, identifying those people who will attack a public figure is our nation's highest-stakes behavioral prediction, one that affects everyone.

At some point during our not so distant past, the conditions surrounding being famous changed. There is a part of that change that makes public life in Western society more challenging than it ever was before. It is the part that every prominent person, from the local politician to the beauty queen to the radio talk-show host to the internationally known media figure, must consider at some time. With fame there are hassles that some say come with the territory, but where did anyone sign on to the idea that if you do very well you will be at risk of being killed for it? To answer that, we must go back to the infancy of the media age.

Performers, politicians, and sports figures have long been admired and even loved, but that love used to be contained and distant, relegated to a part of the mind and heart reserved for people one didn't know personally. It was, emotionally speaking, a one-way street, because feelings could be displayed to the public figure only as part of an acceptable function, like voting, sending letters, or seeing a show. Except for applauding louder or longer than others, members of an audience didn't seek to make themselves known personally to performers.

Before the 1940s, if one woman in an audience stood up and shrieked at the top of her lungs throughout an entire show she'd have been carted off to an asylum. By the midforties, however, entire audiences behaved like that, screaming, tearing at their clothes and hair, leaving their seats to board the stage. On December 30, 1942, while Frank Sinatra sang at the Paramount Theater in New York, the behavior of the audience changed, and a part of our relationship to well-known people changed forever. Psychiatrists and psychologists of the day struggled to explain the phenomenon. They recalled medieval dance crazes, spoke of "mass frustrated love" and "mass hypnosis." Though none of these theories explained what happened, the media age did bring a type of mass hypnosis into American life. It affects all of us to some degree, and some of us to a great degree.

Before the advent of mass media, a young girl might have admired a performer from afar, and it would have been acceptable to have a passing crush. It would not have been acceptable if she pursued the performer to his home, or if she had to be restrained by police. It would not have been acceptable to skip school in order to wait for hours outside a hotel and then try to tear pieces of clothing from the passing star.

Yet that unhealthy behavior became "normal" in the Sinatra days. In fact, audience behavior that surprised everyone in 1942 was expected two years later when Sinatra appeared again at the Paramount Theater. This time, the thirty thousand screaming bobby-soxed fans were joined by a troop of reporters. Expecting a commotion, *450* police officers were assigned to that one theater, and it appeared that society had learned to deal with this phenomenon. It had not.

During the engagement, an eighteen-year-old named Alexander Ivanovich Dorogokupetz stood up in the theater and threw an egg that hit Sinatra in the face. The show stopped, and for a moment, a brief moment, Sinatra was not the star. Now it was Dorogokupetz mobbed by audience members and Dorogokupetz who had to be escorted out by police. Society had not learned to deal with this, and still hasn't. Dorogokupetz told police: "I vowed to put an end to this monotony of two years of consecutive swooning. It felt good." Saddled with the least American of names, he had tried to make one for himself in the most American way, and but for his choice of a weapon, he would probably be as famous today as Frank Sinatra.

Elements in society were pioneering the skills of manipulating emotion and behavior in ways that had never been possible before: electronic ways. The media were institutionalizing idolatry. Around that time, the world met a teenager named Elizabeth Taylor, who began an excursion through public life that defines the celebrity idol as we know it today. A lesser-known teenager of the forties named Ruth Steinhagen would define the anti-idol as we know it today.

Ruth particularly liked a ballplayer named Eddie Waitkus. He was more exclusively hers than Frank Sinatra, who belonged to everyone. Even though they'd never met, Ruth devoted her life to Eddie. He was of Lithuanian descent, so she tried to learn that language. He was number 36 on the Chicago Cubs, so she became obsessed with that number, buying every record she could find that was produced in 1936. She collected press clippings about Eddie, slept with his picture under her pillow, attended every game she could, and sent him letter after letter, even though he never responded. At dinner each evening, Ruth arranged the chairs so that there was an empty one facing hers. She told her sister, "Eddie is in that chair."

Many of Ruth's friends had crushes on baseball players, and while her parents were glad at first that she too had an idol, they became concerned about her behavior. They took her to two psychiatrists, and her mother was glad to hear them report that nothing was wrong with her — except that she should forget about Waitkus (which is a little like saying nothing was wrong with John Hinckley except that he should forget about Jodie Foster). Of course, Ruth did not forget about Waitkus, even for a moment, and when he was traded to the Philadelphia Phillies, she stated that she could not live if he moved away from Chicago.

She began to discuss suicide with one of her girlfriends and then set out to buy a gun. She wanted a pistol, but because a permit was required, she went to a pawnshop and bought a rifle instead.

In the first week of June 1949, Ruth had decided on something better than suicide. She told her friend Joyce to "watch for the fireworks on Tuesday," the day she checked into the Edgewater Beach Hotel in Chicago, knowing from the Phillies' schedule that Eddie would be staying there. She brought along a suitcase filled with Eddie memorabilia, including the ticket stubs from fifty games she'd attended. She also brought the rifle.

In her room, Ruth wrote a letter to her parents ("I hope you understand things. I love you. Things will work out for the best") but crumpled it up and threw it in the trash. She then wrote a note to Eddie:

> Mr. Waitkus, we're not acquainted, but I have something of importance to speak to you about. I think it would be to your advantage to let me explain it to you. As I'm leaving the hotel the day after tomorrow, I'd appreciate it greatly if you could see me as soon as possible. My name is Ruth Anne Burns, and I'm in room

1297-A. I realize this is a little out of the ordinary, but as I said, it's rather important. Please come soon. I won't take up much of your time. *I promise.*

Ruth tipped a bellman three dollars to deliver the note. On reading it, Eddie thought she was probably just another "Baseball Annie" (what we'd today call a groupie), and he agreed to visit her. Ruth put a knife in her skirt pocket, intending to stab Eddie in the heart as he entered her room, but he hurried past her, sat down in a chair, and asked, "So what's all this about?"

"Wait a minute. I have a surprise for you," Ruth said, and then went to the closet and took out the rifle. "For two years, you have been bothering me, and now you are going to die." Ruth fired one shot into Eddie's chest. It punctured a lung and lodged just under his heart. (Waitkus survived and even returned to professional sports. I found an old baseball card of his. Under the heading "My Greatest Thrill in Baseball," it reads, "In 1949, I was shot by a deranged girl.")

The things Ruth said and did after the shooting were extraordinary in 1949, but no longer. She explained to police:

> I liked him a great deal and knew I could never have him, and if I couldn't have him neither could anybody else. *I've always wanted to be in the limelight. I wanted attention and publicity for once. My dreams have come true.*

Ruth was eloquently expressing a sentiment all too familiar to modern-day Americans. In describing the aftermath of the shooting, she said:

> Nobody came out of their rooms. You would think they would all come rushing out. I got mad. I kept telling them I shot Eddie Waitkus, but they didn't know who Eddie Waitkus was. After that, the police came, but I was burning because nobody was coming out of those other rooms. Nobody seemed to want me much. I could've walked right out of that place and nobody would have come after me.

At nineteen years old, Ruth felt it was better to be wanted by the police than not to be wanted at all. About twenty years later, a young woman named Valerie Solanas apparently felt the same way. An aspiring actress and writer, Solanas carried a gun into the headquarters of Andy Warhol and shot the famous artist. Soon after, Solanas walked up to a cop in Times Square and said, "The police are looking for me." She added proudly, "They want me." (It was Andy Warhol who gave us the quote that is itself an icon of the media age: "In the future everyone will be world-famous for fifteen minutes." Ironically, Valerie Solanas got her fifteen minutes at Warhol's expense. She got another ninety minutes last year, when an entire film was made about her life.)

The Solanas attack occurred in 1968, and we were already jaded, but back when Ruth Steinhagen shot Eddie Waitkus, this kind of thing was nothing short of remarkable. When Ruth told her mother that she intended to get a gun and shoot Eddie Waitkus, her mother replied, "You can't do that. Women don't do those things." Mrs. Steinhagen would be proved wrong by Ruth, and by Valerie Solanas, and more recently by Squeaky Fromme and Sara Jane Moore (both of whom attempted to kill President Gerald Ford).

Due to Ruth's choice of target, hers was not a shot heard round the world, though it did make her the first in a long line of media-age public-figure stalkers and attackers, some famous, many others not famous.

Experts decided Ruth was insane, and she was committed to a mental facility. Three years later, experts decided she had regained her sanity, and she was freed. Still alive today, Ruth Steinhagen is the senior member of a uniquely American minority. It's not that other nations haven't had their share of assassination, but killings rooted in some idealistic or political expediency are a far cry from shooting a stranger just to get "attention and publicity for once."

There is also the uniquely American choice of targets. In the thirties and forties, baseball players and statesmen were the most prominent and adored idols. By the time Joe DiMaggio married Marilyn Monroe, the torch of idolatry had been passed from sports to entertainment. Twenty-six years later, an actor became president, and a media addict (John Hinckley) shot him, claiming an obsession with a film actress (Jodie Foster). After a long courtship, the marriage between violence and entertainment was consummated.

Idolizing heroes and falling for their seductive appeal is normal in America, but what is a mild drug to most is a poison for some people. To learn more about that poison, I sought a meeting with an unlikely expert in the field, Robert Bardo, the man who killed Rebecca Schaeffer.

To visit him I had to pass through two metal detectors and follow a prison escort down a series of long green corridors, each ending at a locked steel gate that, after careful scrutiny, a guard would let us through. Finally I was shown into a small concrete cell with two benches anchored to the floor. My escort said he'd be back soon, then closed and locked the cell door. Even with the certainty that one will be let out, being locked in a prison cell is like being locked in a prison cell; it feels awful.

Waiting for Bardo, I thought of Robert Ressler, the FBI agent who'd spent much of his career at the Behavioral Sciences Unit studying and interviewing America's most prolific killers. Sitting in the cell reminded me of Ressler's final prison meeting with Edmund Kemper, a man who'd brutally killed ten people, several of whom he had decapitated. Kemper was literally a giant, six foot nine inches tall and more than three hundred pounds. At the end of a four-hour interview, Ressler pressed the call button for the guard to come and get him out. Some time went by, but no guard. About fifteen minutes later, he pressed the button again, and then again. Still no guard. Kemper must have intuitively detected Ressler's concern, because on the tape of their interview he can be heard to say, "Relax, they're changing shifts, feeding the guys in the secure areas. Might be fifteen, twenty minutes before they come and get you."

After a thoughtful pause, Kemper added, "If I went apeshit in here, you'd be in a lot of trouble. I could screw your head off and place it on the table to greet the guard."

Kemper was correct. Against his terrific size advantage and experience at killing, Ressler didn't stand a chance. Kemper, who had endured a long abstinence from his compulsive habit of murder, now had a live one: a famous FBI agent. Ressler warned the killer that he'd be in big trouble if he murdered a federal official, but Kemper, already serving seven life terms, scoffed, "What would they do, cut off my TV privileges?"

There followed a thirty-minute contest of fear and courage, with Ressler using his impressive behavioral insight to keep Kemper off balance. At one point in their high-stakes debate, Kemper acknowledged that if he killed Ressler, he would have to spend some time in "the hole," but he added that it would be a small price to pay for the prestige of "offing an FBI agent."

One of Ressler's several gambits: "You don't seriously think I'd come in here without some way to defend myself, do you?"

Kemper knew better: "They don't let anybody bring guns in here." That was true, but Ressler suggested that FBI agents had special privileges and that a gun might not be the only weapon available to him.

Kemper didn't bite. "What have you got, a poison pen?" So it went until guards arrived, thankfully before Kemper put his ruminations into action. As Kemper was walked out, he put one of his enormous hands on Ressler's shoulder. "You know I was just kidding, don't you?" But Kemper wasn't just kidding. He was feeding on a favorite delicacy of serial killers: human fear.

The murderer who soon joined me in the cell had been after different rewards: attention and fame. With a young man's light stubble from a few days of not shaving and his prematurely receding hair a mess, Robert Bardo was not menacing like Kemper. In fact, he was the image of an awkward teenager. In another life (and in his previous life) he'd have been the guy dressed in a white apron sweeping the floor in the back of a drive-through restaurant. Robert Bardo was, as he put it, "a geek."

Because I had studied him extensively when I consulted on his prosecution, meeting Bardo was like meeting a character from a book I'd read. I knew most of the lines he might speak, but the young man in front of me was a far more human incarnation than court transcripts or psychiatric reports could ever conjure, more human, perhaps, than I wanted him to be.

The power he'd discharged in one terrible second on the steps of

Rebecca Schaeffer's apartment wasn't in that cell with us. He didn't have the confidence to intimidate anyone, nor did he have those dead-cold murderer's eyes that intimidate all on their own. In fact, he was reluctant to even look at me. We both knew what a murderous thing he'd done, and he knew very well from the trial exactly how I felt about it.

Bardo had been asked a great many questions since the killing and he was used to that, so I decided to let him speak first, to follow rather than lead him. As it turned out, that took a lot of patience. For about fifteen minutes, we just sat there, him with his head down, me counting on the idea that he wouldn't be able to pass up the attention I was withholding.

The otherwise quiet cell was occasionally filled with the clang of some distant gate being slammed. (Noise is one of the few things that roams freely in a prison; the concrete walls that keep out so much carry it into every corner.)

Bardo finally looked up at me and studied my face intently. "Arthur Jackson asked me to give you a message." (Jackson was the obsessed stalker who had brutally stabbed actress Theresa Saldana. After I testified against Jackson in court, he condemned me to "burn in hell.")

"He wants you to meet with him too."

"Not today," I replied.

"Then why do you want to talk to me?"

"Because you have something to contribute," I answered.

"I do want to help other people avoid what happened to Rebecca," he said.

That choice of words implied some distance from his crime, which I didn't want to grant him.

"Nothing just happened to Rebecca. You make it seem as if she had an accident."

"No, no. I killed her. I shot her, and I want to help others not get killed by someone like me."

"That sounds like you think there is someone else like you."

He seemed surprised that it wasn't obvious. "There is. I mean there are . . . many people like me."

He was quiet for a long while before he continued: "I'm not a monster. On television they always want to portray me as someone frightening."

I looked at him and nodded. We'd been together for nearly a half hour, and I had not asked him a single question.

"I was someone frightening, of course, but I'm not now. That video of me telling how I shot Rebecca makes me look like the worst assassin of all, and I'm not the worst." He was concerned about his public image, about how he stacked up against his peers.

Like nearly all modern-day assassins, Bardo had studied those who came before him. After Mark Chapman went to prison for killing John Lennon, Bardo wrote to him and asked why he had done it. Chapman, the famous assassin, and Bardo, the apprentice, had a brief correspondence. "If he told me not to do my crime," Bardo said, "that would not have overridden my emotions. Emotions are the key, out-of-balance emotions. Emotionally healthy people do not harm others."

Bardo had also studied everything he could find on the Arthur Jackson case. Jackson had hired a private detective to locate his victim, so Bardo did too. Jackson used a knife, so on one of his earlier trips to kill Schaeffer, Bardo brought one along. Jackson traveled thousands of miles in pursuit of his target, sometimes in a crisscross fashion — as do nearly all assassins — and Bardo did too. They started off a continent apart but ended up living in the same building.

In a videotaped interview done by the defense months before Bardo knew I was working on the case, he revealed the extent of his research into public-figure attack. Describing the lack of security he had encountered around Rebecca Schaeffer, he said: "It's not like she had Gavin de Becker or anything."

Now, in offering me advice, Bardo hoped to distinguish himself from other assassins. He would become, he thought, the anti-assassin, helping famous people avoid danger. Of course, he was now famous himself, a fact that carried him to an almost too ironic comment on public life: "All the fame that I have achieved from this results in me getting death threats and harassment. The media says things about me that aren't even true. I have no control over them invading my privacy, bringing up my case over and over again on TV so they can make money off it. They portray me in ways I never saw myself."

He didn't like reporters calling him a loner, but the description was accurate. Bardo had no friends, and had never even kissed a girl romantically. (Almost certainly, he never will.) A lack of healthy intimacy is a common feature of many assassins. John Hinckley didn't ever attain a developed romantic relationship; nor did Arthur Jackson, nor did Arthur Bremer, who shot presidential candidate George Wallace.

Bremer was a virgin who sought to change that in the weeks before his crime. Knowing he would soon be dead or in prison for life, he hired a prostitute, but their sexual encounter ended awkwardly. In his diary he wrote, "Though I'm still a virgin, I'm thankful to Alga for giving me a peek at what it's like."

Bizarre though it may seem, the greatest intimacy most assassins attain is with those they attack. Through stalking, they come to know their victims more closely than they know others in their lives, and through shooting them, they become partners of sorts. Bremer's diary shows increasing intimacy with his first victim of choice, President Richard Nixon. As he stalked the president from state to state, the diary references move from "the President" to "he" to "Nixon" to "Nixy," and ultimately to "Nixy-boy."

Those who attack with knives have even more intimacy, as is disturbingly described in multiple-murderer Jack Henry Abbott's book *In the Belly of the Beast.* Of one of his murder victims, he wrote: "You can feel his life trembling through the knife in your hand. It almost overcomes you, the gentleness of the feeling at the center of a coarse act of murder."

Bardo's coarse act of murder was, with the saddest irony, inflicted on the only girl who ever gave him any positive attention. Rebecca Schaeffer had sent a kind reply to one of his letters.

> Bardo: It was a personal postcard where she wrote, "Robert, dash, your letter was the nicest, most real letter I ever received." She underlined "real." She wrote, "Please take care," and drew a heart sign and then "Rebecca." That's what propelled me to want to get some more answers from her.

GdeB: So what advice would you offer other famous people?

Bardo: Be careful about what you write. If you do answer fan mail, don't let it be so overglowing. That's not the way to be with a fan, because it makes it seem like they're the only one, and that's how I felt. I felt I was the only one.

Like other assassins, Bardo had stalked several famous people, including a client of mine whom he decided was too inaccessible. He gave up on her and switched his attention to Rebecca Schaeffer. For assassins, it is the act and not the target, the destination, not the journey, that matters.

Because targets are interchangeable, I asked Bardo how the security precautions taken by some public figures affected his choice. He said, "If I read in an article that they have security and they have bodyguards, it makes you look at that celebrity different and makes a person like me stand back. It kind of stands against this hope of a romantic relationship."

Though Bardo's defense tried to sell the idea that he expected a romantic relationship with Rebecca Schaeffer, he never really did. Bardo expected exactly what he got, an unenthusiastic reception and ultimately a rejection. He used that rejection as an excuse to do what he had long wanted to do: release his terrible anger against women, against his family, and against the rest of us.

Of course, to care about being rejected by a total stranger, one must first come to care about that stranger. Bardo did this by obsessing on each of his various targets. Even today in prison, he is still doing it, focusing intently on two women. One is a singer, and the other is someone who was not famous when he first heard of her but is very famous now: Marcia Clark, the prosecutor who sent him to prison for life. In a letter Bardo wrote to me, he explained: "Twice, the *Daily Journal* has profiled Marcia Clark. . . . I learned a lot. Turn to page two to give you an idea." Page 2 was a lengthy list of personal facts about Marcia Clark and her family.

It is a convoluted irony of the media age that Marcia Clark prosecuted a regular citizen who stalked and killed a famous person, then prosecuted a famous person (O. J. Simpson) who stalked and killed a regular citizen, then became famous herself, and is now the focus of a stalker.

■ ■ ■

Media-age assassins are not unlike another uniquely American icon: the daredevil. If you understand Evel Kneivel, you can understand Robert Bardo. Like those of a daredevil, all of an assassin's worth and accomplishment derive from one act, one moment. This is also true for most heroes, but assassins and daredevils are not people who rise courageously to meet some emergency. The assassin and the daredevil create their own emergencies.

The daredevil fantasizes about the glory of accomplishing his stunt, the fame that waits for him on the other side of the canyon. The media have portrayed the daredevil as a courageous hero, but what if someone got the motorcycle, painted it special, got the colorful leather pants and jacket, got the ramps, notified the press, got all set up at the canyon . . . and then didn't do it? Suddenly he's not cool and special; he's pathetic. Now he's a guy whose silly name and goofy accessories add up to geek, not hero. The whole thing loses its luster if he doesn't do it.

Arthur Bremer wrote, "I want a big shot and not a little fat noise. I am tired of writing about it, about what I was going to do, about what I failed to do, about what I failed to do again and again. It bothers me that there are about 30 guys in prison now who threatened the Pres and we never heard a thing about them."

Assassins, you see, do not fear they are going to jail — *they fear they are going to fail,* and Bardo was no different. He had gotten all the components together: He had studied other assassins, he had researched his target, made his plan, gotten the gun, written the letters to be found after the attack. But like the daredevil, he was just a guy who worked at Jack in the Box until he made that jump, until the wheels left the ground, until he killed someone famous. Everything that goes with fame was waiting for him on the other side of the canyon, where, in his words, he'd finally be "a peer" with celebrities.

When he found Rebecca Schaeffer and was face-to-face with

her, he had all the credentials of an assassin, but he couldn't pick up his prize until he shot her. Since he was fourteen years old, he had known what he wanted to be when he grew up, and he got there on the steps of Rebecca Schaeffer's apartment building. Robert Bardo was a career assassin, a killer for whom the victim was secondary to the act.

Some people put years into their heroic accomplishments; assassins do not. While stalking Richard Nixon, Bremer wrote, "I'm as important as the start of WWI. I just need the little opening, and a second of time." Such narcissism is a central feature of every assassin, and like many of their characteristics, it is in us all to some degree. In his Pulitzer Prize–winning book *The Denial of Death,* Ernest Becker observes that narcissism is universal. Becker says every child's "whole organism shouts the claim of his natural narcissism. It is too all-absorbing and relentless to be an aberration, it expresses the heart of the creature: the desire to stand out, to be the one in creation." Becker says we all look for heroics in our lives, adding that in some people "it is a screaming for glory as uncritical and reflexive as the howling of a dog."

But the howls for glory of assassins had been unanswered in their mundane pre-attack lives. The assassin might be weird or unusual, but we cannot say we don't understand his motives, his goal. He wants what Americans want: recognition, and he wants what all people want: significance. People who don't get that feeling in childhood seek ways to get it in adulthood. It is as if they have been malnourished for a lifetime and seek to fix it with one huge meal.

The same search for significance is part of the motivation for the young gang member who kills, because violence is the fastest way to get identity. Murderer Jack Henry Abbott describes the "involuntary pride and exhilaration all convicts feel when they are chained up hand and foot like dangerous animals. The world has focused on us for a moment. We are somebody capable of threatening the world."

Ernest Becker writes, "The urge to heroism is natural, and to admit it honest. For everyone to admit it would probably release such pent-up force as to be devastating to society."

Well, Bremer, Hinckley, and Bardo all admitted it, with devastating results. Each first aspired to make it in Hollywood but gave that up for a faster, easier route to identity. They knew that with a single act of fraudulent heroism, with one single shot, they could be forever linked to their famous targets.

▪ ▪ ▪

Like all endeavors, assassination is reached by a certain protocol, certain hoops one jumps through. Many of these are detectable, observable hoops that leave a trail we can follow. Assassins teach each other, each learning something from the ones before. When I worked on the Bardo case, I was struck by the fact that he did so many things that Hinckley had done before him. The two young men had early life experiences with some similarities, and that's no surprise, but the similarities of the choices they made later are nothing short of remarkable. For example, Hinckley knew that Mark Chapman had brought along a copy of *Catcher in the Rye* on his trip to murder John Lennon, so he brought one with him on his trip to shoot President Reagan. Bardo brought the same book along when he killed Rebecca Schaeffer, later telling me he read it "to find out how it had made Chapman kill John Lennon."

Look at this list of things that John Hinckley did before shooting President Reagan:

- Wrote letters to an actress
- Wrote songs
- Took a job in a restaurant
- Read *Catcher in the Rye*
- Crisscrossed the country
- Stalked public figures other than his final target
- Traveled to Hollywood
- Kept a diary
- Studied other assassins
- Visited the Dakota building in New York City to see the place where John Lennon was murdered
- Considered an attention-getting suicide
- Sold off his possessions
- Wrote letters to be found after the attack
- Took a bus to the attack location

- Stalked his final target at more than one site before the attack
- Brought along *Catcher in the Rye*
- Didn't shoot at the first opportunity
- Left the scene after the first encounter
- Waited about a half hour and then shot his target

Amazingly, Bardo also did every one of the things on this list. There are more than thirty striking similarities in the behavior of the two men. The predictability of pre-attack behaviors of assassins was confirmed by the work of Park Dietz, the psychiatrist and sociologist who first came to national attention as the lead prosecution expert in the Hinckley case. In 1982, when I was on the President's Advisory Board at the Department of Justice, I proposed a research project to study people who threaten and stalk public figures. Dietz was the expert we chose to run the project. From this and his other pioneering work, he assembled ten behaviors common to modern assassins. Nearly every one of them:

1) Displayed some mental disorder
2) Researched the target or victim
3) Created a diary, journal, or record
4) Obtained a weapon
5) Communicated inappropriately with *some* public figure, though not necessarily the one attacked
6) Displayed an exaggerated idea of self (grandiosity, narcissism)
7) Exhibited random travel
8) Identified with a stalker or assassin
9) Had the ability to circumvent ordinary security
10) Made repeated approaches to some public figure

In protecting public figures, my office focuses on those who might try to kill clients, of course, but also those who might harm clients in other ways, such as through harassment or stalking. In evaluating cases, we consider 150 pre-incident indicators beyond those covered above.

If we had to choose just one PIN we'd want to be aware of above all others, it would be the one we call ability belief. This is a person's belief that he can accomplish a public-figure attack. Without it, he cannot. In fact, to do anything, each of us must first believe on some level that we can do it. Accordingly, society's highest-stakes question might be: "Do you believe you can succeed at shooting the president?" Would-be assassins won't always answer this question truthfully, of course, nor will society always get the opportunity to ask it, but to the degree it can be measured, ability belief is the preeminent pre-incident indicator for assassination.

If the truthful answer is "No, what with all those Secret Service agents and special arrangements, I couldn't get within a mile of the guy," the person cannot shoot the president. Of course, this isn't a permanently reliable predictor, because ability belief can be influenced and changed.

If, for example, I believe I could not possibly dive into the ocean from a 200-foot-high cliff, then I cannot. But a coach might influence my belief. Encouragement, teaching of skills that are part of the dive, taking of lesser dives — first from 20 feet, then 30, then 50 — would all act to change my ability belief. No single influence is more powerful than social proof, seeing someone else succeed at the thing you might have initially believed you could not do. Seeing a diver propel himself off an Acapulco cliff, sail down into the Pacific, and then emerge safely dramatically influences my belief that it can be done, and that I could do it.

Similarly, the enormous media attention showered on those who attack public figures bolsters ability belief in others. It says, "You see, it can be done." Little wonder that in the period following a widely publicized attack, the risk of other attacks goes up dramatically. It is precisely because one encourages another that public-figure attacks cluster (President Ford — two within two weeks; President Clinton — two within six weeks).

Society appears to be promoting two very different messages:

1) It is nearly impossible to successfully attack a public figure, and if you do it and survive, you will be a pariah, despised, reviled, and forgotten.

2) It is very easy to successfully attack a public figure, and if you do it, you'll not only survive, but you'll be the center of international attention.

Since we are discussing what amounts to a form of advertising, information following a public-figure attack could be presented quite differently than it is now. Law-enforcement personnel speaking with the press about a criminal who has been apprehended have tended to describe the arrest in terms of their victory over a dangerous, powerful, well-armed, and clever adversary: "Investigators found three forty-five-caliber handguns and more than two hundred rounds of ammunition in his hotel room. Since the perpetrator is a skilled marksman, it was touch and go when we stormed the building."

This attaches to the criminal a kind of persona doubtless attractive to many who might consider undertaking a similar crime. I have recommended a different approach on my cases, one that casts the offender in a far less glamorous light. Imagine this press conference following the arrest of a person who was planning an assassination:

Reporter: Would you describe the man as a loner?
Federal agent: More of a loser, actually.
Reporter: Did he put up any resistance when taken into custody?
Federal agent: No, we found him hiding in the bathroom — in the clothes hamper.
Reporter: Could he have succeeded in the assassination?
Federal agent: I doubt it very much. He's never succeeded at anything else.

Ideally, the agent would always switch the focus to the people and special methods that act in opposition to assassins, keeping the focus off the criminal.

Federal agent: I want to commend the eight-man team of special agents whose investigative work and application of new technologies made the apprehension possible so rapidly.

I propose that we don't show the bullets on the bureau in the seedy hotel room; show instead the dirty underwear and socks on the bathroom floor. I propose that we don't arrange photo opportunities that show the offender being escorted by ten federal agents from a helicopter to a motorcade of waiting cars. Show him instead in a mangy T-shirt, handcuffed to a pipe in some gloomy corridor, watched by one guard, and a woman at that. Not many identity-seeking would-be assassins would see those images and say, "Yeah, that's the life for me!"

Conversely, guarded by federal agents (just like the president), whisked into waiting helicopters (just like the president), his childhood home shown on TV (just like the president), the type of gun he owned fired on the news by munitions experts extolling its killing power, the plans he made described as "meticulous" — these presentations promote the glorious aspects of assassination and other media crimes. Getting caught for some awful violence should be the start of oblivion, not the biggest day of one's life.

But it was the biggest day in the life of accused Oklahoma City bomber Timothy McVeigh, who was paraded in front of the waiting press surrounded by FBI agents, rushed to a motorcade, and then whisked away in a two-helicopter armada. We saw this even more with accused Unabomber Ted Kaczynski, whose close-up appeared on the covers of *Time, U.S. News & World Report,* and *Newsweek* (twice). The cover text of all three described Kaczynski as a "genius."

Reporters usually refer to assassins with triple names, like Mark David Chapman, Lee Harvey Oswald, Arthur Richard Jackson. One might come to believe that assassins actually used these pretentious triple names in their pre-attack lives; they didn't. They were Mark, Lee, and Arthur.

I propose promoting the least glamorous incarnation of their names. Call a criminal Ted Smith instead of Theodore Bryant Smith. Better still, find some nickname used in his pre-attack life:

> Federal agent: His name is Theodore Smith, but he was known as Chubby Ted.

Our culture presents many role models, but few get as much hoopla and glory as the assassin. Those who have succeeded (and even some of those who failed) are among the most famous people in American lore. John Wilkes Booth survives history with more fame than all but a few other Americans of his time.

The tragically symbiotic relationship between assassins and television news is understandable: Assassins give great video — very visual, very dramatic. Assassins will not sue you no matter what you say about them, and they provide the story feature most desired by news producers: extendability. There will be more information, more interviews with neighbors and experts, more pictures from the high school yearbook. There will be a trial with the flavor of a horse race between lawyers (made famous just for the occasion), and there will be the drama of waiting for the verdict. Best of all, there will be that video of the attack, again and again.

The problem, however, is that that video may be a commercial for assassination. As surely as Procter & Gamble ever pushed toothpaste, the approach of television news pushes public-figure attack.

Way back in 1911, criminologist Arthur MacDonald wrote, "The most dangerous criminals are the assassins of rulers." He suggested that "newspapers, magazines and authors of books cease to publish the names of criminals. If this not be done voluntarily, let it be made a misdemeanor to do so. This would lessen the hope for glory, renown or notoriety, which is a great incentive to such crimes."

MacDonald would be disappointed to see that media-age assassins end up with virtual network shows, but he would not be surprised. After all, the early morning mist of mass-media hype was already thick even in his day. In 1912 a man named John Shrank attempted to kill Theodore Roosevelt. While he was in jail, his bail was abruptly raised because "motion picture men" had planned to pay it and secure his release long enough to restage the assassination attempt for newsreels. Objecting to the movie, the prosecutor told the court he was concerned about "the demoralizing effect such a picture film would have. It would tend to make a hero out of this man, and I don't propose that the young shall be allowed to worship him as a hero." Probably not realizing they were pioneering a new genre, the frustrated motion-picture men picked out a building that resembled the jail and filmed an actor who looked like Shrank emerging between two bogus deputy sheriffs.

■ ■ ■

No discussion of assassination would be complete without exploring the precautions that can be taken to prevent these attacks. First, of course, just as with any danger, one must learn that a hazard exists. In the Bardo case, for example, there were many warnings: Over a two-year period he had sent Rebecca Schaeffer a stream of inappropriate letters through her agents in New York and Los Angeles. When Bardo showed up at the studio where her show was taped, it was a studio security guard who told him which stage she was on. Bardo himself said, "It was way too easy."

On one of his visits to the studio, he explained to the chief of security that he was in love with Rebecca Schaeffer and had traveled from Arizona to see her. After telling Bardo the actress didn't want to see him, the security chief personally drove him back to the motel where he was staying. Unfortunately, even having seen (though perhaps not recognized) several obvious warning signs, the security chief didn't see to it that Rebecca Schaeffer was informed about the "lovesick" man who had been pursuing her for two years and had just traveled hundreds of miles by bus to meet her.

After the shooting, the security chief explained his meeting with Bardo to reporters: "I thought he was just lovesick. We get a hundred in a year, people trying to get in, fans writing letters." To the security chief, it was a matter of handling some fan according to what he called "standard procedure," but to Bardo, it was a powerful and emotional event.

Bardo: I had problems with the security at the studio and the feeling I had toward them, I just put it on Ms. Schaeffer.

GdeB: What was that feeling?

Bardo: It was anger, extreme anger, because they said, "No, you can't come in, get out of here, get away from this place!" They said, "She's not interested, she doesn't want to be bothered," and I just felt that she was the one that I would discuss that with personally in an encounter.

GdeB: But she didn't say that, did she?

Bardo: No, but I felt, I perceived that that's what she was like.

The security chief's account continues: "[Bardo was] terribly insistent on being let in. 'Rebecca Schaeffer' was every other word. 'I gotta see her. I love her.' Something was definitely wrong mentally. There was something haywire going on, but I didn't perceive it as potentially violent."

In an unanswered refrain often heard after preventable tragedies, the security chief added, "What more could I have done?"

About two weeks after Rebecca Schaeffer was killed, there was another much-publicized stalking incident that answers the question. It involved a would-be assailant I'll call Steven Janoff. He had once pursued a client of mine, and though our evaluation determined he did not likely pose a hazard to our client, we were concerned that he might be dangerous to a costar on our client's television show. We met with that actress and told her about the case. Police and studio security warned the pursuer off, assuming that would resolve the matter. It didn't, of course.

About a year later, the actress was in rehearsing for a play. One day she saw a man outside the theater who caught her attention, and she couldn't shake the feeling that he might be the person we had warned her about, so she called us. After some inquiry, we confirmed to her that Steven Janoff was indeed the man she had seen, and that he was there in pursuit of her.

She and her representatives asked for and then exactly followed our recommendations. She stopped using the front entrance to the theater for her rehearsal visits, the box office was provided with Janoff's photo and some guidance on what to do if he showed up, she agreed to have a security person with her, and she applied several other strategies we designed to limit the likelihood of an unwanted encounter.

For five days, Janoff stalked the actress, but because of her precautions, he was unable to encounter her. Janoff had purchased a ticket for the opening night of her play, though he wasn't patient enough to wait till then. One afternoon he walked right up to the box office, where an employee recognized him and sent out a call to police. Janoff produced a handgun and demanded to see the actress. The employee, hoping the gun was not loaded, ran off. Janoff turned the gun on himself, announcing that he would pull the trigger unless the actress was brought to him. After a four-hour standoff with police, he was taken into custody.

Not only did it turn out that the gun was loaded, but Janoff had a collection of other firearms back at his hotel room.

■ ■ ■

The Janoff case shows the enormous improvements the entertainment industry has made to address the safety of media figures. Several theatrical agencies, movie studios, and management firms now routinely have inappropriate communications and visits professionally evaluated. Unlike in the Bardo case, media figures are now more likely to be informed of inappropriate pursuit. These and other improvements have brought clear results: Successful attacks against media figures have been sharply reduced in recent years.

I wish I could say the same for professional sports, which brings to mind the murder attempt on the young tennis star Monica Seles. Though it certainly won't be the last attack on a sports figure, with a little effort it could be the last one facilitated by negligence.

Before I give you some little-known details about the Seles case, I want to discuss something about the hazards public figures face that is relevant to your safety. It is the myth that violence cannot be prevented. John Kennedy once made the point that assassins could not be stopped because "all anyone has to do is be willing to trade his life for the President's." Kennedy's oft-quoted opinion is glib, but entirely wrong. In fact, assassination not only can be prevented, it is prevented far more often than it succeeds. Though assassins have a few advantages over their victims, there are many more factors working against them. Literally thousands of opportunities exist for them to fail, and only one slender opportunity exists for them to succeed. It is not the type of crime a person can practice — both literally and figuratively, an assassin has one shot at success.

Like John Kennedy, people who apply a fatalistic attitude to their own safety (e.g., "Burglary cannot be prevented; someone can always find a way in") often do so as an excuse not to take reasonable precautions. Yes, a committed criminal might well be difficult to stop, but the absence of precautions makes you vulnerable to the uncommitted criminal.

In the Seles case, everybody knew that it made sense for her to have security at her public appearances in Europe. Because she was deeply enmeshed in the continent's greatest conflict, the Serbs versus the Croats, her public appearances frequently brought political demonstrations. She routinely had bodyguards at her tournaments, as she did at the 1993 Citizen Tournament in Germany.

Nevertheless, soon after arriving on the court, one of history's most brilliant athletes lay on her back, bleeding from a serious injury. Though ostensibly protected by two bodyguards, she had fallen victim to a knife attack, the most preventable of all assassination methods. Why did the bodyguards fail and assailant Gunter Parche succeed?

One of the two bodyguards, Manfred, answers my question in his statement to the police, but he begins with the wrong words: "*I am a telecommunications worker.* I have a side job for the private guard firm at the tennis grounds."

Presumably, a star tennis player could fairly have the expectation that the bodyguards assigned to her would in fact be bodyguards, professionals with some relevant training and experience. She might fairly expect that they would have at least discussed the possibility of a safety hazard, maybe even discussed what they would do should one present itself.

But none of that happened, and the promoters did not tell her that the people they had assigned to guard her life were unqualified part-timers. She had to learn that when Gunter Parche plunged the knife into her back and then raised his arm to do it again.

The second bodyguard's name is Henry, and his statement too begins with the wrong words: "*My main job is as a loader at Hamburg harbor.* I have a side job where I am in charge of security at the tennis grounds. At this tournament, my job was specifically to accompany and look after Monica Seles."

Amazingly, both men reported that they took special notice of assailant Gunter Parche prior to the stabbing. Henry pegged the attacker quite accurately: "Call it a sixth sense or whatever, I cannot explain it, but I noticed the man. Something told me that something was not quite right with this man. He was swaying instead of walking. I cannot explain it in more detail. I just had an uneasy feeling when I saw the man. As I said, I cannot explain it in more detail."

Though he clearly had an intuition about the assailant, his main message appears to be that he "cannot explain it."

Rather than tell anyone about his concerns, Henry decided instead to put down a coffee cup (which he was holding in his hand even though he was on a protective detail for the most controversial figure in world tennis) and stroll over to do I don't know what, and he didn't know what. Of course, he had taken only a few steps by the time the attack had started and finished.

It is perhaps not fair to criticize Henry and Manfred, for they know not what they do. That, however, is exactly my point.

While Seles was recovering from the knife wound, tennis promoters set out to promote the idea that such attacks cannot be prevented. Here is promoter Jerry Diamond telling interviewers on CNN that screening for weapons with metal detectors would never work in tennis: "When you are working in an enclosed facility where you've got walls and a ceiling and a roof, yeah, all those things are possible. But a metal detector is not going to deter anyone who is determined to go in that direction."

His statement that weapons screening can't work for tennis because some facilities lack walls and ceilings makes no sense. When I heard it, I was offended that someone would throw around life-and-death opinions with such misplaced confidence. Though he later called weapons screening "ludicrous," Mr. Diamond has throughout his career managed to screen every single spectator for something far smaller than a weapon: a tiny piece of paper, the ticket he sold them.

He doesn't know, I imagine, that most television shows now have metal-detector screening for audiences. Why? Because if they didn't, some armed person with the intent of harming a TV star could get a ticket and get within immediate reach of his target, just like Robert Bardo did when he visited Rebecca Schaeffer's TV show carrying a concealed knife, and just like Parche did at the Citizen Tournament. When you screen audience members, you don't have to worry about what is in people's heads because you know what is in their purses and pockets.

Weapons screening is good enough for courthouses, airlines, TV shows, city halls, concerts, high schools, even the Superbowl (no ceiling!), but somehow, a businessman tells us, it can't work for tennis. Of course, it's convenient to see it Mr. Diamond's way, because if attacks are unpreventable, then he and other promoters have no duty to try to prevent them.

Questioned by reporters about security weaknesses in professional tennis, another spokesperson explained that since tournaments occur all over the world, security precautions cannot be standardized. Really? Everywhere in the world they require that each tennis ball must bounce 135 to 147 centimeters when dropped from 2.5 meters. Everywhere in the world the courts are required to be exactly 23.8 meters long and 8.2 meters wide, with service courts that extend exactly 6.4 meters from the net to the service line. This sounds like standardization to me, and yet they asked how could you possibly have a standard credential and access-control system in all those countries? Well, you'd just have to go to the trouble of implementing one.

After the Seles attack, the Women's Tennis Council publicized that they'd enhanced security, yet they didn't require promoters to take two obvious steps: the use of metal detectors for screening spectators, and the installation of clear plastic audience barricades (like those at hockey games). Weak security improvements — including those you might make in your own life — are sometimes worse than doing nothing because they give false peace of mind and convince people that safety is being addressed when it is not. Poorly designed security fools everyone . . . except the attacker.

▪ ▪ ▪

When people hear about some public-figure stalker, they may think the case can be added to a list that consists of Chapman and Hinckley and those few others they recall. In fact, each is added to a far longer list. My office has managed more than twenty thousand cases, and only a quarter of one percent have ever become public. Several individual clients of mine have received as many as ten thousand letters a week from members of the general public, some of which meet the criteria for review by our Threat Assessment and Management (TAM) staff. Death threats, stalking, bizarre demands, and persistent pursuit are all part of public life in America. Our work carries us to an underside of this culture that most people would not believe exists, but it does exist, just out of view, just below the surface. Here is a brief sampling of the kinds of cases we encountered in one two-year period:

- A woman wrote more than six thousand death threats to a client because he was "marrying the wrong person."
- A man sent a client of ours a dead coyote, which the sender had killed "because it was beautiful like you."
- A man sent several letters each day to the actress with whom he hoped to have a romantic relationship. Six times a week, he walked miles to his local post office to see if a reply had arrived. Over eight years, he sent the actress more than *twelve thousand* letters, one of which included a photo of him with the inscription "Can you see the gun in this picture?" We were waiting for him when he showed up at her home.
- A man who was obsessed with becoming famous shaved off one eyebrow, half his head and half his beard, then traveled cross-country in pursuit of a famous actor. He arrived in the actor's hometown and went directly to a sporting goods store, where he priced a rifle and scope. He was arrested the night be-

fore our client made a major public appearance. When I interviewed the stalker, he told me that "whoever kills Caesar becomes a great man."

- A man sent a famous singer a picture of a heart pierced by a knife. Six months later, he was at her gate to "serenade her to kingdom come."

And then there were those who committed terrible crimes against others, influenced by delusions involving some distant public figure:

- A man attacked a teenage girl with a knife because he thought she was the famous model he was obsessed with.
- A teenage girl killed her parents and said she was ordered to do it by a movie star.
- In one case that became very public, a man named Ralph Nau had sinister delusions involving four different famous women, all clients of our office. He focused primarily on one whom he believed was an evil impostor. He killed a dog and sent the teeth to one of our clients. Later he traveled more than thirty thousand miles to destinations around the world in search of her. (He knew where the "impostor" lived but didn't go there.) Once, he attended a concert given by the "impostor," unaware that all the seats around him were occupied by TAM agents. We investigated ways to get him incarcerated or hospitalized, but he went to work reliably and never broke the law. He worked at a veterinary clinic, so even the killing of the dog could not be proven to be criminal. We monitored him closely every day for three years, after which he returned to his family home. I notified his father that references in some of his six hundred letters convinced us he would likely be dangerous to someone in his family. Within a few months he had killed his eight-year-old half-brother with an ax. The boy was preventing him from watching something very important on television: a signal about my client that he felt was being sent to him. (Even though he confessed to the killing, Nau was acquitted on a technicality. Every few months he is able to petition the court to release him from a mental hospital, and every few months we stand ready to testify against him.)

Given the number of cases evaluated by our TAM office — a virtual assembly line of madness and danger — I have had to be mindful of the need to keep a human connection between protector and pursuer, for only then are predictions likely to be accurate. Members of my staff who work on assessments put together a profile on each case. At some point, we began to refer to individuals under assessment as "profiles." This became part of a growing terminology unique to our work, some of which I've shared with you in this book. For example, those people who believe they are the Messiah, Captain Kirk, or Marilyn Monroe are described as DEL-ID cases (for delusions of identity). Those who believe they are married to one of our clients are called SPOUSE-DEL (for spousal delusion). Those who feel they are acting under the direction of God or voices or devices installed in their brains are known as OUTCON cases (short for "outside control").

I used to be concerned that this vernacular would dehumanize and depersonalize our assessments, but as we met more and more pursuers, came to know their lives more closely and understand their torment and the tragedy for their families, this concern evaporated. One can't help being profoundly affected by close involvement with people whose lives are a twisted chain of police encounters, hospitalization, relentless pursuit by imagined enemies, perceived betrayal by their loved ones, restlessness that moves them to new places, only to be restless there and move again, and above all, loneliness.

No, there is no chance that my office will get too far from the human side of our assessment work. We can't forget the young man who broke out of a mental hospital, mailed a final letter to a distant public figure he "loved," and then committed suicide. We can't forget those who killed others and somehow involved a media figure in their crime. Above all, we cannot and will not forget those who might try to harm our clients.

▪ ▪ ▪

In their search for attention and identity, most assassins go, as Park Dietz has put it, "to the people who have the most identity to spare:

famous people." Assassins know that when someone kills or attempts to kill a famous person in America, it is the grandest of all media events. A television reporter will stand with his camera crew just a few feet from another reporter standing with her camera crew, and invariably they will each call the crime "a senseless act."

But assassination is anything but senseless to the perpetrator, and those reporters are part of the sense it makes. The literally millions of dollars spent videotaping every single walk a president takes to and from a car or helicopter makes sense too. Some call it "the assassination watch," and electronic news organizations have obviously concluded that the cost of all those crews and all those satellite-dish vans, all that equipment and all that wasted videotape, is worth the images they'll get if somebody starts firing a gun. Thus, television and the assassin have invested in the same crime, and every few years they together collect the profit from it.

Remember Arthur Bremer, who set out to assassinate President Nixon but later settled on presidential candidate George Wallace? He weighed his act in terms that would make Nielsen proud. In his journal (which he always intended to publish after he became famous), Bremer worried about his ratings: "If something big in Nam flares up, [my attack] won't get more than three minutes on network T.V. news."

These senseless acts make perfect sense.

▪ 14 ▪

EXTREME HAZARDS

"In ourselves our safety must be sought.
By our own right hand it must be wrought."
— *William Wordsworth*

All of us will encounter people in our lives who alarm us or might pose some hazard, but as you've seen, a prominent public figure can have literally hundreds of people seeking unwanted encounters. I am not talking about fans; I am talking about people who feel they are under orders from God to harm a famous person, or who believe they are destined to marry a particular star, or who believe some media figure is being held hostage, and on and on. These cases have lessons any of us can benefit from. I want to present one that will demonstrate that even the most extreme safety hazards are manageable.

This book has explored obsessions, death threats, stalking, mental illness, child abuse, multiple shootings, and children who kill their parents. Amazingly, there is one case that brings all these elements together, a virtual hall of fame of American violence.

▪ ▪ ▪

At about four P.M. on July 20, 1983, I was at a hotel in Los Angeles to meet with a client who was finishing a public appearance event. As I crossed the lobby, I was waved over by one of several people assigned to my client from my company's Protective Security Division (PSD). He told me about an important radio call from our office that he suggested I take in one of our cars. As always, I found the cars lined up, drivers at the ready, fully prepared for an "unscheduled departure," our euphemism for an emergency.

The report I received was an alarming one; it would clear my schedule for that day and for the thirty days that followed: "Police in Jennings County, Louisiana, have discovered the bodies of five people brutally murdered. The lead suspect is Michael Perry."

▪ ▪ ▪

It was not the first time I'd heard that name. Michael Perry was among thousands of mentally ill pursuers my office had under assessment, but one of the very few we placed in the highest hazard category. The radio call was personal to me because the public figure Perry was obsessed with was not only a longtime client, she was also a dear friend.

The client Perry was obsessed with is an internationally known recording artist and film actress. She already had a team of PSD agents who'd been assigned to her home for about a year. The precaution of full-time bodyguards had been undertaken in part because we predicted that Perry might show up and in part because of another murderous stalker (Ralph Nau). The radio crackled with bulletins between my office and the security personnel at my client's house in Malibu. Someone from our Threat Assessment and Management division (TAM) was already speaking with local police, and a meeting was scheduled for me at the FBI field office.

Alarming reports are not uncommon for major media figures, but usually the more you learn about a situation the less serious it turns out to be. The exact opposite happened in the Michael Perry case. While one person from TAM reviewed our files on Perry, another gathered information from police in Jennings County, Louisiana.

To insulate clients from the routine management of safety issues, I maintain a policy of not telling them about particular cases unless there is something they must personally do. The Perry matter had reached that point and here is what I intended to tell my client: Perry had been obsessed with her for about two years. He was an accomplished survivalist who had been to Los Angeles several times in pursuit of her. Perry's parents were among the homicide victims, and a high-powered rifle and at least two handguns were missing from their home. Perry had had more than enough time to reach Los Angeles. He had recently told a psychiatrist that my client was "evil and should be killed."

Before making that call, however, I was informed of one more detail that changed everything. Based on what I learned about a few words Perry had written on a sheet of paper found at the murder scene, I did something I'd never done before and haven't done since, even though clients have faced very serious hazards. I called my client and asked her to pack for a few days because I'd be there within a half hour to pick her up and take her to a hotel. Given what I now knew, I didn't feel we could adequately protect her at her home, even with a team of bodyguards.

By the time I got to my client's neighborhood, the street had been closed by police, and a sheriff's helicopter was buzzing loudly overhead. Within minutes, I was answering my client's anxious questions as we drove away from her home followed closely by a PSD backup car. We'd be met at the hotel by two more PSD people. We would enter through a loading dock and be taken upstairs via a service elevator. A room near my client's suite was being modified to serve as a security command center.

Two people from my office had already left Los Angeles bound for Louisiana. By the time they got to the murder scene the next morning, the bodies had been removed, but photos revealed a gruesome aspect of the homicides: Perry had shot out his parents' eyes with a shotgun. He had also killed an infant nephew in the same house, and then broken into another house and killed two more people.

In the living room of his parents' house, we saw that he'd fired several shotgun blasts into a wall heater. The damaged heater was a mystery we'd solve the next day, along with why he had shot out the eyes of his victims, but at that point, we were looking past these details in search of a single sheet of paper.

Near where the bodies were found was a small pad printed up as a promotion for a local dry cleaner. On the top page was a collection of names, some crossed out then rewritten, some intersected by lines that connected them to other names, some circled, some underlined, some in a column, others separated into groups of three or four. The names and lines were Perry's efforts to narrow down to ten the number of people he intended to kill. Some were in Louisiana, one in Texas, one in Washington, D.C., and one in Malibu (the one that concerned me most). Little could any of these people have known that they were part of a bizarre contest between the enemies of Michael Perry. Little could they have known that in a small, dingy house in Louisiana, a man sitting with the bodies of three relatives he'd just shot was calmly and studiously weighing whether they would live or die.

Perry wrote the word *sky* near the names of those he'd killed already, and he crossed out some others that didn't make his top ten. When he was done, my client's name remained. Now I had to find Michael Perry.

His list not only brought us to the humid bayou, but started my excavation of Perry's history. In the weeks that followed, I would come to know his family and the people of Jennings County very well, come to know his schizophrenic sister, the doctors he'd told about his plan to kill people in "groups of ten," the coroner who would later Fed Ex us plaster casts of Perry's shoe prints from the murder scene, the neighbor boy who told us how Perry had decapitated his dog, the librarian who had lent Perry the books on survivalism that made him so hard to catch. I would soon know Michael Perry better than anyone else had ever wanted to know him.

▪ ▪ ▪

While people from my office began their second day in Louisiana, others quickly hustled my client from the hotel to a safe house we rented out of state. Others pursued leads in California, Nevada, Texas, Washington, D.C., New York, and even Africa. In Louisiana, Jennings County's small sheriff's department placed all three of its investigators on the Michael Perry case; my office added another fourteen people to the search.

Grace and Chester Perry had long ago predicted that their son would someday kill them. Whenever he was in town, his mother locked herself in the house, and he was rarely allowed in unless his father was home. They kept family guns hidden, paid Perry money to leave whenever he visited, and slept easier when he was off on one of his trips to California (looking for my client). It is unclear exactly when he got angry enough to orphan himself, but it may have been at seven years old, when, according to him, his mother pushed him against the wall heater in their home. Certainly the disfiguring and (to him) shameful burns on his legs daily reminded him of that incident. The shotgun blasts at the heater were a too-little, too-late revenge that had waited more than twenty years.

As Michael Perry grew up, stories about him were always making the rounds, and neighbors had given up trying to figure out why he did the bizarre things he did. For example, he liked to be called by the nickname Crab, but then hired a lawyer to legally change his name to Eye. Everybody thought it was just another of his senseless ideas, but it did make sense. Michael Perry hadn't been the only six-year-old whose father came home from work and questioned him about his various transgressions of the day, such as riding his bike in the street. He was, however, probably the only one whose father knew the details of each and every misdeed. Perry's father had been so uncannily accurate because a neighbor had agreed to watch the boy from her porch and then report his activities to Chester.

His father told Michael: "When I go to work, I leave my eyes at home." Perry spent twenty-eight years trying to hide from the scrutiny of those eyes; he even tried to symbolically become an Eye. Then, on July 19, 1983, he closed his father's eyes forever.

The Perry house was built on foot-high stilts, and a child might predictably fear what was under there, as many fear what is beneath the bed. But unlike those of most children, Perry's fears were not soothed, and they grew into an elaborate delusion that dead bodies were rising from a chamber beneath the floor.

With so much to occupy his pathology right at home, why did Perry's mind wander to a famous woman who lived 1,500 miles away? Why did he believe he would find his peace by killing her? I would know soon enough.

There was another prominent woman on his list: Sandra Day

O'Connor, who'd just been appointed to the U.S. Supreme Court. Why did she get Perry's attention? "Because no woman should be above a man," he later explained.

He was used to powerful women; he'd been raised, as nearly all children are, by the most powerful woman in the world: his mother. Her power was misused, he felt, and his anger over it consumed him. Though the burns from the heater were long healed, Perry still wrapped his legs in Ace bandages and never bared them in public. After returning from one of his stalking trips to Malibu, he beat his mother so badly that he was arrested and committed to a mental hospital. He quickly escaped and went right back to her house. Sheriff's deputies found him there, but his mother refused to let them take Perry back into custody. They persisted, but she resisted and she prevailed. The next time deputies came to her home, the strong and domineering woman would be dead.

Within a day of the murders, sociologist Walt Risler, a pioneering thinker in the field of predicting violence and a full-time consultant to our office for more than a decade, was on his way to Louisiana. There he interviewed family members, reviewed Perry's writings, and studied other evidence. Risler found the murder scene to be fertile ground for just the kind of madness deciphering he was so expert at. In a crib in the living room, Perry had piled an assortment of items: a crucifix, a pillow, three family photos facedown, a wall plaque of the Virgin Mary, and a ceramic crab. This was a shrine of meaning to only Michael Perry until Risler began putting the pieces together.

It was fair to assume that Perry was in one of three places or somewhere between them: still in Louisiana in pursuit of local victims on his list; in Washington, D.C., stalking Sandra Day O'Connor; or in Malibu, likely in the thousands of acres of wilderness behind my client's home. Predicting that he might act out violently was simple; we'd done that even before the murders. The difficult questions to answer were how he would go about encountering his victims and how patient he would be.

One late night, sitting in my office reviewing case material for the hundredth time, I noted a report indicating that a book written by expert tracker Tom Brown was missing from the Jennings County Library. We knew that Perry had once checked out another book by Brown called *The Search.* Did Perry use the information in these books to escape detection while he lived secretly in the hills behind my client's home? Could he be just a few feet off a path as we walked obliviously by him? I knew whom to ask.

Tom Brown had authored more than a dozen books on tracking and on nature, and he had been called in to search for dangerous men before. He was not anxious to do it again, but in an hour-long phone call, I convinced the wary and reluctant tracker to fly to Los Angeles and help us find Michael Perry. I picked him up at the airport, a wiry man with the quiet seriousness of Clint Eastwood. As I drove him to a waiting helicopter, he asked me questions about Perry: What kind of food does he like? Does he eat meat? Does he smoke? Tell me about his shoes. What kind of clothes does he wear? Tell me what his hair is like.

Soon after arriving in Los Angeles, Brown was high above the Malibu hills surrounding my client's home, looking for any sign of Perry. Some firemen who had been shown a picture of Perry told us about a makeshift camp where they'd seen him some months before, and Tom overflew the area, pointing out spots that PSD agents then checked out on foot or horseback. When he searched on the ground, he was accompanied by armed PSD agents, and during the few days they spent together, he taught them some of what he knew about tracking. Brown was an absolute marvel. He could tell you where a person had walked, slept, even paused. His intuition was informed by a subtle and sometimes odd series of signals: bent weeds, unsettled pebbles, shadows in the dust, and other details most people would look right past.

Brown explained to me, "When somebody moves something in your house, you notice it. When somebody moves something in the woods, I notice it."

In a backpack, one of the PSD agents carried a plaster cast of a shoe print taken from the dirt outside the murder scene. Occasionally

Brown would ask to have it brought out and he'd compare it to some small ridge or depression in the dust.

One afternoon after I dropped Brown back at his hotel for a brief rest, I was told by radio that a Malibu resident a mile or so from my client's home had reported that a strange man had knocked on the door and asked questions about "the magic movie star." He had headed up the hill on foot. I sped back to my client's house, knowing I'd get there before someone who was walking. When I arrived, several sheriff's deputies had joined two PSD people. We waited for about thirty minutes, and then the dogs began barking and running up the side of a hill.

Everyone followed the dogs, and soon we could clearly see a man crawling through the brush. Some sheriff's deputies ran around behind him, and a police helicopter descended on him from above. In a flash of everyone's adrenaline, the intruder was on the ground, handcuffed and scuffling. I rushed up the hill to identify him for the deputies, hoping the search for Michael Perry had just ended. He was lifted up and seated on the dirt looking right at me, and I recognized him immediately — but he wasn't Michael Perry. He was Warren P., *another* mentally ill pursuer whom we had interviewed years before and heard from occasionally. He was a lovesick man who hoped to marry my client.

Though worthy of assessment, Warren was without sinister intent; he was more of a tragic figure than a dangerous one. His bad luck had carried him through years of effort and across thousands of miles, finally getting him to my client's home, the mecca of his romantic delusions, but on the worst possible afternoon for a visit. As he was walked to one of the sheriff's cars, he just kept repeating, "I had no idea the security would be this tight."

Late the next night, three PSD agents searching the area around my client's property using some of Tom Brown's techniques found a suspicious-looking trail. They took me there, and shone their flashlights parallel to the ground, showing me the patterns in the dust. I confess I didn't see what they saw, but we all followed along, through a gully and into the dark brush. We were silent, hoping to find Perry and on some level hoping not to. Ahead of us we saw what even I could tell was a shelter built of gathered wood and twigs. We moved toward it, and as we got closer we could see that nobody was there.

Inside we found evidence that it was indeed the home of someone pursuing my client: Amid the filthy clothes we found the sleeve of one of her record albums. There was also a fork, some matches, and a crude weapon called a bola made from two rocks tied to the end of a length of rope. As we crawled out of the hut, we could see through a clearing directly to where my client drove by each day on her way to and from home. If Michael Perry lived here, he likely surveilled her from this spot.

It did not take long before we heard the sounds of someone moving toward us through the brush. In the moonlight, we held our breath and watched a man approach. He had a mess of dark hair, more than I thought Perry could have grown in the time he'd been at large. The man was wearing a crown on his head made of twigs and leaves. Pounced on from all sides, he yelled out, "I'm the king, I'm the king!" as he was handcuffed. It wasn't Perry, but still *another* mentally ill pursuer. This one was here to watch over my client, his "queen."

(Those two obsessed men living in my client's orbit during the Perry case make clear just how menacing public life can be. The next time you see one of those frequent tabloid reports about some star's being stalked by a "crazed fan," you'll know how silly the hype is — you could choose almost any star almost any day and that story would be true. All that makes it "news" is that a tabloid needed a headline.)

Just as we might come upon Michael Perry in Malibu at any moment, Walt Risler and our investigator might find him in the reeds along the marshy waterways around Jennings County. Or some lucky (or, if not careful, unlucky) state trooper might find him speeding in Chester Perry's Oldsmobile down the highway, or the U.S. Supreme Court police might find him wandering the halls of the historic building in search of Sandra Day O'Connor.

Walt Risler, swimming deepest in the waters of Perry's delusions, concluded that Washington, D.C., and Malibu were a Perry-esque Sodom and Gomorrah. Weighing everything he'd learned about the case, Risler predicted that Perry was on his way to the nation's capital to kill Justice O'Connor. Based on this, I made contact with a seasoned Washington, D.C., homicide investigator named Tom Kilcullen and filled him in on the case and Risler's opinion. Kilcullen was a creative thinker who followed up on several leads in the Washington area.

Our efforts in Malibu continued with daily interviews of people who might have seen Perry. We asked local shopkeepers to keep us informed of anyone inquiring about my client, and we urged special attentiveness at the Malibu library. That's because a search of Grace and Chester Perry's phone records had revealed that their son had called them collect from there a few times during one of his visits to California. Another call on those records was more chilling. Six months earlier, there'd been a small newspaper report about my client's frequenting a particular Beverly Hills shop. The phone records revealed that Perry had called his parents from the phone booth right outside that shop. We were dealing with a capable stalker.

To learn what Perry might know about his own manhunt, I reviewed newspaper stories about the case. Scanning *USA Today* during those weeks was interesting because I would come to a headline like "Suspect in Five Murders . . . ," and it wouldn't be Perry; "Mass Killer Still at Large . . . ," and it wouldn't be Perry; "Man Wanted for Family Slayings . . . ," and it wouldn't be Perry. Only in America.

For eleven days, teams in different parts of the country looked for a man who hated to be looked at, until July 31, when Risler's prediction proved correct. Police in Washington, D.C., received a call from a sleazy hotel: A guest had reportedly stolen a radio from another guest. An officer was dispatched to question the two derelict oddballs who'd been annoying each other, and he concluded that nothing illegal had happened. The minor dispute call would be over once the officer completed the routine step of checking each man for any arrest warrants. He asked them to wait a moment while the results of the computer search came over his radio. The unimportant matter became the most important of that officer's career because standing patiently in front of him was mass murderer Michael Perry.

Within an hour, Detective Kilcullen called me and offered to let me talk to Perry, who was now in his custody. Just that quickly, the murderous stalker who had dominated my thoughts every moment for almost two weeks was on the other end of the phone, ready to chat.

Without preparation, I stumbled into an interview with the nation's most wanted killer. We knew he'd been to my client's home, so I first asked him about that. He lied without hesitation, sounding like a fast-talking, streetwise con man.

Perry: I don't think I've ever been to her house, sir. I don't think so. I really don't.

GdeB: Really?

Perry: Right. I really don't.

GdeB: Have you ever been to California at all?

Perry: Well, I just went swimming at the beach, you know, and did some camping; that's all.

Then, without my even asking, he told me how my client fit in to his reasons for killing.

Perry: When she was in that movie, and whenever she turned around, she had quite a different face, you know. She looked like my mother back in 1961, you know, the face that my mother had. It was 1961, my mother walked into the room, and I was up way before anyone else. And my mother walked in and she had this ugly-looking face, and I looked at this, and she turned her head and rubbed her shoulder. And that face in that movie reminded me of 1961. It ruined the whole thing, you know.

Perhaps he was recalling the day of the heater incident, burned into his memory as it was burned into his skin. He then quickly changed the subject and again denied ever having been to my client's home. It's common for criminals to avoid giving information someone wants, often precisely because it's wanted, but then he just gave up the lie and described the entrance to my client's home exactly.

Perry: You know they had like a little drive-in theater deal [the gate intercom], you know, you push the button. And a red light [part of the security program]. And I had the impression that the house might have had an underground shelter, and it's a big place. And I rang the bell, and there was a camera out in front and everything. I didn't get that girl's attention, and she didn't get mine, either. I just said, "This can't be the place," you know, due to respect that this was such an ancient place. That's a strong, strong feeling.

Perry became quiet. When he next spoke, it was about the nature of obsession itself. In his unsophisticated way, he described the inside of his experience as accurately as any psychiatrist could hope to.

Perry: I really don't want to bring it up. It passed my mind. She kind of creeped up, and *nothing, nothing had ever stuck to my mind like that.* And even, you know, even today, even today, even today . . .

He drifted off into silence, and I waited quietly for him to speak again.

Perry: On her special, on HBO, I saw her eyes change color. Her eyes change color a lot.

GdeB: What was that like?

Perry: I didn't like it at all. That girl might be a witch, you know. She may do some damage to me if she hears me saying this. I'm saying what I saw. It did look like my mother. I don't want to mess with it because I know it was a relief whenever I forgot about it. I weighed the fact that she was a movie star, and realistically speaking, her address being in a magazine is not right. So I'm kind of scared of this girl if I met her. Of course, I don't know what it would be like. I know it's a touchy situation with this girl. I've stayed up many nights thinking about it.

GdeB: What if you had seen her at the house?

Perry: I never did, and anyway, she has a boyfriend. But you know, she asked of me and so I did, so that's about it, but I don't want to get too personal. I'm under arrest right now, I just want you to know that. They called the folks back home, and there's been some sort of big accident, some theft or something like that, which I didn't do.

Perry got quiet again. It was clear that the man who'd tried to exorcise one of his demons by shooting his mother in the face still wasn't free of it.

GdeB: You don't like this whole subject, do you?

Perry: No, I don't. The bad thing about it was that she turned around and had that ugly face. The face was completely different from the one she had had. I mean, it was a disaster that she looked like her. It was terrible, you know, and I turned off the TV and I left. I don't want to talk too much about it because man, it took a lot of my time after I saw that. I said, "This is too much." It took a lot of my time, and I didn't want it anymore.

His voice drifted off and then he hung up. I sat at my desk in disbelief. The emergency that had consumed nearly every hour of every person in my company had just ended, not with a stakeout or a gunfight or a SWAT team, but with a phone call. The man I had tried to know and understand through every means I could find had just told me outright why he had stalked my client and why he wanted to kill her. I walked into the TAM office, which was bustling with activity regarding the case, and said, "I just got off the phone with Michael Perry." That didn't make sense to anybody, but it wasn't funny enough to be a joke.

I flew to D.C. the next morning to learn anything of relevance to the case and to gain information that would help with the prosecution. Since our next job would be to help ensure that Perry was convicted, I'd been in regular touch with the Jennings County prosecutor, who was meeting me in D.C.

When I arrived, Kilcullen told me Perry's car had been found and was being held at a nearby tow yard. We drove over together to look at it and see what evidence it held.

Chester Perry's green Oldsmobile was dusty from its long drive. An officer looked in the window at the front seat and then recoiled a bit. "It's covered in blood," he said. Sure enough, there was a dark, pulpy liquid sticking to the fabric upholstery. As we opened the door,

I saw watermelon seeds on the floor; it wasn't blood on the seat, it was watermelon juice. Rather than pause to eat somewhere, Perry had bought a watermelon and eaten it with his right hand as he sped along the highway toward D.C.

Perry had chosen to stay at a cheap little place called the Annex Hotel, which was about a mile and a half from the Supreme Court. When we went there, it became clear what he had spent most of his money on. He had turned Room 136 into something that stunned us all, a bizarre museum of the media age, a work of pop art that connected violence and madness and television. Into that tiny room, Perry had crammed nine television sets, all plugged in, all tuned to static. On one, he had scrawled the words "My Body" in red marker. Several of the sets had giant eyes drawn on the screens. One had my client's name written boldly along the side.

The Louisiana detective in charge of the Perry homicides, Irwin Trahan, came to D.C. to transport Perry back home for trial. Often, such prisoners are flown on commercial planes or on "Con Air" — the nickname for the U.S. Marshals' jet fleet — but Trahan and his partner had decided to drive Perry back to Louisiana. This unusual trio sped along the same highways Perry had driven to get to D.C. Checking into motels along the way, the detectives took turns staying awake to watch Perry, who didn't sleep at all. At the close of their two-day trip, Perry asked them to pass a message to me. It was about my client: "You better keep an eye on her twenty-four hours a day."

In an irony I wouldn't recognize for many years, Perry also told the detectives that if his case ever went before the U.S. Supreme Court and Judge Sandra Day O'Connor, "I wouldn't have a chance then, because that's a woman." (His case did eventually go before the Supreme Court.)

A while after Perry was back in Louisiana, we arranged for Walt Risler to interview him in jail to follow up on his sinister warnings about my client. An agitated Perry explained to him, "Tell her to stay away from Greece. That's all I want to say to you now, man. I'm feeling sick, so sick; my head is just filled with vomit."

To keep the interview from ending, Risler asked about one of

Perry's favorite topics: television. Perry responded: "Man, TV is really fucked up lately. I don't know what it means. After a while it got so that the only sense I could make of television was by watching channels with nothing on. I could read them and make more sense than what was happening on the programs."

He then asked his attorney to leave so he could speak with Risler in private. He took Risler's hands in his and explained that if he didn't get out of jail, there would be hell to pay. If he was executed, it would trigger the explosion of an atomic missile hidden in the swamps near town. "So you see, getting me out of here is important to everyone. I'm just trying to save lives."

Perry stood up to end the interview: "Oh, man, my head is filled with vomit. You can just see how fucked up my head is, can't you, from the things I think?"

Perry was not faking insanity — this was the real thing.

▪ ▪ ▪

When I got back to Los Angeles, there was a kind letter from Justice O'Connor thanking me for my help and lamenting the fact that "there are people in this country who are sufficiently unstable to constitute genuine threats to others."

A few years later, after the Supreme Court adopted the MOSAIC program I designed, I met with Justice O'Connor in her office. Michael Perry, by then convicted of the five murders and sentenced to death, had come back into her life in an interesting way. Prison officials ordered doctors to give Perry medication so that he would be lucid enough to know what was happening on the day he was executed. The doctors refused, reasoning that since the medication was being given just so he could be killed, it was not in their patient's best interest. The matter went all the way to the Supreme Court, and in one of history's most impartial decisions, the justices ruled that the murderer who had stalked one of them could not be forced to take medication just to be executed. Michael Perry is alive today because of that ruling.

▪ ▪ ▪

The Perry case shows that even the most public of crimes are motivated by the most personal issues. Though the odds are overwhelming that you'll never appear on the death list of some mass killer, I've discussed the case here to add to your understanding of violence, and to reveal the human truth in the sensational stories we see in the news. Reports of such murders on TV, presented in one dimension without perspective and without the kind of detail you've just read, usually do little more than add unwarranted fear to people's lives. And people hardly need more of that.

15

THE GIFT OF FEAR

"Fears are educated into us, and can, if we wish, be educated out."

— *Karl A. Menninger*

We all know there are plenty of reasons to fear people from time to time. The question is, what are those times? Far too many people are walking around in a constant state of vigilance, their intuition misinformed about what really poses danger. It needn't be so. When you honor accurate intuitive signals and evaluate them without denial (believing that either the favorable or the unfavorable outcome is possible), you need not be wary, for you will come to trust that you'll be notified if there is something worthy of your attention. Fear will gain credibility because it won't be applied wastefully. When you accept the survival signal as a welcome message and quickly evaluate the environment or situation, fear stops in an instant. Thus, trusting intuition is the exact opposite of living in fear. In fact, the role of fear in your life lessens as your mind and body come to know that you will listen to the quiet wind chime, and have no need for Klaxons.

Real fear is a signal intended to be very brief, a mere servant of intuition. But though few would argue that extended, unanswered fear is destructive, millions choose to stay there. They may have forgotten or never learned that fear is not an emotion like sadness or happiness, either of which might last a long while. It is not a state, like anxiety. True fear is a survival signal that sounds only in the presence of danger, yet unwarranted fear has assumed a power over us that it holds over no other creature on earth. In *The Denial of Death,*

Ernest Becker explains that "animals, in order to survive, have had to be protected by fear responses." Some Darwinians believe that the early humans who were most afraid were most likely to survive. The result, says Becker, "is the emergence of man as we know him: a hyperanxious animal who constantly invents reasons for anxiety even when there are none." It need not be this way.

I learned this again on a recent visit to Fiji, where there is less fear in the entire republic than there is at some intersections in Los Angeles. One morning, on a peaceful, hospitable island called Vanua Levu, I took a few-mile walk down the main road. It was lined on both sides with low ferns. Occasionally, over the sound of the quiet ocean to my left, I'd hear an approaching car or truck. Heading back toward the plantation where I was staying, I closed my eyes for a moment as I walked. Without thinking at first, I just kept them closed because I had an intuitive assurance that walking down the middle of this road with my eyes closed was a safe thing to do. When I analyzed this odd feeling, I found it to be accurate: The island has no dangerous animals and no assaultive crime; I would feel the ferns touch my legs if I angled to either side of the road, and I'd hear an approaching vehicle in plenty of time to simply open my eyes. To my surprise, before the next car came along, I had walked more than a mile with my eyes closed, trusting that my senses and intuition were quietly vigilant.

When it comes to survival signals, our minds have already done their best work by the time we try to figure things out. In effect, we've reached the finish line and handily won the race before even hearing the starting pistol — if we just listen without debate.

Admittedly, that blind walk was in Fiji, but what about in a big American city? Not long ago, I was in an elevator with an elderly woman who was heading down to an underground parking garage after business hours. Her keys were protruding through her fingers to form a weapon (which also displayed her fear). She was afraid of me when I got into the elevator as she is likely afraid of all men she encounters when she is in that vulnerable situation.

I understand her fear and it saddens me that millions of people feel it so often. The problem, however, is that if one feels fear of all people all the time, there is no signal reserved for the times when it's really needed. A man who gets into the elevator on another floor (and hence wasn't following her), a man who gives her no undue attention, who presses a button for a floor other than the one she has selected, who is dressed appropriately, who is calm, who stands a suitable distance from her, is not likely to hurt her without giving some signal. Fear of him is a waste, so don't create it.

I strongly recommend caution and precaution, but many people believe — and we are even taught — that we must be extra alert to be safe. In fact, this usually decreases the likelihood of perceiving hazard and thus reduces safety. Alertly looking around while thinking, "Someone could jump out from behind *that* hedge; maybe there's someone hiding in *that* car" replaces perception of what actually is happening with imaginings of what could happen. We are far more open to every signal when we don't focus on the expectation of specific signals.

You might think a small animal that runs across a field in a darting crisscross fashion is fearful even though there isn't any danger. In fact, scurrying is a strategy, a precaution, not a reaction to a fear signal. Precautions are constructive, whereas remaining in a state of fear is destructive. It can also lead to panic, and panic itself is usually more dangerous than the outcome we dread. Rock climbers and long-distance ocean swimmers will tell you it isn't the mountain or the water that kills — it is panic.

Meg is a woman who works with violently inclined mental patients every day. She rarely feels fear at her job, but away from work, she tells me, she feels panic every night as she walks from her car to her apartment. When I offer the unusual suggestion that she'd actually be safer if she relaxed during that walk, she says, "That's ridiculous. If I relaxed, I'd probably get killed." She argues that she must be acutely alert to every possible risk. Possibilities, I explain, are in the mind, while safety is enhanced by perception of what is outside the mind, perception of what *is* happening, not what might happen.

But Meg insists that her nightly fear will save her life, and even as she steadfastly defends the value of her terror, I know she wants to be free of it.

GdeB: When do you feel the fear?

Meg: As I park my car.

GdeB: Is it the same every night?

Meg: Yes, and then if I hear a noise or something, it gets ten times worse. So I have to stay extra alert. Living in Los Angeles, I have to stay alert all the time.

(Note her reference to Los Angeles — a satellite.)

I explain that if she's scared to death every night, focused intently on what might happen, then no signal is reserved for when there actually is risk that needs her attention. Ideally, when there is fear, we look around, follow the fear, ask what we are perceiving. If we are looking for some specific, expected danger, we are less likely to see the unexpected danger. I urge that she pay relaxed attention to her environment rather than paying rapt attention to her imagination.

I know Meg is feeling anxious, and that is a signal of something, though not danger in this case. I ask her what risks she faces as she walks from her car each night.

Meg: Isn't that a dumb question coming from you? I mean, there are so many risks. Los Angeles is a very dangerous city, not a place I'd choose to live.

GdeB: But you do choose to live here.

Meg: No, I have to; I'm trapped by this job. I have to live here, and it's so dangerous, people are killed here all the time, and I know that, so I'm afraid when I walk to my apartment, terrified, actually, and I should be!

GdeB: Certainly anything could happen to anyone anytime, but since you've made that walk more than a thousand times without injury, the terror you feel is likely a signal of something other than danger. How do you normally communicate with yourself?

An agitated Meg says she doesn't understand my question, but that she doesn't want to discuss it anymore — she'll think about it overnight. When she calls the following afternoon, she not only understands my question about how she communicates with herself, but has found her answer. She agrees that her intuition is indeed communicating something to her, and it isn't imminent danger; it is that she does not want to stay in Los Angeles or in her job. Her nightly walk from her car into her apartment is simply the venue for her inner voice to speak most loudly.

■ ■ ■

Every day, my work brings me into close contact with people who are afraid, anxious, or just worrying. My first duty is to figure out which it is. If it's real fear they feel, there is important information for me to glean, possibly relevant to safety.

There are two rules about fear that, if you accept them, can improve your use of it, reduce its frequency, and literally transform your experience of life. That's a big claim, I know, but don't be "afraid" to consider it with an open mind.

RULE #1. THE VERY FACT THAT YOU FEAR SOMETHING IS SOLID EVIDENCE THAT IT IS NOT HAPPENING.

Fear summons powerful predictive resources that tell us what might come next. It is that which might come next that we fear — what might happen, not what is happening now. An absurdly literal example helps demonstrate this: As you stand near the edge of a high cliff, you might fear getting too close. If you stand right at the edge, you no longer fear getting too close, you now fear falling. Edward Gorey gives us his dark-humored but accurate take on the fact that if you do fall, you no longer fear falling — you fear landing:

The Suicide, as she is falling,
Illuminated by the moon,
Regrets her act, and finds appalling
The thought she will be dead so soon.

Panic, the great enemy of survival, can be perceived as an unmanageable kaleidoscope of fears. It can be reduced through embracing the second rule:

RULE #2. WHAT YOU FEAR IS RARELY WHAT YOU THINK YOU FEAR — IT IS WHAT YOU *LINK* TO FEAR.

Take anything about which you have ever felt profound fear and link it to each of the possible outcomes. When it is real fear, it will either be in the presence of danger, or it will link to pain or death. When we get a fear signal, our intuition has already made many connections. To best respond, bring the links into consciousness and follow them to their high-stakes destination — if they lead there. When we focus on one link only, say, fear of someone walking toward us on a dark street instead of fear of being harmed by someone walking toward us on a dark street, the fear is wasted. That's because many people will approach us — only a very few might harm us.

Surveys have shown that ranking very close to the fear of death is the fear of public speaking. Why would someone feel profound fear, deep in his or her stomach, about public speaking, which is so far from death? Because it isn't so far from death when we link it. Those who fear public speaking actually fear the loss of identity that attaches to performing badly, and that is firmly rooted in our survival needs. For all social animals, from ants to antelopes, identity is the pass card to inclusion, and inclusion is the key to survival. If a baby loses its identity as the child of its parents, a possible outcome is abandonment. For a human infant, that means death. As adults, without our identity as a member of the tribe or village, community or culture, a likely outcome is banishment and death.

So the fear of getting up and addressing five hundred people at the annual convention of professionals in your field is not just the fear of embarrassment — it is linked to the fear of being perceived as incompetent, which is linked to the fear of loss of employment, loss of home, loss of family, your ability to contribute to society, your value, in short, your identity and your life. Linking an unwarranted fear to its ultimate terrible destination usually helps alleviate that fear. Though you may find that public speaking can link to death, you'll see that it would be a long and unlikely trip.

Apply these two rules to the fear that a burglar might crash into your living room. First, the fear itself can actually be perceived as good news, because it confirms that the dreaded outcome is not occurring right now. Since life has plenty of hazards that come upon us without warning, we could welcome fear with "Thank you, God, for a signal I can act on." More often, however, we apply denial first, trying to see if perhaps we can just think it away.

Remember, fear says something might happen. If it does happen, we stop fearing it and start to respond to it, manage it, surrender to it; or we start to fear the next outcome we predict might be coming. If a burglar does crash into the living room, we no longer fear that possibility; we now fear what he might do next. Whatever that may be, while we fear it, it is not happening.

■ ■ ■

Let's go one step deeper in this exploration of fear: In the 1960s there was a study done that sought to determine which single word has the greatest psychological impact on people. Researchers tested reactions to words like *spider, snake, death, rape, incest, murder.* It was the word *shark* that elicited the greatest fear response. But why do sharks, which human beings come in contact with so rarely, frighten us so profoundly?

The seeming randomness of their strike is part of it. So is the lack of warning, the fact that such a large creature can approach silently and separate body from soul so dispassionately. To the shark, we are without identity, we are no more than meat, and to human beings the loss of identity is a type of death all by itself. In his book *Great White Shark,* Jean-Michel Cousteau calls the shark "the most frightening animal on earth," but there is, of course, an animal far more dangerous.

Scientists marvel at the predatory competence of the great white, praising its speed, brute strength, sensory acuity, and apparent determination, but man is a predator of far more spectacular ability. The shark does not have dexterity, guile, deceit, cleverness, or disguise. It also does not have our brutality, for man does things to man that sharks could not dream of doing. Deep in our cells, we know this, so occasional fear of another human being is natural.

As with the shark attack, randomness and lack of warning are the attributes of human violence we fear most, but you now know that human violence is rarely random and rarely without warning. Admittedly, danger from humans is more complicated than danger from sharks; after all, everything you need to know about how to be safe from sharks can be spoken in five words: Don't go in the ocean. Everything you need to know about how to be safe from people is in you too, enhanced by a lifetime of experience (and hopefully better organized by this book).

We may choose to sit in the movie theater indulging in the fear of unlikely dangers now and again, but our fear of people, which can be a blessing, is often misplaced. Since we live every day with the most frightening animal on earth, understanding how fear works can dramatically improve our lives.

People use the word *fear* rather loosely, but to put it in its proper relation to panic, worry, and anxiety, recall the overwhelming fear that possessed Kelly when she knew her rapist intended to kill her. Though people say of a frightening experience, "I was petrified," aside from those times when being still is a strategy, real fear is not paralyzing — it is energizing. Rodney Fox learned this when he faced one of man's deepest fears: "I was suddenly aware of moving through the water faster than I ever had before. Then I realized I was being pulled down by a shark which had hold of my chest." As the powerful predator took him from the surface, a far more powerful force compelled Rodney to caress the shark's head and face, searching for its eyes. He plunged his thumbs deep into the only soft tissue he found. The shark let go of him immediately, but Rodney embraced it and held on tight so it couldn't turn around for another strike. After what seemed like a long ride downward, he kicked away from it and swam through a cloud of red to the surface.

Fear was pumping blood into Rodney's arms and legs and using them to do things he would never have done on his own. He would never have decided to fight with a great white shark, but because fear didn't give it a second thought, he survived.

Rodney's wild, reckless action and Kelly's quiet, breathless action were both fueled by the same coiled-up energy: real fear. Take a moment to conjure that feeling and recognize how different it is from worry, anxiety, and panic. Even the strongest worry could not get you to fight with a shark, or follow your would-be murderer silently down a hallway.

▪ ▪ ▪

Recently I was asked to speak to a group of corporate employees about their safety, but as is often the case, it quickly became a discussion about fear. Before I began, several people said, "Please talk to Celia, she's been looking forward to this meeting for weeks." Celia, it turned out, was eager to tell me about her dread of being followed, a topic her co-workers had heard a lot about. When people come to me in fear (of a stranger, a co-worker, a spouse, a fan), my first step is always to determine if it actually is a fear as opposed to a worry or a phobia. This is fairly simple since, as I noted above, real fear occurs in the presence of danger and will always easily link to pain or death.

To learn if Celia was reacting to a fear signal (which is not voluntary) or if she was worrying (which is voluntary), I asked if she feared being followed right then, right in the room where we sat.

She laughed. "No, of course not. I fear it when I'm walking alone from my office to my car at night. I park in a big gated lot, and mine is always the only car left because I work the latest, and the lot is empty and it's dead silent." Since she had given me no indication of actual risk, her dread was not the fear signal of nature but the worry only humans indulge in.

To get her to link the fear, I asked what about being followed scared her. "Well, it's not the following that scares me, it's the being caught. I'm afraid somebody will grab me from behind and pull me into a car. They could do anything to me, since I'm the last one here." She launched this satellite about working the latest several times.

Since worry is a choice, people do it because it serves them in some way. The worry about public speaking may serve its host by giving him or her an excuse never to speak in public, or an excuse to cancel or to do poorly ("because I was so scared"). But how did Celia's worry serve Celia? People will always tell you what the real issue is, and in fact, Celia already had.

I asked why she couldn't just leave work earlier each evening: "If I did, everybody would think I was lazy." So Celia was concerned about losing her identity as the employee who always worked the longest. Her frequent discussions of hazard and fear were guaranteed to quickly carry any conversation to the fact that she worked the latest. And that is how the worry served her.

The wise words of FDR, "The only thing we have to fear is fear itself," might be amended by nature to "There is nothing to fear unless and until you feel fear." Worry, wariness, anxiety, and concern all have a purpose, but they are not fear. So any time your dreaded outcome cannot be reasonably linked to pain or death and it isn't a signal in the presence of danger, then it really shouldn't be confused with fear. It may well be something worth trying to understand and manage, but worry will not bring solutions. It will more likely distract you from finding solutions.

In the original form of the word, to worry someone else was to harass, strangle, or choke them. Likewise, to worry oneself is a form of self-harassment. To give it less of a role in our lives, we must understand what it really is.

Worry is the fear we manufacture — it is not authentic. If you choose to worry about something, have at it, but do so knowing it's a choice. Most often, we worry because it provides some secondary reward. There are many variations, but a few of the most popular follow.

- Worry is a way to avoid change; when we worry, we don't do anything about the matter.
- Worry is a way to avoid admitting powerlessness over something, since worry feels like we're doing something. (Prayer also makes us feel like we're doing something, and even the most committed agnostic will admit that prayer is more productive than worry.)
- Worry is a cloying way to have connection with others, the idea being that to worry about someone shows love. The other side of this is the belief that not worrying about someone means you don't care about them. As many worried-about people will tell you, worry is a poor substitute for love or for taking loving action.
- Worry is a protection against future disappointment. After taking an important test, for example, a student might worry about

> whether he failed. If he can feel the experience of failure now, rehearse it, so to speak, by worrying about it, then failing won't feel as bad when it happens. But there's an interesting trade-off: Since he can't do anything about it at this point anyway, would he rather spend two days worrying and then learn he failed, or spend those same two days *not* worrying, and then learn he failed? Perhaps most importantly, would he want to learn he had passed the test and spent two days of anxiety for nothing?

In *Emotional Intelligence,* Daniel Goleman concludes that worrying is a sort of "magical amulet" that some people feel wards off danger. They believe that worrying about something will stop it from happening. He also correctly notes that most of what people worry about has a low probability of occurring, because we tend to take action about those things we feel are likely to occur. This means that very often the mere fact that you are worrying about something is a predictor that it isn't likely to happen!

▪ ▪ ▪

The relationship between real fear and worry is analogous to the relationship between pain and suffering. Pain and fear are necessary and valuable components of life. Suffering and worry are destructive and unnecessary components of life. (Great humanitarians, remember, have worked to end suffering, not pain.)

After decades of seeing worry in all its forms, I've concluded that it hurts people much more than it helps. It interrupts clear thinking, wastes time, and shortens life. When worrying, ask yourself, "How does this serve me?" and you may well find that the cost of worrying is greater than the cost of changing. To be freer of fear and yet still get its gift, there are three goals to strive for. They aren't easy to reach, but it's worth trying:

1) When you feel fear, listen.
2) When you don't feel fear, don't manufacture it.
3) If you find yourself creating worry, explore and discover why.

▪ ▪ ▪

Just as some people are quick to predict the worst, there are others who are reluctant to accept that they might actually be in some danger. This is often caused by the false belief that if we identify and name risk, that somehow invites or causes it to happen. This thinking says: If we don't see it and don't accept it, it is prevented from happening. Only human beings can look directly at something, have all the information they need to make an accurate prediction, perhaps even momentarily make the accurate prediction, and then say that it isn't so.

One of my clients is a corporation whose New York headquarters has an excellent safety and security program. All doors into their suite of offices are kept locked. Adjacent to each entry door is a plate over which employees wave a magnetic card to gain ready access. The president of the firm asked me to speak to an employee, Arlene, who persistently refused to carry her access card. She complained that the cards scare people because they bring to mind the need for security. (Call this fear of fear.) Yes, she agreed, since many employees work late at night, there is a need for a security program, but the cards and locked doors should be replaced with a guard in the lobby because "the cards make the place seem like an armed camp, and they scare people."

Trying to link this fear of the cards to pain or death, I asked Arlene what it is that people fear. "The cards increase the danger," she explained, "because their presence says there's something here worth taking."

Could it be, I asked, that the cards actually reduce fear and risk since their use means that the offices are not accessible to just anyone off the street? No, she told me, people don't think that way. "They'd rather not be reminded of the risk." Arlene explained that metal detectors at airports conjure the specter of hijacking as opposed to reassuring people. Tamper-proof packaging does not add comfort, it adds apprehension, and, she noted, "It's just an invitation to tamper."

At the end of her confident presentation about human nature and why the cards scared people, I asked if she agreed that there could be hazard to employees if the doors were left unlocked. "Of course I do. I was assaulted one night when I worked late at my last job. The doors weren't kept locked there, and this guy walked right in. There was nobody else in the whole building — so don't tell me about danger!"

With that story, Arlene revealed who was afraid of the cards. She also clearly stated her philosophy for managing her fear: "*Don't tell me about danger.*" Later, after questioning me extensively about safety in her apartment, and on the subway, and while shopping, and when dating, she agreed to use the cards.

▪ ▪ ▪

Occasionally, we answer fears that aren't calling; other times we ignore those that are, and sometimes, like physician Bill McKenna, we fall somewhere in the middle.

"My wife, Linda, was on a business trip, so I took the girls out to dinner. We got home late; I made sure they got to sleep and then got into bed myself. As I was dozing off I heard a noise downstairs which for some reason really scared me. It wasn't that it was loud, and I don't even recall exactly what it sounded like, but I absolutely couldn't shake it. So I got out of bed and went downstairs to be sure everything was all right. I made a quick walk around and then went back to bed. A half hour later, I heard a sound so quiet that I still don't know how it woke me; it was the sound of someone else's breathing. I turned on the light, and there was this guy standing in the middle of the room with my gun in his hand and our CD player under his arm."

If Bill's mission on his walk downstairs was "to be sure everything was all right," as he put it, then he succeeded admirably. If, though, it was to answer the survival signal — to accept the gift of fear — he failed. When he heard that noise downstairs, if he had consciously linked the fear he felt to its possible dangerous outcomes — as his intuition had already done — he would have recognized that the stakes were high, and he might have conducted his search with the goal of finding risk as opposed to the goal of finding nothing.

Had he responded to his fear with respect, he would have found the intruder before the intruder found his gun. If he had said, in effect, "Since I feel fear, I know there is some reason, so what is it?"

then he could have brought into consciousness what his intuition already knew and what he later told me: The living room light was on when he got home, the cat had somehow gotten outside and was waiting on the porch, an unusual old car was parked near his driveway, its engine clinking as it cooled, and on and on. Only in the context of all these factors did that noise, which would have been inconsequential at another time, cause fear.

Bill McKenna and his daughters (four and five years old) were held at gunpoint by the intruder for more than an hour. The man let the girls sit on the floor of the master bedroom and watch a videotape of *Beauty and the Beast.* He told Bill that he needed time to make what he called "the most difficult decision of my life." He asked, "Have you ever had a really tough problem?" and Bill nodded.

Bill told me he was alert until the intruder left, but that he did not feel any fear whatsoever. "When someone's already got you at gunpoint, it's too late for fear. I had more important things to focus on, like keeping the girls calm by showing them that I was okay — and keeping this guy calm. Anyway, my fear had come and gone, and after a while, that guy had come and gone too."

Bill's lack of dread, just like his original fear on hearing the noise, made sense. First, the burglar did not bring a gun with him, so he was not an intruder who expected or was prepared to kill. Second, his goal was fairly lightweight theft, as evidenced by the CD player he'd taken. Finally, he spoke his conscience when he said he was weighing "the most difficult decision" of his life. A man willing to kill would have little need to discuss his personal exploration of right and wrong with his intended victims. In fact, he would dehumanize and distance his victims, certainly not bring them into his deliberations.

The intruder not only left, but he left the CD player. He did the family another favor too: He took the gun, which now won't be available to some more dangerous intruder in the future. (Bill is not replacing it.) Bill let the girls watch the rest of the movie before putting them back to bed. They still recall the night the "policeman with the gun" visited, and it is not a traumatic story they tell. They didn't sense fear in Bill because, just as he told me, he didn't feel it.

Real fear is objective, but it's clear that we are not. Meg was afraid of being killed, and Celia was afraid of being followed, even when there was nobody there. Arlene was afraid of access cards even though they added to her safety. Bill was not afraid of an intruder even when the man was standing in his bedroom with a gun. This all proves, as I noted early in the book, that we have odd ways of evaluating risk. Smoking kills more people every day than lightning does in a decade, but there are people who calm their fear of being struck by lightning during a storm — by smoking a cigarette. It isn't logical, but logic and anxiety rarely go together.

I recently met a middle-aged couple from Florida who had just obtained licenses to carry concealed handguns. The man explained why: "Because if some guy walks into a restaurant and opens fire, like happened at Luby's in Texas, I want to be in a position to save lives."

Of course, there are plenty of things he could carry on his belt that would be far more likely to save lives in a restaurant. An injection of adrenaline would treat anaphylactic shock (the potentially lethal allergic reaction to certain foods). Or he could carry a small sharp tube to give emergency tracheotomies to people who are choking to death. When I asked him if he carried one of those, he said, "I could never stick something into a person's throat!" But he could send a piece of lead into a person's flesh like a rocket.

Statistically speaking, the man and his wife are far more likely to shoot each other than to shoot some criminal, but his anxiety wasn't caused by fear of death — if it were, he would shed the excess forty pounds likely to bring on a heart attack. His anxiety is caused by fear of people, and by the belief that he cannot predict violence. *Anxiety, unlike real fear, is always caused by uncertainty.*

It is caused, ultimately, by predictions in which you have little confidence. When you predict that you will be fired from your job and you are certain the prediction is correct, you don't have anxiety about being fired. You might have anxiety about the things you can't predict with certainty, such as the ramifications of losing the job. Predictions in which you have high confidence free you to respond, adjust, feel sadness, accept, prepare, or to do whatever is needed. Accordingly, anxiety is reduced by improving your predictions, thus increasing your certainty. It's worth doing, because the word *anxiety,* like *worry,* stems from a root that means "to choke," and that is just what it does to us.

Our imaginations can be the fertile soil in which worry and anxiety grow from seeds to weeds, but when we assume the imagined outcome is a sure thing, we are in conflict with what Proust called an inexorable law: "Only that which is absent can be imagined." In other words, what you imagine — just like what you fear — is not happening.

■ ■ ■

Donna is a twenty-nine-year-old filmmaker from New York who courageously left her job and drove to Los Angeles hoping to make significant documentaries. She used her brightness and enthusiasm to get a meeting with a prominent film executive. About ten miles from the meeting, her old car decided it wasn't going to take her any farther, and she was stuck directly in the center of the street. Immediately, she linked being late to all of its worst possible outcomes: "I will miss the meeting, and they won't agree to reschedule. If you keep someone like this waiting, your chances of a career are nil, so I'll be unable to pay the rent, I'll be tossed out of my apartment, I'll end up on welfare," and on and on. Because this type of imaginative linking builds a scenario one step at a time, it feels like logic, but it is just an impersonation of logic. It is also one of our dumbest creative exercises.

A passing car carrying a man and woman slowed to look at Donna, and the man called out an offer of help. Donna waved them on. Very stressed, she got out of her car and ran down the street looking for a service station, along the way adding inventive chapters to the story of her financial ruin. She noticed the same car driving alongside her, but she just kept running. Reaching a pay phone, she called the studio executive's office and explained she'd be late. As she predicted, they told her the meeting could not be rescheduled. The career that she envisioned ended in that phone booth.

Donna slumped and started crying just as that same car pulled up slowly toward the phone booth. Even though these people had been following her, she wasn't afraid. The man stayed in the car while the woman got out and tapped on the glass, saying, "Is that you?" Through tears, Donna looked up to see the face of Jeanette, a friend with whom she'd shared an apartment in college.

Jeanette and her boyfriend rushed Donna to the meeting (she didn't get the job) and then took her to lunch. Within a few weeks, Donna and Jeanette were partners in a new business of finding art and antiques around the world for resale in America. They became so successful that within two years, Donna had saved enough money to co-finance her first documentary film.

Amid all of Donna's creative projections when her car broke down, she hadn't included the possibility that it would lead to a reunion with an old friend with whom she'd form a business that would take her around the world and give her the resources to make her own films.

Few of us predict that unexpected, undesired events will lead to great things, but very often we'd be more accurate if we did. The history of invention is filled with perceived failures that became unpredicted successes (à la James Watt's failure to get a pump working and his inadvertent success at inventing the vacuum). I have gotten great benefits from taking the voice of skepticism that I used to apply to my intuition and applying it instead to the dreaded outcomes I imagined were coming. Worry will almost always buckle under a vigorous interrogation.

If you can bring yourself to apply your imagination to finding the possible favorable outcomes of undesired developments, even if only as an exercise, you'll see that it fosters creativity. This suggestion is much more than a way to find the silver lining our grandmothers encouraged us to look for. I include it in this book because creativity is linked to intuition, and intuition is the way out of the most serious challenges you might face. Albert Einstein said that when you follow intuition, "The solutions come to you, and you don't know how or why."

A young man named Andrew had promised to take a much-anticipated date to a particular movie she wanted to see. At first he couldn't locate a theater showing it, and once he found where it was playing, he couldn't get tickets. He and the thus-far-unimpressed girl waited in line for a second-choice film, which they learned after forty minutes of standing was also sold out. Andrew's date was a failure, and his hopes of what young men hope for were dashed. He was, predictably, very disappointed, and he was also annoyed at the hassle of trying to see a film. He did not immediately say to himself, "Maybe this discouraging evening will compel me to develop a new computerized phone-in system through which moviegoers can choose the film they want to see, learn where it's playing, and actually purchase the tickets in advance."

But that's exactly what Andrew Jarecki did, founding MovieFone (which you may know as 777-FILM), the innovative service used each week by millions of people in cities all over America. (He also married that date.)

Having told so many stories of risk and harm, I share some with more favorable outcomes to make this point: Worry is a choice, and the creative genius we apply to it can be used differently, also by choice. This truth is mildly interesting when the stakes are low, like worrying about a job interview or a date, but in the situations with the highest stakes, this same truth can save your life.

▪ ▪ ▪

I've spent much of my career trying to make accurate predictions of which bad thing might happen next. Admittedly, this skill has been a powerful asset, because people are eager to hear forecasts of every possible tragedy. Just one indication of this is the fact that television in large cities devotes as much as forty hours a day to telling us about those who have fallen prey to some disaster and to exploring what calamities may be coming: "NEW STUDY REVEALS THAT CELLULAR PHONES CAN KILL YOU. LEARN THE FACTS AT ELEVEN!" "CONTAMINATED TURKEY DINNER KILLS THREE! COULD YOUR FAMILY BE NEXT!?"

Silly and alarming news promos are of more than passing interest to me because understanding how they work is central to understanding how fear works in our culture. We watch attentively because our survival requires us to learn about things that may hurt us. That's why we slow down at the scene of a terrible car accident. It isn't out of some unnatural perversion; it is to learn. Most times, we draw a lesson: "He was probably drunk"; "They must have tried to pass"; "Those little sports cars are sure dangerous"; "That intersection is blind." Our theory is stored away, perhaps to save our lives another day.

Ernest Becker explains that "man's fears are fashioned out of the ways in which he perceives the world." Animals know what to fear by instinct, "but an animal who has no instinct [man] has no programmed fears." Well, the local news has programmed them for us, and the audience is virtually guaranteed by one of the strongest forces in nature — our will to survive. Local news rarely provides new or relevant information about safety, but its urgent delivery mimics importance and thus gets our attention, much as someone would if they burst into your home and yelled, "Don't go outside or you'll be killed! Listen to me to save your life!" That's the way local television news works as a business. Fear has a rightful place in our lives, but it isn't the marketplace.

(On a personal note, even though I have a professional interest in hazard and risk, I never watch the local television news and haven't for years. Try this and you'll likely find better things to do before going to sleep than looking at thirty minutes of disturbing images presented with artificial urgency and the usually false implication that it's critical for you to see it.)

Electronic scare tactics come in several forms. When news is scarce, they march out an update on some old story. You might recall the bizarre kidnapping of a busload of schoolchildren in a California town called Chowchilla. The perpetrators buried the bus — with the children inside — in a massive ditch at a rock quarry. The story ended with the rescue of the twenty-six children and the arrest of the kidnappers. A year later came the update: All the same footage was shown, the original incident was told again in its entirety, and a reporter walked down a Chowchilla street offering this foreboding wrap-up: "But the people of this little town still awaken in the night, worried that it could all happen again."

They do? Worried that what could all happen again — another

mass kidnapping with a busload of their children buried in a rock quarry? I don't think so. These often ridiculous summaries are used to give news stories significance, or to leave them uncertain and thus open for still further stories, e.g., "Whether more will die remains to be seen." In the world of local news, frightening stories never end. We rarely hear the words "And that's that."

Local news has several favorite phrases, one of which is "Police made a gruesome discovery today in [name of local city]." The satellite age has increased the library of available shocking footage, so that now, if there wasn't a something grisly in your town, you might hear, "Police made a gruesome discovery today in Reno," or Chicago, or Miami, or even Caracas. It may not be local, but it is gruesome, and there's some footage, so what the hell. Whether they go back in time to find something shocking or go around the planet, in neither case is the information necessarily valuable or relevant to your life. Local news has become little more than what *Information Anxiety* author Richard Saul Wurman calls "a list of inexorable deaths, accidents, and catastrophes — the violent wallpaper of our lives."

I discuss all this here as much more than a pet peeve. Understanding how the television news works and what it does to you is directly relevant to your safety and well-being. First, the fear of crime is itself a form of victimization. But there is a much more practical issue involved: Being exposed to constant alarm and urgency shell shocks us to the point that it becomes impossible to separate the survival signal from the sound bite. Because it's sensationalism and not informationalism, we get a distorted view of what actually poses a hazard to us.

Imagine a widely televised report: "Dolphin attacks swimmer!" Such a story would make a new connection in the minds of literally millions of people: Dolphins are dangerous to man (which they are not). Though unusual animal-attack stories are good news fodder, humans are not the favored prey of any predator. (We are somewhat bony, low on meat, and smart as the dickens.) The point is that your survival brilliance is wasted when you focus on unlikely risks.

Unfortunately, just giving a criminal hazard a name gives it a place in our minds and gives us another reason to feel unwarranted fear of people. Think back to the so-called freeway shootings in Los Angeles. Though television news was full of interviews with motorists pointing out bullet holes in their windshields, the fact is that there were fewer freeway shootings that year than there had been the year before. There was no trend, no rash of attacks, no criminal fad, nothing any different than what had happened before or has happened since. But we don't hear anything these days about freeway shootings. Are there no more hot days and angry armed motorists stuck in slow traffic? Have freeway shootings really stopped, or have the reports stopped because that story is an episode from last season?

The only real trend is the way local news finds two similar stories with some striking visuals or an overly excited interview, gives the risk a name, and repeats it for a while with different victims. When such a crime succeeds, the local news will tell people how it was done. Thus, supposedly new forms of criminal violence can indeed become fads — through the very same method that other fads do: It's called advertising.

A serious-looking news celebrity tells of the most current danger we simply must know about to save our lives: "I'm standing at the scene of the latest follow-home robbery to hit this posh westside neighborhood, part of a growing trend of random attacks. How can you avoid this terror?" This will be followed by a list of cautions, some of them so obvious as to be comical (e.g., "Don't let strangers into your car"). There will be an interview with someone seriously billed as a "follow-home robbery expert." Then suddenly one day you'd think such robberies had just stopped, because local television will move on to the next criminal hazard. Soon it will be "Robbers who hide out in your purse until you get home!" followed by a checklist of warning signs to look out for: "Purse feels extra heavy; purse difficult to close; unusual sounds coming from purse . . ."

Though television news would have us think differently, the important question is not how we might die, but rather "How shall we live?" and that is up to us.

▪ ▪ ▪

In my life and work, I've seen the darkest parts of the human soul. (At least I hope they are the darkest.) That has helped me see more clearly the brightness of the human spirit. Feeling the sting of violence myself has helped me feel more keenly the hand of human kindness.

Given the frenzy and the power of the various violence industries, the fact that most Americans live without being violent is a sign of something wonderful in us. In resisting both the darker sides of our species and the darker sides of our heritage, it is everyday Americans, not the icons of big-screen vengeance, who are the real heroes. Abraham Lincoln referred to the "better angels of our nature," and they must surely exist, for most of us make it through every day with decency and cooperation.

Having spent years preparing for the worst, I have finally arrived at this wisdom: Though the world is a dangerous place, it is also a safe place. You and I have survived some extraordinary risks, particularly given that every day we move in, around, and through powerful machines that could kill us without missing a cylinder: jet airplanes, subways, buses, escalators, elevators, motorcycles, cars—conveyances that carry a few of us to injury but most of us to the destinations we have in mind. We are surrounded by toxic chemicals, and our homes are hooked up to explosive gases and lethal currents of electricity.

Most frightening of all, we live among armed and often angry countrymen. Taken together, these things make every day a high-stakes obstacle course our ancestors would shudder at, but the fact is we are usually delivered through it. Still, rather than be amazed at the wonder of it all, millions of people are actually looking for things to worry about.

Near the end of his life, Mark Twain wisely said, "I have had a great many troubles, but most of them never happened."

▪ ▪ ▪

You now know a great deal about predicting and avoiding violence, from the dangers posed by strangers to the brutality inflicted on friends and family members, from the everyday violence that can touch anyone to the extraordinary crimes that will touch only a few. With your intuition better informed, I hope you will have less unwarranted fear of people. I hope you'll harness and respect your ability to recognize survival signals. Most important, I hope you'll see hazard only in those stormclouds where it exists and live life more fully in the clear skies between them.

ACKNOWLEDGMENTS

When you learn the way I have, you have many teachers to thank for many lessons. In the interest of space, I won't list all that I learned from my agent and dear friend Kathy Robbins, or from my exceptional editor and coach, Bill Phillips. I'll say only that what they've taught me is certainly apparent to the people who read and commented on my early drafts: the passionate Erika Holzer, the logical Ted Calhoun, the intuitive Eric Eisner, the encouraging Sam Merrill, the light-hearted Harvey Miller, the legal-minded Madeleine Schachter, the honest Rod Lurie, the protective Victoria Principal, the supportive Kate Bales, Betsy Uhrig, Lara Harris, David Joliffe, Linden Gross, Allison Burnett, and my compulsively accurate chief-researcher, Connie Nitzschner. Thanks to you all.

Thanks to Charles Hayward, whose support I felt from start to finish, and to Sarah Crichton and Peter Benedek.

When it comes to following spears into the jungle, I have been blessed with three great guides: Park Dietz, Walt Risler, and John Monahan. Thanks to each of you for the light of your intellect and experience.

Thanks to Bryan Vosekuill and Dr. Robert Fein at the U.S. Secret Service for bringing me along on your exploration of new ideas.

Your *Exceptional Case Study Project* is itself exceptional, and will reduce the risks in the world's most dangerous job: president of the United States.

Thanks to Attorney General Janet Reno and Director Eduardo Gonzalez at the U.S. Marshals Service for your encouragement on MOSAIC, and to Steve Weston and his staff at the California State Police Special Investigations Unit, to Robert Ressler, Clinton Van Zandt, Jim Wright and Roy Hazlewood from the FBI Behavioral Sciences Unit, to several unnamed colleagues at the Central Intelligence Agency, to Dennis Chapas and his staff at the U.S. Supreme Court, to Sheriff Sherman Block, Assistant Sheriff Mike Graham, and Lt. Sue Tyler at the L.A. County Sheriff's Department for your enthusiasm and support, to John White and Jim MacMurray at LAPD, to Steven Devlin at Boston University, Jim Perotti at Yale University, William Zimmerman and Richard Lopez at the U.S. Capitol Police, to Thomas Taylor of the National Governor's Security Association. Thanks to my friend Robert Martin, who conceived of and founded LAPD's Threat Management Unit.

To those who attended my firm's first Threat Assessment and Management Conference way back in 1983: Walt Risler, Mike Carrington, Cappy Gagnon, Bill Mattman, Burton Katz, and Pierce Brooks. You put me through a college of sorts, and I am grateful.

Thanks to the extraordinary friends whose lessons run throughout this book: Linda Shoemaker, Arthur Shurlock, Rosemary Clooney, Miguel, Gabriel, Monsita, Raphael and Maria Ferrer, Jeanne Martin, Gina Martin, Stan Freberg, Donna & Donna Freberg, Michael Gregory, Pamela, Portland and Morgan Mason, Peter, Alice, Andrea and Tom Lassally, Cortney Callahan, Gregory Orr, Cher, Joan Rivers, Allan Carr, Brooke Shields, Dr. Harry Glassman, Jennifer Grey, Michael Fox and Tracy Pollan, Ren, Ed Begley Jr., Tom Hanks and Rita Wilson, Tony and Becky Robbins, Nina Tassler, Jerry Levine, Jeff Goldblum, Lesley Ann Warren, Laura Dern, Ron Taft, Jaime Frankfurt, Jim Miller, David Viscott, Tom Nolan, Mark Bryan, Lisa

Gordon, Garry Shandling, Tom & Lynne Scott, Eric and Tanya Idle, Andrew and Nancy Jarecki.

And to other teachers of life lessons: Beatriz Foster, Jeff Jacobs, Norman Lear, Walt Zifkin, Norman Brokaw, Darrell Wright, Bill Sammeth, Bruce King, Sandy Litvak, Harry Grossman, Bob Weintzen, Michael Cantrell, Roger Davies, Jim Chafee, Gary Beer, Linden Gross, John Wilson, Walt Decuir, James "Chips" Stewart, Francis Pizzuli, Stephen Pollan, Donna Kail, Lisa Gaeta, Peggy Garrity, and Barbara Newman. A special thanks to Richard Berendzen, for courage and encouragement.

And thanks to those who taught me adult lessons about family violence and who work so hard to reduce it: Scott Gordon, Marcia Clark, Chris Darden, Gil Garcetti, Bill Hodgman, Carol Arnett, Casey Gwinn, Tom Sirkel, Betty Fisher, and to all the members of the Victory Over Violence Board. To the Goldman family, and to Peter Gelblum and Daniel Petrocelli: thanks for having me on your team.

And to a few friends who are important life-models for me and many others: Oprah Winfrey, Robert Redford, Tina Turner, Michael Eisner. Each of you has taught me so much about honor, integrity and responsibility.

Thanks to Steven Spielberg, Barbra Streisand, Meryl Streep, Steve Martin, Tom Hanks, and the too-few others who have proven that movies can teach more than just clever new ways to kill bad guys who are holding hostages in a skyscraper, aircraft carrier, airport, airplane, train, subway, or bus.

And thanks for your courage to: Theresa Saldana, Cheryle Randall, Ruben and Lisa Blades, Jackie Dyer, and Olivia Newton-John.

Thanks to my co-workers at Gavin de Becker, Incorporated: Michael LaFever, David Batza, Tracy Spencer, Michael Kolb, Michelle Taylor, Robert Martin, David Falconer, Jo Ann Ugolini, John Jackson, Hank Rivera, Jeff Marquart, Raquel Rimando. And to those of you whose work is non-public: RNI, GCO, BMI, MDE, GPO, RGA, TJA, RMR, SMR, SAB, MVA, BWA, SBA, WHA, NLI, JHA, JJC, KKI, GTO, SMN, SMA, APR, ALI, ESO, MMI, SMN, JDE. You and your staffs have been part of something important, and I am amazed at your ability, professionalism, dedication and results. Mostly, I am proud to be on your team.

To my friends in Fiji: I came to study you, and then I came to love you.

This book would not have been written without Charlie Rose, who introduced me to Richard Berendzen and Sherwin Nuland, and who introduces us all to so many extraordinary writers.

Finally, my gratitude and love to Michelle Pfeiffer, who is either my dear friend or the best actress in the world (or both), to Shaun Cassidy (*mi hermano*), for twenty-four years of friendship and encouragement, and to Carrie Fisher, who thanked me at the end of one of her books by saying: "without whom these acknowledgments would never have been possible." Carrie: without you, these acknowledgments would never have been possible.

And of course, thanks to Kelly.

▪ APPENDIX ONE ▪

SIGNALS AND PREDICTIVE STRATEGIES

PINS (pre-incident indicators)
FORCED TEAMING
LOAN SHARKING
TOO MANY DETAILS
UNSOLICITED PROMISES
TYPECASTING
DISCOUNTING THE WORD "NO"
THE INTERVIEW
RULE OF OPPOSITES
LIST THREE ALTERNATIVE PREDICTIONS
JACA (Justification, Alternatives, Consequences, Ability)
RICE (Reliability, Importance, Cost, Effectiveness)

THE MESSENGERS OF INTUITION

Nagging feelings
Persistent thoughts
Humor
Wonder
Anxiety
Curiosity
Hunches
Gut feelings
Doubt
Hesitation
Suspicion
Apprehension
Fear

▪ APPENDIX TWO ▪

HELP-GIVING RESOURCES

National Domestic Violence Hotline:

1-800-799-SAFE. This hotline provides information, support, and referral to battered women's shelters in your area.

Impact:

Full-contact self-defense training for women using padded instructors who pose as assailants. Courses teach verbal skills to avoid confrontation, ways to make victimization less likely, and techniques designed specifically for the physical advantages women bring to self-defense. Available in most major American cities. For additional information, call IMPACT at 1-800-345-5425.

Big Brothers/Big Sisters of America:

Call 215-567-7000 for a number in your area and details on how these exceptional mentoring programs work.

Alanon Family Groups:

Help families affected by alcoholism and addiction. Special groups for children and teens are available in most areas. Alanon is reached through directory assistance or through a local office of Alcoholics Anonymous. Or call 1-800-344-2666 (in Canada: 1-800-443-4525). Internet Web page: www.al-anon.alateen.org.

National Victim Center, *INFOLINK* Program:

Call 1-800-FYI-CALL for comprehensive information and referrals to more than eight thousand victim-assistance programs across the nation. Each caller can receive up to five of the seventy information bulletins free of charge. All *INFOLINK* bulletins are available on the Internet at www.nvc.org.

CIVITAS Initiative:

A nonprofit organization whose mission is to discover and broadly communicate real-world solutions to problems impeding the optimal development of children. CIVITAS partners with public and private institutions to support innovations in any area that will have a systemic impact on the health and welfare of maltreated children. If you are interested in investing in the healthy development of children, please call or write:

CIVITAS Initiative
16 East Pearson
Chicago, IL 60611
312-915-6484
http://www.bcm.tmc.edu/civitas

Victory Over Violence:

The official advisory board to the Domestic Violence Council, an organization of people from the entertainment industry, business, and government dedicated to increasing public awareness and providing direct support to families fleeing from domestic violence. Among its many projects, VOV funds nursing care for women and children at shelters, provides art therapy for children, coordinates cosmetic-surgery programs for women disfigured by domestic violence injuries, and provides children's play areas at district attorney's offices so women can give crime reports without being overheard by their young children. We welcome your help, financial and otherwise.

VICTORY OVER VIOLENCE BOARD

Victoria Principal, Co-chair
Gavin de Becker, Co-chair

Ed Begley Jr.
Roseanne Donnelly
Carrie Fisher
Jeff Goldblum
Jennifer Grey
Stephanie Kopfliesch
Jerry McGee
Michelle Pfeiffer
John Strozdas
Lesley Ann Warren
Laura Dern
Betty Fischer
Mark Fleischer
Dr. Harry Glassman
David E. Kelley
Marlee Matlin
Rosie O'Donnell
Meg Ryan
Caroline Thompson

Scott Gordon, Linda Ikeda-Vogel
Co-chairs, Domestic Violence Council

Carol Arnett
Executive Director, Domestic Violence Council

Victory Over Violence
3175 West 6th Street
Los Angeles, CA 90020

▪ APPENDIX THREE ▪

GUN SAFETY

For some people, banning handguns is the psychological equivalent of government-imposed castration, so let me be clear: I am not challenging our so-called right to bear arms (in whose name, by the way, more Americans have died at home than have died at war). And I am not advocating gun control. I am advocating something far more practical, something we might call *bullet control.*

I propose that we hold gun manufacturers to the same product-liability standards we require for every other consumer product. Imagine if caustic drain opener were sold in easy-pour, flip-top, pistol-grip dispensers made attractive to children by the endorsement of celebrities. Now, drain openers can hurt people, but they aren't made for that purpose. Handguns are made precisely for that purpose, so shouldn't manufacturers be required to build in safety features that have been technologically practical for decades? Even electric drills have safety triggers, yet revolvers do not.

Guns could have components that inhibit firing by children, or technologies that allow operation only in the hands of the owner (with a coded ring or wristband, for example, or a combination lock built into the gun). In the meantime, it's easier to shoot most handguns than it is to open a bottle of children's vitamins.

Speaking of tamper-proof containers, the design of billions of bottles of consumer products was changed after the deaths of eight people from poisoned Tylenol — a tragedy completely beyond the control of the manufacturer — while gun makers knowingly and enthusiastically produce products that kill five hundred Americans *each week,* and we don't require a single safety feature. Does it make sense to you that manufacturers who sell products specifically designed to inflict tissue damage, to do it efficiently, rapidly, portably, and lethally, have fewer safety requirements than virtually every other product you use?

Gun companies will say their buyers understand and accept the risks of firearms, but that doesn't answer for the forty New Yorkers killed by stray bullets in one year alone, or for all the other people who will become unwilling consumers of ammunition.

To be certain the gun manufacturers have no misunderstanding, let me do right now what I hope more Americans will do, which is to put them on notice:

> I, for one, do not accept the avoidable risks posed by your products. As a potential victim, I do not sign on to any implied agreement with Colt or Smith & Wesson or Ruger, and I hold you entirely accountable for your failure to build in child-safe and other locking features that would clearly and predictably reduce deaths.

Some gun owners explain that they needn't lock their weapons because they don't have children. Well, other people do have children, and they will visit your home one day. The plumber who answers your weekend emergency will bring along his bored nine-year-old son, and he will find your gun.

The other oft-quoted reason for not locking guns is that they must be ready to fire immediately in an emergency, perhaps in the middle of the night. Imagine being in the deepest sleep and then a split second later finding yourself driving a truck as it careens down a dark highway at seventy miles per hour. That is the condition gun advocates vigorously insist remain available to them, the ability to sit up in bed and start firing bullets into the dark without pausing to operate a safety lock. An Associated Press story described one gun owner who didn't even have to sit up in bed; she just reached under her pillow, took her .38 in hand, and, thinking it was her asthma medicine, shot herself in the face.

Every year in California alone close to 100,000 guns are stolen. The people of my state more than make up for the loss by purchasing 650,000 guns each year. Little wonder that in a typical week, almost a thousand Californians are shot. The majority survive to tell about their ordeal, so that those who hear the awful tales can rush out . . . and buy guns. There's a lot to think about here, but my main point is that those stolen guns would be worthless and harmless if a locking system made them inoperable.

In the meantime, if you own a gun, you can do something the manufacturers have neglected to do: lock it, not just the cabinet or the closet or the drawer, but the gun itself. This paragraph is a survival signal for some child, because that is who will likely find the gun that the owner felt certain was too high to reach or too hard to fire.

Gun locks are available at gun stores and many sporting-goods stores. Though not marketed specifically for guns, many types of padlocks can be placed through the trigger guard behind the trigger of revolvers. An excellent one for this purpose is the Sesamee lock manufactured by Corbin, which is available at many hardware stores. An advantage of this lock is that if the gun is found by an intruder and aimed at you, the lock is clearly visible to you on the gun. The Corbin Sesamee lock also allows the buyer to program in his or her own combination, making rapid removal easy if one knows the combination.

▪ APPENDIX FOUR ▪

WORKPLACE VIOLENCE

Understanding & Preventing Workplace Violence is a series of videotapes that provide advanced training for managers of government agencies, large corporations, and universities. They are not intended for the general public. The program includes interviews with perpetrators and victims of major acts of violence in the workplace. Co-written by Park Dietz and Gavin de Becker (both of whom are extensively interviewed), it received the Mercury Video Awards Gold Medal for best training tape and was rated by the Employee Assistance Association of America at 100 out of 100 points.

Narrated by Efrem Zimbalist Jr. and produced by Emmy-nominated filmmaker Gregory Orr, the program covers such topics as predicting violent behavior, the warning signs of workplace violence, the legal issues, pre-employment screening, and the termination process. Topics were guided by an advisory board of representatives from Kraft Foods, the Walt Disney Company, the United States Marshals Service, Pfizer, and Target Stores.

Originally sold for $1,750 (with proceeds benefiting the National Victims Center), the eight-part, four-hour series can be purchased for $875 through:

Video Distribution
3727 West Magnolia Boulevard, Suite 162
Burbank, CA 91510-7711

▪ APPENDIX FIVE ▪

GAVIN DE BECKER, INCORPORATED

Gavin de Becker, Incorporated, provides consultation and support to public figures, government agencies, corporations, and others who face high-stakes predictions of violence. The forty-six-member firm advises media figures on safety and privacy. The Protective Security Division (PSD) provides logistical support, advance work, and protective coverage for public figures.

The Threat Assessment and Management Division (TAM) evaluates and assesses inappropriate, alarming, and threatening communications. It provides expert-witness consultation and testimony on court cases that involve stalking, threats, and the foreseeability or prevention of violence. It also develops artificial intuition systems, which currently include:

MOSAIC-2: Used by government agencies to evaluate inappropriate communications to public officials.

MOSAIC-3: Used to evaluate threats to judges and prosecutors.

MOSAIC-5: Used by corporations, universities, and other large organizations for evaluation of angry current or former employees who might pose a hazard to others in the workplace.

MOSAIC-10: Used to assess risks to reproductive health facilities.

MOSAIC-20: Used by police and prosecutorial agencies to determine which domestic violence situations are most likely to escalate.

MOSAIC-50: Used to evaluate which child-abuse cases are most likely to escalate.

(Note: MOSAIC 2, 3, and 10 are available to government agencies only.)

Gavin de Becker, Incorporated, provides advanced training on the assessment of threats, case management, and the prediction of violent behavior to police departments, prosecutors, state and federal agencies, large corporations, and universities. One-, two-, and three-day courses are taught at Boulder Creek, the firm's eighteen-acre training facility just outside Los Angeles.

Gavin de Becker, Incorporated
11684 Ventura Boulevard, Suite 440
Studio City, CA 91604

Fax: 818-506-0426

On-line address: INFOLINE@GDBINC.COM

Regular citizens facing high-stakes predictions involving stalkers, angry employees, or abusive spouses can learn about assessment resources through the Gavin de Becker, Incorporated, Web page: WWW.GDEBINC.COM.

▪ APPENDIX SIX ▪

THE ELEMENTS OF PREDICTION

1) *MEASURABILITY OF OUTCOME*
   4 obvious, clear
   3 discoverable and shared definition
   1 discoverable, but fluid or inconsistent
   0 not measurable/undiscoverable

2) *VANTAGE*
   3 perspective view
   2 proxy view
   0 obstructed or no view

3) *IMMINENCE*
   4 imminent
   2 foreseeable
   0 remote

4) *CONTEXT*
   3 fully revealed
   0 concealed

5) *PRE-INCIDENT INDICATORS*
   5 several, reliable, detectable
   3 few, reliable, detectable
   0 unreliable or undetectable

6) *EXPERIENCE*
   5 extensive with both outcomes
   3 with both outcomes
   2 with one outcome
   0 elemental/partial/irrelevant

7) *COMPARABLE EVENTS*
   4 substantively comparable
   1 comparable
   0 not comparable

8) *OBJECTIVITY*
   2 believes either outcome is possible
   0 believes only one outcome or neither outcome is possible

9) *INVESTMENT*
   3 invested in outcome
   1 emotionally invested in outcome
   0 uninvested in outcome

10) *REPLICABILITY*
   5 easily replicable
   2 replicable by sample or proxy
   0 impractical or not replicable

11) *KNOWLEDGE*
   2 relevant and accurate
   0 partial or inaccurate

This scale helps determine if a given prediction can be made successfully (which is distinct from whether it will be made successfully). To evaluate a prediction, answer the eleven questions described in chapter 6 by selecting from the range of possible answers above. Then add up the total points.

22 or lower:	Not reliably predictable, a matter of chance
23–27:	Low likelihood of success
28–32:	Predictable
32 or higher:	Highly predictable

Note: The vantage question asks if the person making the prediction is in a position to observe the pre-incident indicators and context. If you can observe the situation and pre-incident indicators directly, then you have a Perspective View, but if you can only observe them through some medium (such as reports or other evidence), select Proxy View.

Following are some popular predictions, scored on the assumption that the person answering the question cares about the outcome and is as objective as possible:

WHO WILL WIN THE OSCAR? (predicted by film historian Rod Lurie)	22	mere chance
WILL A THREATENER WHO IS KNOWN AND IDENTIFIED SHOW UP IN THE PRESIDENT'S ENVIRONMENT WITH A WEAPON? (predicted by Bryan Vosekuill and Robert Fein of the U.S. Secret Service)	33	highly predictable
WILL A GOOD FRIEND DEFAULT ON A LOAN? (predicted by the lender, who frequently lends money to friends)	33	highly predictable
WILL THE DOG IN FRONT OF ME ATTACK ME? (predicted by dog behavior experts Jim and Leah Canino)	34	highly predictable
WILL A PUBLISHER BE INTERESTED IN A GIVEN BOOK IDEA? (predicted by literary agent Kathy Robbins)	37	highly predictable
HOW WILL A GIVEN BOOK SELL? (predicted by editor Bill Phillips at the time of paying advance to author)	29	predictable
WILL A GIVEN GUEST DO WELL ON A TALK SHOW NEXT WEEK? (predicted by Peter Lassally, executive producer of *The Tonight Show Starring*	30	predictable

Johnny Carson and *The Late Show Starring David Letterman*)

WILL A GIVEN STAND-UP COMEDIAN DO WELL ON A TALK SHOW NEXT WEEK? (predicted by Peter Lassally)	36	highly predictable

(This prediction ranks higher than that of a regular guest because we all share a common definition of what it means for a comedian to do well: The audience laughs. The definition of what it means for a regular guest to do well is more fluid — the audience could be informed, amused, or moved. This prediction also scores higher because a comedian's performance can be replicated with another audience first.)

WILL THERE BE A MAJOR EARTHQUAKE IN LOS ANGELES THIS YEAR? (predicted by geologist Gregory Dern)	22	mere chance
WILL THE PLANE I AM ON CRASH? (predicted by Tom Nolan, member "Million Mile Club," while flying smoothly cross-country)	24	low-success prediction
WILL MY SIX-YEAR-OLD LIKE A PARTICULAR FOOD? (predicted by Lisa Gordon, parent)	34	highly predictable
WILL I QUIT SMOKING NEXT WEEK? (predicted by a smoker who has quit in the past but started again)	35	highly predictable
WHICH PASSENGER BOARDING A FLIGHT, IF ANY, WILL ATTEMPT TO HIJACK THE PLANE? (predicted by the ticket agent)	19	mere chance

WHICH PERSON IN THE FRONT ROW, IF ANY, WILL LEAVE HIS SEAT

AND TRY TO GET ON STAGE DURING A CONCERT? (predicted during show by Jeff Marquart, professional bodyguard trained in "AMMO," Audience Management, Monitoring, and Observation)	33	highly predictable
WILL A GIVEN EMPLOYEE WHO KNOWS HE IS TO BE FIRED GO ON A SHOOTING SPREE? (predicted by David Batza, director of TAM at Gavin de Becker, Incorporated)	35	highly predictable
WILL AN ABUSIVE HUSBAND ESCALATE HIS VIOLENCE WHEN HE LEARNS HIS WIFE HAS FILED FOR DIVORCE? (predicted by his wife)	35	highly predictable

APPENDIX SEVEN

QUESTIONS FOR YOUR CHILD'S SCHOOL

- Do you have a policy manual or teacher's handbook? May I have a copy or review it here?
- Is the safety of students the first item addressed in the policy or handbook? If not, why not?
- Is the safety of students addressed at all?
- Are there policies addressing violence, weapons, drug use, sexual abuse, child-on-child sexual abuse, unauthorized visitors?
- Are background investigations performed on all staff?
- What areas are reviewed during these background inquiries?
- Who gathers the information?
- Who in administration reviews the information and determines the suitability for employment?
- What are the criteria for disqualifying an applicant?
- Does the screening process apply to all employees (teachers, janitors, lunchroom staff, security personnel, part-time employees, etc.)?
- Is there a nurse on-site at all times while children are present (including before and after school)?
- What is the nurse's education or training?
- Can my child call me at any time?
- May I visit my child at any time?
- What is your criteria for when to contact parents?
- What are the parent notification procedures?
- What are the student pick-up procedures?

- How is it determined that someone other than me can pick up my child?
- How does the school address special situations (custody disputes, child kidnapping concerns, etc.)?
- Are older children separated from younger children during recess, lunch, restroom breaks, etc.?
- Are acts of violence or criminality at the school documented? Are statistics maintained?
- May I review the statistics?
- What violence or criminality has occurred at the school during the last three years?
- Is there a regular briefing of teachers and administrators to discuss safety and security issues?
- Are teachers formally notified when a child with a history of serious misconduct is introduced to their class?
- What is the student-to-teacher ratio in class? During recess? During meals?
- How are students supervised during visits to the restroom?
- Will I be informed of teacher misconduct that might have an impact on the safety or well-being of my child?
- Are there security personnel on the premises?
- Are security personnel provided with written policies and guidelines?
- Is student safety the first issue addressed in the security policies and guidelines material? If not, why not?
- Is there a special background investigation conducted on security personnel, and what does it encompass?
- Is there any control over who can enter the grounds?
- If there is an emergency in a classroom, how does the teacher summon help?
- If there is an emergency on the playground, how does the teacher summon help?
- What are the policies and procedures covering emergencies (fire, civil unrest, earthquake, violent intruder, etc.)?
- How often are emergency drills performed?
- What procedures are followed when a child is injured?
- What hospital would my child be transported to in the event of a serious injury?
- Can I designate a different hospital? A specific family doctor?

- What police station responds to the school?
- Who is the school's liaison at the police department?

The school should have a ready answer to every one of these questions. Just the process of asking these questions (which can be done in writing) will identify those areas that have not been considered or thoroughly addressed by the school's officials.

RECOMMENDED READING

Abbot, Jack Henry. *In the Belly of the Beast: Letters from Prison.* New York: Random House, 1991.

Becker, Ernest. *The Denial of Death.* New York: Free Press, 1985.

Berendzen, Richard and Laura Palmer. *Come Here: A Man Copes with the Aftermath of Childhood Sexual Abuse.* New York: Random House, 1993.

Bingham, Roger and Carl Byker. *The Human Quest.* Princeton, NJ: Films for the Humanities and Sciences, 1995. Videocassette series.

Blankenhorn, David. *Fatherless America: Confronting Our Most Urgent Social Problem.* New York: Basic, 1995.

Branden, Nathaniel. *Honoring the Self: The Psychology of Confidence and Respect.* New York: Bantam, 1985.

Burke, James. *The Day the Universe Changed.* Boston: Little, Brown, 1995.

Clinton, Hillary Rodham. *It Takes a Village: And Other Lessons Children Teach Us.* New York: Simon and Schuster, 1996.

Dutton, Donald and Susan K. Golant. *The Batterer: A Psychological Profile.* New York: Basic, 1995.

Faludi, Susan. *Backlash: The Undeclared War Against American Women.* New York: Crown, 1991.

Fein, Ellen and Sherrie Schneider. *The Rules.* New York: Warner, 1995.

Goleman, Daniel. *Emotional Intelligence: Why It Can Matter More Than IQ.* New York: Bantam, 1995.

Gorey, Edward. *Amphigorey.* New York: Putnam, 1980.

Gross, Linden. *To Have or To Harm: True Stories of Stalkers and Their Victims.* New York: Warner, 1994.

Hare, Robert D. *Without Conscience: The Disturbing World of the Psychopaths Among Us.* New York: Pocket, 1995.

Jones, Ann R. and Susan Schechter. *When Love Goes Wrong: What to Do When You Can't Do Anything Right.* New York: HarperCollins, 1993.

Konner, Melvin. *Why the Reckless Survive: And Other Secrets of Human Nature.* New York: Viking, 1990.

Larson, Erik. *Lethal Passage: The Journey of a Gun.* New York: Crown, 1994.

Miller, Alice. *Banished Knowledge: Facing Childhood Injury.* New York: Doubleday, 1990.

Miller, Alice. *The Drama of the Gifted Child: The Search for the True Self.* New York: Basic, 1994.

Miller, Alice. *Thou Shalt Not Be Aware: Society's Betrayal of the Child.* New York: NAL-Dutton, 1991.

Miller, Alice. *The Untouched Key: Tracing Childhood Trauma in Creativity and Destructiveness.* New York: Doubleday, 1990.

Monahan, John. *Predicting Violent Behavior: An Assessment of Clinical Techniques.* Beverly Hills, CA: Sage, 1981.

Mones, Paul. *When a Child Kills.* New York: Pocket, 1992.

Morris, Desmond. *Bodytalk: The Meaning of Human Gestures.* New York: Crown, 1995.

Peck, M. Scott. *The Road Less Traveled: A New Psychology of Love, Traditional Values and Spiritual Growth.* New York: Simon and Schuster, 1993.

Pipher, Mary. *Reviving Ophelia: Saving the Selves of Adolescent Girls.* New York: Ballantine, 1995.

Ressler, Robert and Tom Schachtman. *Whoever Fights Monsters . . . : A Brilliant FBI Detective's Career-Long War Against Serial Killers.* New York: St. Martin's, 1993.

Schaum, Melita and Karen Parrish. *Stalked!: Breaking the Silence on the Crime Epidemic of the Nineties.* New York: Pocket, 1995.

Schickel, Richard. *Intimate Strangers: The Culture of Celebrity.* New York: Doubleday, 1985.

Snortland, Ellen. *Beauty Bites Beast: Awakening the Warrior Within Women and Girls.* Pasadena, CA: Trilogy Books, 1996.

Sulloway, Frank J. *Born to Rebel.* New York: David McKay, 1996.

Wrangham, Richard and Dale Peterson. *Demonic Males: Apes and the Origins of Human Violence.* Boston: Houghton Mifflin, 1996.

Wright, Robert. *The Moral Animal.* New York: Random House, 1995.

Wurman, Richard Saul. *Information Anxiety: What to Do When Information Doesn't Tell You What You Need to Know.* New York: Bantam, 1990.

Zunin, Leonard and Natalie Zunin. *Contact: The First Four Minutes.* Ballantine, 1986.

INDEX

Abbott, Jack Henry, 241, 244
ability, perceived, 95, 130, 156
See also JACA elements
ability belief, 246
abuse minimization, 175
acceptance and the word no, 201
See also discounting the word no
Ackerman, Diane, 27
African hunter-gatherers, 44
Against All Odds (film), 196
alcohol abuse, 174, 226
alternatives, perceived, 94–95, 130, 156
See also JACA elements
anger, 94
and assassins, 242
and righteous indignation, 167
and teenage murderers, 219
in young boys, 226–227
animals, 94
danger senses of, 79
dog behavior, 90
kangaroos, 36–37, 40
predators, 47
sharks, 283–285
anonymous calls, 81, 113–114
anxiety
and denial, 10–11
and fear, 281, 291–292
messenger of intuition, 73, 306
threats to kill, 103
apologies, 124–125
apprehension, 73, 306
and threats, 118
Arnett, Carol, 189
arsonists, 12
artificial intuition, 20, 313–314
See also MOSAIC software
assassins, 22–23, 23–24, 43, 98–99, 118, 231
media attention to, 247, 248–251
media names for, 249
precautions against, 251–253
attachment, language of, 92–93, 131
attention seeking, language of, 92–93

baby-sitter choices, 76–77
Bardo, Robert, 43, 46, 49, 237–244, 245–246, 251–252
battered children, 176–177
See also child abuse
battered women, 9, 173, 176
shelters for, 181, 190–192
battering syndrome, 178
Batza, David, 319
Becker, Ernest, 244, 278, 295
beginner's luck, 28
Begley, Ed, Jr., 308
behavioral predictions, 12, 80
rule of opposites in, 83
Bender, Theresa, 186

Bergman, Ingmar, quoted, 88
Black, Laura, 141–142, 147
blame it on others, 175
Blankenhorn, David, 225
bodyguards, 254–255, 263
body language, 92
  and cars, 39
Bodytalk (Morris), 92
bomb threats, 110–111
bookends, 177
Booth, John Wilkes, 250
Born to Rebel (Sulloway), 229
Bosket, Willie, 218
brain, 32
  as stagehand, 27
Branden, Nathaniel, 183
Bremer, Arthur, 241, 243, 244, 260
Brothers, Leslie, quoted, 57
Brown, Tom, 267–268
bullet control, 309
bullying, 174
Burke, David, 144–145, 167
Burke, James, 32, 37, 97

California Forestry Association, 71–72
Canino, Jim, 90, 317
Canino, Leah, 317
Cantrell, Michael, 34–36, 73
capital punishment, 9–10
Carson, Johnny, 131–133
Carson, Michael, 213
Carson, Suzan, 213
caution and precaution, 279
Central Intelligence Agency, 36–37
Chaney, Connie, 187
Chapman, Mark, 240, 245, 249
charm, 67
Cheers (TV series), 196
child abuse, 175–177, 224, 229–230
  baby-sitters and, 77–78
  heredity factor, 179
  and neglect, 49
  and parricide, 220
  statistics for, 9
  and violence, 221, 224, 225
  See also battered children
children
  primary caregivers of, 227–228
  at school, 12, 221–224
  and violence, 53
choices
  battered women, 178–179
  and spousal selection, 183
CIVITAS Initiative, 307
Clark, Marcia, 43, 242
Clinton, Bill, 53
coconut falling vignette, 106–107
cognitive processes, 26
Coming of Age in Samoa (Mead), 43–44
communication
  explicit rejection, 198–201
  instruments of, 109
  and intuition, 281
  threats, 104
comparisons
  and predictions, 68
  with violent people, 175
compartmentalization, 10
con artists, 55
conduct control strategies, 127
conflict, technology of, 11
Connally, John, 87
consequences, perceived, 95, 130, 156
  See also JACA elements
context, 69
  versus content, 106
  of details, 58–59
  and prediction of gravity, 80
  threats of violence, 104–106
control, 129, 136
  date stalkers, 207
  money and, 179–180
  rape as, 6
Coppola, Meredith, 172
court orders. *See* restraining orders
Cousteau, Jean-Michel, 283
crime of passion, 183–184
criminal-justice system, 11
curiosity, 73, 306
  and intuition, 28

danger
  and physical strength, 181
  warding off, 287
Darden, Christopher, 176
daredevils, 243
dark humor, 71–73
date stalking, 33–34, 188, 194–209

David and Goliath, 94
Davis, Tammy Marie, 186
The Day the Universe Changed (Burke), 32
death, fear of, 282
death threats, 22, 23, 28–29, 112
  prediction of, 108
de Becker, Gavin, 240, 312
  business description, 21–22
  childhood of, 20–21, 50–51
  at George Washington University, 107
  See also Gavin de Becker, Incorporated
deceptive smiles, 57
defenses
  descriptions of excuses, 184
  against forced teaming, 55–56
  against too many details, 59
Demonic Males (Wrangham, Peterson), 43
denial, 10, 23, 41
  and workplace violence, 145
The Denial of Death (Becker), 244, 277
Department of Justice, 12, 187–188, 246
Dern, Gregory, 318
Dern, Laura, 308
DETACH management plan, 206
Diamond, Jerry, 255–256
Dietz, Park, 147–148, 154, 216, 246, 259, 312
difficult childhoods, 48–49, 219–221, 226–230
dignity domino, 162
DiMaggio, Joe, 236
directness in terminating employees, 164–165
discounting the word no, 67, 201, 305
domestic violence, 172–193
  faxes from abusive men, 176
  management of, 181
Domestic Violence Council, Los Angeles, 173, 180, 189
Domestic Violence Division, Nashville Police Department, 52
Donnelly, Roseanne, 308
Dorogokupetz, Alexander Ivanovich
  threw an egg at Frank Sinatra, 233
doubt, 73, 306
  as messenger of intuition, 61
The Drama of the Gifted Child (Miller), 227
drug abuse, 174
  by parents, 225
  suicide attempts, 215
  by teenagers, 215
Dyer, Teak, 157–158

earthquake prediction, 101
Eckman, Paul, quoted, 57
Einstein, Albert, quoted, 43, 293
electronic scare tactics, 294–296
embarrassment, 174
  terminating employees, 162, 167
Emotional Intelligence (Goleman), 49, 218, 287
Employee Assistance Association of America, 312
employee fear, management of, 9
employee terminations, 16, 144, 162–167
  behavior prediction, 82, 84
  and violence, 148–151
employment interviews, 159–161
encouragement, 247
entitlement, language of, 92–93, 131
extortion, 114–117
extreme emotions, 175

facsimile bombs and stalkers, 23
family murderers, 219
Farley, Richard, 141–142, 167
Fatherless America (Blankenhorn), 225
fathers, role of, 225
fear, 5–7, 11, 73, 306
  of crime, 296
  management of, 23
  of public speaking, 282
  rules about, 281–283
  of spouse, 175
  as survival signal, 277
  versus worry, 285–287
Federal Aviation Administration, 136–137
feeling of apprehension, 4
Fein, Robert, 317
feminine intuition, 12
firearms. *See* guns

Fischer, Betty, 308
Fisher, Carrie, 216, 308
Fitzgerald, F. Scott, quoted, 131
Fleischer, Mark, 308
forced teaming, 55–56, 67, 305
Ford, Gerald, 236
foresight and hindsight, 18
Foster, Jodie, 234, 237
Fox, Rodney, 283–284
fraudulent heroism, 244–245
freeway shootings, 297
Freud, Sigmund, quoted, 43
Fromme, Squeaky, 236

Garcetti, Gil, 180
Garmanian, Rodney, 157–158
Gavin de Becker, Incorporated, 313–314
  Protective Security Division (PSD), 261–263, 267–268, 313
  Threat Assessment and Management Division (TAM), 257–259, 262, 313
Gein, Ed, 47
Gelenter, David, 72
gender issue
  intuition, 12
  offer of help, 63–64
genetic factors and children, 229
Glassman, Dr. Harry, 308
Goldblum, Jeff, 308
Goldman, Ron, 173
Goldman family, 172
Goleman, Daniel, 49, 218, 287
Goodall, Jane, 15
Gordon, Scott, 173, 176, 308
Gordon, Lisa, 318
Gorey, Edward, quoted, 57, 281
Gottesman, Irving, 229
The Graduate (film), 195–196
grandiosity, language of, 92–93
gravity prediction, 78–80
Great White Shark (Cousteau), 283
Grey, Jennifer, 308
Gross, Linda, 192
Gross, Linden, 186
guns, 11
  and assassins, 252–253
  safety and, 309–311
  in workplace, 142–143
  See also weapons
gut feelings, 13, 26, 71, 73, 306

harassment, 128–129, 140, 142
Hare, Robert D., 81
hazard assessment state, 25
hearing sense and survival, 68–69
heroism, 244–245
hesitation, 73, 306
Hicklin, Jim, 134–139, 147
hijacking, 32, 87
Hillside Strangler, 12
Hinckley, John, 234, 236, 245–246
hindsight *versus* foresight, 33
Hoffman, Dustin, 195–196, 200
Hollywood definitions of romance, 195–196
homicide prevention centers, 181
homicides, 43
  prediction of, 101–102
  spousal abuse, 186–190
  women in workplace, 9
Honoring the Self (Branden), 183
hostile employees, 83–84
hotlines
  Alanon, 306
  Big Brothers/Big Sisters, 306
  Domestic Violence Council, 180
  IMPACT, 306
  National Domestic Violence, 306
  National Victim Center, *INFOLINK* Program, 307
House of Games (Mamet film), 55
human behavior
  prediction of, 14–15, 40
  violence prediction and, 42–43
human predators, 47
humor, 306
Humphrey, Nicholas, 43
hunches, 73, 306

identity seeking, language of, 92–93
Ikeda-Vogel, Linda, 308
imagination and prediction, 42
imaginative theories, 13–14
IMPACT self-defense course, 65–66
imposters, 258
impulse behavior prediction, 82

inaccurate information risks, 36–37
inflexibility, 151, 175
Information Anxiety (Wurman), 82
inner voice, 38
insults and typecasting, 60
insurance and prediction, 86
internal guardian, 7
interview, the, 67, 69–70, 305
interviews, pre-employment, 157–161
In the Belly of the Beast (Abbott), 241
intimacy, lack of, 241
intimidation, 174
  versus threat, 108–109
introspection, 43
intuition, 4, 5, 12–14, 23, 28
  of dogs, 29–31
  interpretation of, 70
  versus knowledge retention, 28
  versus logic, 26
  origin of word, 27
  and prediction, 40–41
  process and denial, 41
  puzzles and, 90–91
  and spousal abuse, 175–176
  of women, 174
intuitive abilities, 30
intuitive signals
  anxiety, 71
  apprehension, 71
  curiosity, 71
  denial of, 35–36
  doubt, 71
  fear, 70
  gut feelings, 71
  hesitation, 71
  humor, 71
  hunches, 71
  nagging feelings, 71
  persistent thoughts, 71
  physical sensations, 71
  suspicion, 71
  wonder, 71
intuitive word puzzles, 90–91

JACA elements, 93–97, 130, 138, 141, 143, 305
  difficult employees, 156
jack joke, 149
Jackson, Arthur, 239, 240, 249
Janine, battered woman, 178
Janoff, Steven, 252–253
Jarecki, Andrew, 293–294
jealousy, 174
Joey, 221–223
Judas Priest rock group, 210–217
justification, perceived, 93–94, 130, 141, 156
  See also JACA elements
juvenile detention centers, 225

Kaczynski, Ted, 48, 249
kangaroo attacks, 36–37, 40
karate classes, 11
Keller, Helen, quoted, 179
Kelley, David E., 308
Kelly, 3–6, 57, 73, 283–284
Kemper, Edmund, 237–238
Kennedy, John F., 87, 253–254
key words
  persistence related, 197
  threats of violence, 105–106
kidnapping, 73–74
Kilcullen, Detective, 270, 273
killer was normal and quiet, 47–48
Kneivel, Evel, 243
knowledge retention, 28
knowledge *versus* inaccurate information, 37
Konner, Melvin, 32, 44
Kopfliesch, Stephanie, 308
Kraft Foods, 312
Kroft, Steve, 96
Krueger, Bob, 203
Krueger, Kathleen, 203

Lassally, Peter, 317, 318
Lennon, John, 12, 240, 245
Leonard, China, 40–41, 73
Leonard, Richard, 40–41
letting go, 124–125
Limbaugh, Rush, 93
listening and intuition, 91
Lo, Wayne, 145–147
loan sharking, 67, 305
logic and battered women, 178
love letters and stalkers, 23
Lowery, Shirley, 186

luck and spousal selection, 183
Lurie, Rod, 317

MacDonald, Arthur, quoted, 250
Mace, 11
mail bombs, 71–72
male privilege, 175
Mamet, David, 52–53, 55
Marquart, Jeff, 319
Massey, Jason, 219
mass hypnosis, 232
mass shooters, 142
Matlin, Marlee, 308
McGee, Jerry, 308
McKenna, Bill, 289–290
Mead, Margaret, 43
media figures, 22–23, 131, 134–139, 251–253
  assassinations of, 231–260
  attitudes about, 232–234
media influences
  on children, 216
  and perception, 284–298
  Stained Class record album, 211–213
Menninger, Karl, quoted, 43
mental illness
  and assassins, 268, 275
  genetic predisposition to, 48
messengers of intuition, 73, 306
  levels of, 70
metal detector searches, 11
Mihalko, Dan, 72
Miller, Alice, 227
misplaced fear, 23
Monahan, John, 79, 94, 140
Mones, Paul, 219–220
money as control, 174, 179–180
Monroe, Marilyn, 236
Montgomery, Donna, 186
mood swings, 175
Moore, Demi, 195
Moore, Sara Jane, 236
Morris, Desmond, 92
MOSAIC software, 20, 191–192, 275, 313–314
motive of charm, 56
murderers, 45–46
  inhuman, 44
Murray, Anne, 131
Murray, Betsy, 187
My Sister Sam (TV show), 231
  See also Schaeffer, Rebecca
mystical story, 26

nagging feelings, 73, 306
narcissism, 244
National Alliance of Mental Illness, 48
A Natural History of the Senses (Ackerman), 27
natural psychologists, 43
Nau, Ralph, 258, 262
Navarro, Maria, 186–187
negotiation
  and terminated employees, 163
  and the word no, 62–63, 199–200
Newberry, Steven, 213
niceness, 57
Nixon, Richard, 241, 244, 260
no is a complete sentence, 62–63, 197, 305
  See also discounting the word no
Nolan, Tom, 318
noninformation as information, 48
notes in blood, 23

O'Connor, Sandra Day, 266, 274, 275
O'Donnell, Rosie, 308
Oklahoma City bombing, 9
Orr, Gregory, 312
Oswald, Lee Harvey, 249

Pacewitz, Michael, 213
Palestinians, 95–96
panic, 281
Parche, Gunter, 254–255
parents
  responsibility of, 217–221
  single parent childhood, 225
parricide, 219–220
Peck, M. Scott, 225
pepper spray, 11
perceiving hazards, 279
Perry, Chester, 264, 269, 273
Perry, Grace, 264
Perry, Michael, 262–275

persistence
of John Searing, 131–133
and stalking, 195–196
and success, 121
of Edward Taylor, 134–140
of Tommy, 119–130
unwanted, 123
persistent thoughts, 73, 306
Peterson, Dale, 43
Pfeiffer, Michelle, 308
Pfiel, Steven, 218
Pfizer, 312
Phillips, Bill, 317
PINs. *See* pre-incident indicators
police encounters, 153, 174
date stalkers, 204
police officers, 104
as prediction experts, 34–36
postal workers, 104, 147
poverty, 224
predatory criminals, 51, 57
loan sharking, 60–61
predictability
and human societies, 51
in nature, 46
questions about, 317–319
Predicting Violent Behavior (Monahan), 79, 140
prediction, 23
elements of, 97–101
of future hazards, 112
and gravity, 79–80
and Joey, 223
language of, 90–93
and preparation, 86
resources and philosophies and, 151
and routine behavior, 37–40
skills of, 33
technology of, 11
of violence, 15, 16, 22–23
See also behavioral predictions; violence prediction
prediction elements scale
comparable events, 99, 316
context, 98, 315
experience, 99, 316
imminence, 99, 315
investment, 100, 316
knowledge, 100, 316
measurability of outcome, 97, 315
objectivity, 99–100, 316
pre-incident indicators (PINs), 98–99, 151–153, 305, 315
replicability, 100, 316
vantage, 97, 315
pre-employment checks, 157–158
pre-incident indicators (PINs), 98–99, 209, 305, 315
assassins, 246–247
ideas and actions, 18–19
spousal violence and murder, 174–175
and teenagers, 218–219
teenage suicide attempts, 215
in workplace, 151–153
See also prediction elements scale
preparation and prediction, 86
president as father image, 53
prisons, 11
private detectives, 136
problem employees, 161–162
promises, unsolicited, 61–62
promises and threats, 109
protest masculinity, 225
psychopaths, lack of conscience, 81
public figures
attacks on, 9, 87, 117, 231–232, 247–249
stalking of, 246, 266
public speaking, fear of, 282
pursuers, 22–23
puzzles, 90–91

random violence, 15
rapists, 5, 12, 54
preteens, 221–222
rapport building, 56
Reagan, Ronald, 245
threats against, 50
real truth, 37
recklessness and bravado, 50–51
recognition
and attention, 136
and significance, 244
references, importance of, 157–158

refusing to let go, 124, 129–130, 140, 203
rejection
  explicit, 198–201
  language of, 92–93, 131, 136, 199–200, 242
relationship addiction, 204
Ressler, Robert, 47, 48, 226–227, 237–238
restraining orders, 37
  homicides, 186–190
  spousal abuse, 184–185
  against stalkers, 126, 128, 142, 205
revenge, 92–93, 94
RICE evaluation, 86–87, 305
ridicule and embarrassment, 136
righteous indignation, 167
risk assessment, 32
  personal, 177
  termination meetings, 169
risks of dating, 208
Risler, Walt, 266, 269, 274–275
Rivera, Hilda, 187
The Road Less Traveled (Peck), 225
Robbins, Kathy, 317
Robinson, Floyd, 146
Robinson, Trinka, 146
Rodgers, Bernard, 145–147
romance
  and predicting spousal abuse, 183
Roosevelt, Franklin D., quoted, 286
Roosevelt, Theodore, 250
Ross, Katherine, 195–196
Rowe, Mary, 129–130
rule of opposites, 83, 305
Ryan, Meg, 308

safety and context, 107
safety lessons, 7–8, 56, 261
safety predictions, 68
Saldana, Theresa, 239
satellite details, 113–114, 280
Schaeffer, Rebecca, 43, 49, 231, 237, 240–242, 243–244, 245, 251–252
Scheme Team, 173
schools and security, 224, 320–322
scriptwriters, 148–151
The Search (Brown), 267
Searing, John, 131–133
secure environment, family as, 178
security industry, 12
  and assassins, 242, 251–257
  and fear, 288
  at schools, 222–223
Seles, Monica, 253–254
Self Help (Smiles), 57
Selling Out America's Children (Walsh), 216
serial killers, 5, 48, 69
serial rapists, 69
serial victims, 181
sexual abuse
  by children, 221–222
  by family members, 225
shared experiences, 55
shark attacks, 283–285
Sharpton, Al, 93
Sherill, Pat, 143
shooting sprees, 80, 142–143, 146
Shrank, John, 250–251
signals and intuition, 54, 305–306
silent consent, 197
Simpson, Nicole Brown, 172–173, 180–181
Simpson, O. J., 22, 172–176, 180–181
Sinatra, Frank, 232–233
sinister statements, 84–85
60 Minutes, 96
Smiles, Samuel, 57–58
Solanas, Valerie, 236
Son of Sam killer, 12
spousal abuse, 182–183
Stacey J., 49–50
stalking, 16, 22–23, 131
  categories of, 194
  husbands, 186–187
  prosecution of, 190–192
  suitors, 198, 202–203, 203–206, 208, 209
Standard Gravure plant, 73
Steinhagen, Ruth, 233–236
strangers
  as stalkers, 194
  threats posed by, 23
strong and silent type, 181–182
Strozdas, John, 308
substitute teachers, 37–40

suicide prevention centers, 181
suicides
  after killing spouse, 186–187
  prediction of, 89, 101–102
  reasons for, 211
  and stalkers, 234
Sulloway, Frank, 229
Supreme Court justices, 20
survival senses, 27, 68–69, 79
survival signals, 23
  charm and niceness, 56–58
  discounting the word no, 62–64
  fear, 277
  forced teaming, 55–56
  ignoring, 31
  Kelly, 5–6
  loan sharking, 60–61
  recognized by brain, 27
  too many details, 58–59
  typecasting, 59–60
  unsolicited promise, 61–62
suspicion, 73, 306
Suzuki, Shunryu, quoted, 28
SWAT teams, 11
symbolic violence, 174

Target Stores, 312
Tasers, 11
Taylor, Bob, 71–72, 73
Taylor, Edward, 134–139, 147
Taylor, Elizabeth, 233
termination meetings, 156, 162–169
territorialism, 15
terrorism, 96
Thompson, Caroline, 308
Thompson, Ray, 144–145
Thompson, Robert, 49, 73
threatening phone calls, 13
threats, 17
  assessments of, 105–106
  bomb, 110–111
  extortion, 114–117
  to kill, 103–118
  role of, 23
  of violence, 103–104
TIME syndrome, 150–151
timing, terminating employees,
    165–166
To Have or To Harm (Gross), 186
Tonight Show stalker, 131–133
too many details, 67, 305
Tootsie (film), 200
TRO. *See* restraining orders
trust issues, 4, 58
TV news, 48, 75
  See also media influences
Twain, Mark, quoted, 298
typecasting, 67, 305

Unabomber, 48, 71–72, 249
unconscious knowledge, 26
United States Marshals Service, 312
universal code of violence, 7–8
unsolicited promises, 305
The Untouched Key (Miller), 227
unwanted pursuit. *See* stalking
us *versus* them, 43, 44

Vance, James, 210–217
verbal abuse, 174
Verbrugge, Dr. Joseph, Jr., 40–41
victims
  harassment, 130, 131–133
  how we become, 31
  the interview, 63
  Kelly, 7
  restraining orders, 205
  and stalking, 195
  truths and myths, 47
Victory Over Violence, 307–308
videotapes, 154, 312
vignettes
  airport ticket line, 83–84
  Andrew's movie date, 293–294
  Arlene and security program,
    288–289, 291
  Billy on the airplane, 66–67
  bomb package, 71–72
  Celia and fear, 285–286, 291
  city employee fired, 170
  college roommate telephone call, 26
  convenience store robbery, 25–26,
    27
  Cynthia the substitute schoolteacher,
    37–40
  Donna the filmmaker, 292–293
  employee firing, 141–143
  employee kills boss, 104–105

vignettes *(cont.)*
Ginger the dog, 29–30
hotel guest commits suicide, 89
Iranian restaurant owner, 38–39
Joey the preteen, 223
Katherine and Bryan, 33–34, 206–208
Kelly, 3–6, 57, 73, 283–284
Leonard, China, and operation, 40–41
Lisa's story, 192–193
MacGuard security firm, 157–158
McKenna, Bill, and intruder, 289–290
Meg's fear of death, 279–281, 290–291
Nancy in sports car, 73–74
Oliver and guinea pig, 45–46
persistence, 131–133
police officers, 34–36
Sally and sale of house, 113–114
satellite details, 113–114
sex avoidance, 31–32
stalking, 257–258
Tony the lawyer intern, 28–29
Unabomber package, 72
walking with eyes closed, 278
violence, 140, 174
energy of, 7–8
prediction of, 7, 15, 20, 43, 80
warning signs for, 34
violence in workplace, 141–143, 312
and pre-incident indicators (PINs), 151–153
violent employees, 22–23
Vosekuill, Bryan, 317
VOV. *See* Victory Over Violence

Waitkus, Eddie, 233–236
Walker, Lenore, 191
Wallace, George, 87
Walsh, David, 216
Walt Disney Company, 312
Warhol, Andy, 236
warning signs
date stalkers, 206–208
ignoring, 147
from scriptwriters, 150
violence, 15, 127
See also pre-incident indicators
Warren, Lesley Ann, 308
weapons
of assassins, 241, 248–249, 252–253
as instruments of power, 175
of stalkers, 23
See also guns
weapons screening, 87, 151, 255–256
Westbecher, Joseph, 73
When a Child Kills (Mones), 219
Whoever Fights Monsters . . . (Ressler), 226
Why the Reckless Survive (Konner), 32
Wilson, John, 190
window of opportunity, 49
Without Conscience (Hare), 81
women
and abusive relationships, 176
battered, 173
and communication from men, 58
murders of, 9
personal security of, 64–65
reliance on intuition of, 91
responses to date stalkers, 202–203
and unwanted persistence, 123
See also battered women
Women's Tennis Council, 256
wonder, 73, 306
worry and fear, 284–287
Wrangham, Richard, 43
Wurman, Richard Saul, 82
Wynn, Mark, 52

Zimbalist, Efrem, Jr., 312